BUSINESS ETHICS

PROFILES IN
CIVIC VIRTUE

JAMES E. LIEBIG

The author would like to thank the following for their permission to reprint:

Excerpts from *Habits of the Heart: Individualism and Commitment in American Life* by Robert N. Bellah, with Richard Madsen, William M. Sullivan, Ann Swidler, and Steven M. Tipton. Copyright © 1985 by The University of California Press. Reprinted by permission of The University of California Press.

Excerpts from *An Incomplete Guide to the Future* by Willis W. Harman. Copyright © 1976 by Willis W. Harman. Reprinted by permission of Willis W. Harman.

Excerpts from "Creativity and Intuition in Business," speech given by Willis W. Harman at the Shell "Uncertainty in Management" Seminar, Vevey, Switzerland, June 19, 1986. Reprinted by permission of Willis W. Harman.

Excerpts from material of The World Business Academy. Reprinted by permission of Willis W. Harman.

Library of Congress Cataloging-in-Publication Data

Liebig, James.
    Business ethics : profiles in civic virtue / James Liebig.
        p.   cm.
    Includes bibliographical references.
    ISBN 1-55591-059-9
    1. Business ethics. 2. Businessmen—United States—Biography.
I. Title.
HF5387.L54   1990
338.092'273—dc20
[B]   3 2280 00631 8091   89-29522
                                                                   CIP

ISBN 1-55591-101-3 (pbk.)

Printed in the United States of America

10 9 8 7 6 5 4 3 2 1

Fulcrum Publishing
Golden, Colorado

To all in business leadership who regard their vocation as a high calling and who seek to enhance the development of a just and equitable society in the process of achieving business excellence.

CONTENTS

FOREWORD BY A
BUSINESS LEADER

Vaughn L. Beals, Jr.
Chairman of the Board
Harley-Davidson, Inc.

IF YOUR COMPANY is not already committed to virtuous management as defined by James Liebig, your corporate future is likely at risk. Many American enterprises already have fallen victim to foreign companies managed by these principles. More will fall victim in the future if social costs continue to escalate as a result of unresolved major community problems such as education, health care costs and crime.

In 1983, after five years of struggling to increase the involvement of our employees at Harley-Davidson, our management group concluded that we needed a new vice-president of human resources who would be truly committed to full employee involvement. After considerable thought, I called the one person who, from my prior experience, had the best understanding of such matters—James Liebig, author of this book. Our company and our employees have been daily beneficiaries of his recommendations ever since.

If you have not had the good fortune to know Jim personally or professionally, this book is indeed a godsend. His perspective is not that of a starry eyed theorist but rather that of a people-sensitive manager who has practiced in the real world. He knows what works—and also what doesn't—as illustrated in his selection of 24 corporate examples.

Beginning in the 1960s, there was an increased emphasis on insuring that corporations were managed ethically and in a socially responsible manner. Personally, I believe that the vast majority of American companies are indeed run on an ethical basis; unfortunately, the few that are not are vividly reported in the media.

The movement toward demanding increased social responsibility by business, in my opinion, started off too idealistically, or maybe more properly, it was misinterpreted by professional managers. Certainly every responsible corporation recognizes the need to financially support the social infrastructure of the communities in which it does business, for example, by supporting United Way, hospitals and schools. Some, but far fewer, managements establish an environment that encourages and supports volunteerism. Early proponents of increased corporate social responsibility seemed to be prescribing levels of community support that far exceeded that provided by even the most generous corporations. I was one of many who found it difficult to reconcile these recommendations with the responsibilities of a corporation to its shareholders.

In the last decade a third dimension, in addition to ethics and social responsibility, has been added—the importance of fully involving all employees in the business. This includes not only asking employees to contribute their ideas to the daily operation of the business but involving them in setting the longer range direction of the corporation and sharing the rewards of success with them.

The message of hope in this book is that virtuous management that incorporates these three tenets—ethical management, corporate social responsibility and full employee involvement—is in fact synonymous with the management's and the shareholders' self-interests. World-class quality and productivity, essential to any corporation's long-term success, are simply not achievable in an adversarial environment. Only knowledgeable, well-trained, happy, well-compensated and enthusiastic employees can achieve the levels of quality and productivity required in today's competitive environment.

Even the most pragmatic managers are recognizing that the future viability of their corporations is dependent upon the availability of well-educated high school and college graduates and that the corporation's competitive position can be adversely impacted by out-of-control social costs. As a result, enlightened managements today are markedly increasing their involvement in the community and their financial support of efforts to improve the environment in which they do business. *Business Ethics* should encourage others to adopt these principles of virtuous management in their own self-interests.

Your time will be well rewarded by studying this book. I can't imagine that anyone wouldn't find several ideas in what follows to improve the operation of their company as well as the lives and well-being of their employees. But unless these concepts are put into practice, they simply remain ideas. So the real test is what you do with these ideas in your own company. You will find one outstanding example in this book of how one C.E.O. translated an inspiring message she had heard into real action in her company—for the joint benefit of her employees, stockholders, company and community.

FOREWORD BY AN EDUCATOR

Paul R. Lawrence
Wallace Brett Donham Professor of Organization Behavior
Harvard Business School

BUSINESS ETHICS DEMONSTRATES clearly that not all business men and women have their eyes fixed solely on the bottom line. People in business bring a variety of motives to their worklife, motives that go beyond the purely economic. Some undoubtedly can be classified under the general rubric of "concern for the common good."

This book will appeal to a wide range of readers interested in business and its impact on society. It profiles two dozen contemporary business leaders, 16 in detail, who have exhibited a concern for people and our common life that is integrated with their pursuit of business success. The author's straightforward documentation of the remarkable achievements of these individuals makes for fascinating reading. Now their stories can serve as guides for others.

The author, Jim Liebig, whom I have known as a student and as a businessman, is no stranger to the subject. As a creative participant-observer in progressive business organizations for over three decades, he has witnessed firsthand the human and social benefits, as well as the business results, generated by exemplarily led organizations.

Profiles of business leaders whose interests embrace a concern for the development of people and society infrequently appear in business periodicals. Except in studies of organization behavior, they are not often the subject of case studies used in management education. When they do appear, they are frequently treated as if they were the exception to some obscure but commonly suspected rule. Whether they are or aren't exceptional is difficult to prove.

However, recent responsible research does indicate that such exemplary leadership produces organizations that generate superior business and financial results as well as other benefits.

That the business sector in general has become very influential in our national culture is beyond question. The quality of business leadership can have widespread significance. Those who assume leadership positions in business often exercise power affecting people and communities far beyond the immediate confines of their companies.

The uniqueness of *Business Ethics* lies in its attempt to identify those influences, exposures and experiences that have produced exemplary leaders. In an absolute sense, such an identification in specific situations is, of course, problematic. However, the weight of evidence is convincing that particular human experiences seem to be inordinately productive of a concern for others. Those influences are summarized in a chapter at the end of the book.

Although not a textbook, this volume can be employed appropriately as a resource by those designing courses in management and ethics and as a casebook or as collateral reading for courses in business ethics, corporate social responsibility, organization effectiveness and human resource development.

The final chapters present the author's assessment of what society expects of its business leaders today and what will be required of them in the future. To enhance the objectivity of this assessment, the author uses material from the widely acclaimed works of sociologist Robert Bellah and futurist Willis Harman as standards. This analysis generates reasonable and interesting points for serious consideration.

Business Ethics is a valuable addition to the empirically based literature on business leadership and its growing influence in our evolving culture.

PREFACE

CERTAINLY WHEN ATTENTION to insider trading and other greed-inspired actions by some in business dominates the media, those contemporary business leaders who have been exemplary[1] in their conduct are overlooked. Actions of greed, legal or illegal, when they become known, are usually sensational incidents of the moment and, therefore, more readily reportable. Virtuous behavior, on the other hand, is subtle and unobtrusive, not dramatic, observable only over a period of time.

Take, for example, the case of the founder-chairman of a company who decided early on to share the success of his business with those who made it successful, his employees. To accomplish this, he developed an employee stock ownership plan several decades ago. Today the vast majority of shares are owned by the employees. The company's directors, and thus its officers, must stand for re-election by the employee shareholders annually.

Another example is the new president of a company who considered himself the senior servant of the organization. As the result he turned the imposing and intimidating office he was offered into a conference room. In its place he selected a smaller office, furnished it with a table and chairs, and quietly went about setting an example regarding what he considered to be the true role of the leader.

At one level this book is primarily a series of profiles of very admirable business men and women, the good works they have accomplished and what seems to have motivated their efforts. Underlying the profiles, however, is a thesis that grew out of my experience and observations over some three decades in business. It has become increasingly apparent to me that business is now the dominant and most influential institution in our society. That means that the quality of business leadership has become very important to all of us whether we have recognized it or not. Further, that importance is not limited to the material aspects of life, but includes the moral realm as well.

In interviewing and profiling exemplary businesspeople I wanted to identify the human/social concerns these leaders were addressing, to learn how they were addressing them and to discover the factors responsible for their development as leaders who exhibited "an uncommon concern for the common good."[2]

I found that these talented, highly principled business people covered the philosophical spectrum. They ranged from religious, to nonreligious (even antireligious), to somewhat authoritarian, to democratic, to totally pragmatic. Their one common characteristic was a real concern for the development and well-being of people and the health of human society.

I came to believe that though they might not represent the majority of business leaders, they certainly represent much more than a small minority. Casual reading also informed me that this group of people-minded business men and women is growing. Small items have increasingly appeared in newspapers and magazines around the country reporting significant social contributions being made by companies in their communities and on internal organizational changes enhancing employee status and their participation in making decisions about the management of their work. Such actions bode well for the future.

They need to be seen, however, not as discretionary actions. They have become imperatives in a highly competitive world economy where the energy and imagination of all employees are required for business survival and the support of the public is necessary for the business system to thrive.

In the past, the words *virtue* and *virtuous* were used to describe persons of excellent character who related the common good to their own personal welfare. In short, the two were seen as necessarily interdependent. While working on this book I came to feel that it was important to recapture the concept of virtue, the linking of the common to the individual good. Our contemporary culture seems to have broken them apart, unmindful of the destruction this sundering has wrought. The importance of recapturing the concept of virtue, I believe, lies not just in indicating that virtue is the opposite of greed, but in showing virtue to be the core ingredient of leadership.

Because business has become the primary institution in society, business leadership, not usually subject to democratic accountability, must be marked by virtue, the understanding that business success is directly related to the pursuit of human development and the welfare of society.

The personally centered, broadly visioned, humanly sensitive (thus ethical in a proactive sense) individuals portrayed here are examples of contemporary virtue. Their life stories are magnificently varied, but the results in character of their development show remarkable similarities. The forces that have molded and shaped them have been subtle. No one can positively identify the most significant influences in each of their lives. However, the factors most frequently and consciously identified by the leaders themselves should come as no surprise.

The profiles reveal that the development of virtuous business leadership is a complex matter. It happens over time. It goes far beyond the formal education process, though it certainly involves educational preparation as well. It entails more than learning to crunch numbers or to hone technical skills. It requires an experienced sensitivity to the right of people to fair treatment and to their need to grow and to participate in the common human enterprise which a business is in its essence.

Such a preparation for business leadership surely involves a broader view of the role than currently exists and which often informs business educators. It demands a more comprehensive exposure to the historical, human, social and political aspects of reality than a trendy emphasis on teaching ethics as a mandatory exercise to reluctant students in search of vocational training.

The human and global consequences of business decisions and activities are often more significant than the immediate financial and technical objectives being pursued. Because these are interdependent variables, they all must be understood and wisely considered with equal competence and seriousness.

The business leaders of exemplary virtue you will meet on the pages ahead show how many businesses can and are positively benefitting people and society today. To do so has required a conscious vision and persistent action in every situation. It has been accomplished neither quickly nor by superficial efforts. But the results in many cases have been extraordinary.

These leaders also demonstrate that greed is not a universal norm in American business. In short, they declare that business organizations today can no longer exist for the primary purpose of generating personal wealth for a controlling elite.

My wish is that you, the reader, will share my excitement in getting to know these business men and women and see the promise they hold both for the professionalization of business leadership and for the future of human society.

ACKNOWLEDGMENTS

IN ADDITION TO the business men and women who are profiled in this book and who are mentioned as contributors to those profiles, over six dozen others were involved in getting this work accomplished. The following especially gave me valuable guidance and direct assistance along the way.

James D. Anderson	Richard Logan
Pat Barrentine	Noreen D. Martin
Robert Bellah	Robert McLean III
Wilfred Bockelman	Joan Mills
Richard Broholm	Jitsuo Morikawa
Evelyn Burry	Ronald Nater
Richard Chartier	Ronald Phillips
Edwin Cox	Peter Senge
Willis Harman	John Staton
Fred Herbolzheimer	William Sullivan
Jack Howell	Charlotte Taylor
John James	James Thurber
Muriel James	Stuart Weeks
James Joseph	Gayle Wegner

I am also indebted to Cheryl Dugan and her staff of typists and to Margaret Achter for transcribing innumerable tapes. Eileen Gillis patiently word processed several drafts. Her dedicated efforts ensured that a presentable manuscript would finally emerge.

My wife, Margaret, gave me her normal unobtrusive support and her candid reactions to my ideas. An old and close friend, Alan W. C. Green, stimulated my thinking and provided a critique of my early efforts which measurably improved the final product.

Finally, none of this would have come to fruition without the thoughtful guidance of my publisher, a new and valued friend, Bob Baron, and editor, Carmel Huestis.

To all those named and unnamed who supported me in this effort, my sincere thanks.

THE COMPANIES AND THE PEOPLE

The Allied Companies   Miles Barber
   (diversified services)
CAPSCO Sales, Inc.   Billye Ericksen
   (electronic components distribution)
Carwell Franchise Corporation   Carol B. Green
   (auto rustproofing)
3Com Corporation   L. William Krause
   (computer networking systems)

Control Data Corporation   Norbert R. Berg
   (diversified electronics)
Dahlstrom Manufacturing Co., Inc.   Harold Bolton
   (precision metal fabrications)
GCA Corporation   James E. Gallagher
   (electronic equipment manufacturer)
Graco, Inc.   David A. Koch
   (fluid handling equipment)

Hammermill Paper Company   Albert Duval
   (paper manufacturer and distributor)
The Hanover Insurance Companies   William J. O'Brien
   (casualty insurer)
M. S. Hansson, Inc.   Margaret S. Hansson
   (business development)
Hunter Business Direct, Inc.   Victor L. Hunter
   (business-to-business telemarketing)

Managistics, Inc. (payroll services)   Shirley Parris
Nucor Corporation   F. Kenneth Iverson
   (steel maker/joist manufacturer)

Park Tower Realty Corporation   Veronica W. Hackett
    (commercial real estate developer)
Real Estate Developer   John T. Ferris
    (inventor, social entrepreneur)

Republic Airlines, Inc.   Daniel F. May
    (commercial airline)
Resource Development Group   Bruce Copeland
    (community social resource development)
Schreiber Foods, Inc.   Jack Meng
    (cheese manufacturer)
Eugene B. Shea Associates   Eugene B. Shea
    (placement consultants)

TDIndustries, Inc.   Jack Lowe, Jr.
    (commercial air conditioning)
Texas Utilities Generating Company   Robert Gary
    (public utility)
Townsend and Bottum, Inc.   C. E. (Bill) Bottum, Jr.
    (construction services)
A. O. Wilson Structural Company   Albert O. Wilson, Jr.
    (structural steel fabricator)

BUSINESS ETHICS

Chapter 1

THE VIRTUOUS LEADER LIVES!

THE YEAR IS 1787. The place is Philadelphia. The authors of the Constitution are discussing the qualities required of citizens in a democratic republic. They speak of virtue, mindful of Montesquieu's definition: "The virtuous citizen was one who understood that personal welfare is dependent on the general welfare and could be expected to act accordingly."[3]

The time is the late 1940s. The place is Dallas. The founder and president of a new air conditioning distribution and installation firm is making plans to share the success, management and ownership of his company with his employees.

The time is the early 1970s. The place is Minneapolis. A senior officer of a diversified corporation is developing a new facility to employ persons only able to work part-time, such as mothers of young school-age children, students and the handicapped.

The time is 1980. A new high-tech manufacturing company has just been organized. The firm supplying venture capital has agreed with the founders' requirement that every employee of the new company be included in the organization's stock option and stock purchase plans.

The year is 1988. The place is Milwaukee. It is 7:30 a.m. The employees of a telemarketing firm are meeting to decide what charitable cause should receive this month's grant, which is equal to 10 percent of the company's net profit before taxes.

VIRTUE

As noted in the Preface, the words *virtue* and *virtuous* have lost the significance they once had. At our nation's founding, virtuous

1

persons were those of high ethical standards who pursued the good for the benefit of society as well as for themselves. It is this definition of virtue that is meant to apply here. Virtuous business leaders, therefore, are those leaders who are mindful that the needs and realistic expectations of others in society must be satisfied if their own needs and realistic expectations are to be met.

This book is based on the observation that today the business enterprise system is the dominant institution in America and in the world in general. Concerns related to business effectiveness currently preoccupy governmental and other institutional leaders internationally. In socialist and communist states, no less than in capitalist countries, the success of their economic enterprises is perceived as determining the comparative health of those societies.

Furthermore, the institution of business has become a major determiner of social values, of personal and family priorities, readily observable in our own society. Business values seem to have filled the vacuum left in recent years by the withdrawal of much of the educational system from the value-development arena.

The influence of business on society, however, is not always positive. Inferior products and services, environmental degradation, unsafe physical working conditions and the misutilization and underutilization of human resources are sometimes among its shortcomings.

However, despite sex-oriented advertising and the distorted portrayals of "the good life" and of business tycoons on television, most U.S. companies don't intentionally underwrite the depraving of the American public. Indeed most businesses make many positive nonmaterial, as well as material, contributions to our lives. In addition to providing products and services which meet our needs as well as our wants, businesses generate jobs which often give meaning and purpose to life. Jobs generate income and opportunities to develop social relationships as well. As "community," once determined by the commonality of vocational and residential geography, has seemed to decline for many of us, relationships generated through business involvement have emerged as at least one important element of social connectedness in our fragmented society.

Because of receiving mixed reviews, however, the concern for ethics in business has generated a lively debate. Unlike the professions, business operates under no intrinsic social principles other than self-interest and survival. Historically, ethics in business have been what society decided from time to time was legally and morally right. Where well-delineated legalities ended, however, and during times of social change, what was morally right was often as much obscured as helped by the consideration of situational factors, of what was the lesser or the greater good, and of short-term versus long-term consequences. Hence, the debate regarding business ethics continues unabated.

Whether businesses can legitimately earn profits is not debated here. Every economic enterprise, capitalist or socialist, must develop a surplus in order to maintain the organization's base of resources and for growth. The issue of the morality of downsizing is likewise not intentionally addressed here. The competitiveness and survival of many businesses have recently required drastic, unpopular and often personally distressing actions. How profits and downsizing have been accomplished can involve ethical questions, however. Several examples of how "excess personnel" have been treated are described in the material that follows.

Beyond traditional, narrowly focused debates regarding business ethics, however, lies the broader issue of business social purpose. Though arguable at one level, that business has a social purpose is virtually undeniable, given the role that business has in contemporary society, and whether business has intended it to be that way or not. Whether by assignment or by conscious acceptance, and for better or for worse, American business enterprise profoundly affects each of our lives today.

If this is indeed true, then the human sensitivity and social consciousness of business leaders are very important to each one of us. Further, the preparation of persons to assume business leadership becomes vitally important. Mere vocational training preparing managers to become technically proficient in order to achieve personal success is no longer sufficient. The self-serving excesses of a few Wall Street manipulators, even other actions that are currently "legal" but whose only purpose is to satisfy the appetites of the power-hungry and greedy, provide inappropriate models for emulation and ultimately destroy the moral fabric of society.

As we will see, business leadership practiced responsibly can produce a renaissance. When it is practiced irresponsibly and selfishly, all facets of human society end up losing.

OVERVIEW

In the following chapters, profiles of 24 leaders are offered as evidence, despite headlines to the contrary, that virtue persists in the private sector. Virtue is practiced by thoughtful business persons, who are mindful of the common good, of the needs of people and of society that go beyond the provision of products and services. These profiles describe models, not of finished organizations or of perfect organizational leadership, but of intention and of direction. They are only a few examples among the many virtuous business leaders throughout the United States today. The threads of consistency and the direction of movement seen in these situations inspire confidence that a major leavening of the corporate lump is possible given the appropriate preparation and the will and support of persons in business to do so.

For ease of presentation and analysis, many of these 24 business men and women have been divided into three groups. The assignment of each person to a group could only be roughly done and does not imply their exclusion from another category. Also, there is no intentional ranking of this classification. Rather, the groups are presented in general order of their appearance on the American business stage.

The *Traditionalists* are business leaders who primarily have focused their efforts on personal and corporate philanthropy and volunteerism, that is, on causes in society outside their organizations.

The *Transitionalists* have pursued emerging issues, often employing traditional methods, but frequently involving their organizations directly in those actions.

The *Transformers* are business leaders who are changing, or who have changed, how their businesses are organized, managed, rewarded and, often, owned.

A fourth potential type of virtuous leader is identified in the last chapter. This type combines major attributes of the other three and promises to profoundly alter the relationship between the business system and the society of which it is such a significant part.

Virtuous leaders are persons of honesty, integrity and trust. As popularly defined in business literature today, they are concerned about excellence. Facing the rough-and-tumble of competition, and its ancillary temptations, they must exhibit moral courage. But virtue requires more than techniques and personal integrity. Virtue requires the acceptance of equity in human relationships and a commitment to act accordingly. It involves that core element, the belief system of a person.

But how can virtue be sustained in business management beyond its existence in an exemplary leader here and there? Certainly a supportive context must prevail for virtue to survive. For virtue to become the norm in business a new vision and an inspiring purpose are required for the business system, a vision and purpose that go beyond the sole achievement of private objectives as its ultimate goal. Such a new vision and inspiring purpose do not emanate from eyes and minds fixed solely on the traditional bottom line. They issue from hearts and minds that have wrestled with the reason for "being" itself and from the imagination of those who can visualize how social purposes can be furthered while business objectives are being accomplished. The challenge is essentially spiritual.

The people you will meet in the following pages have involved themselves in the social dynamics of business in a variety of ways. No two stories are alike except that all have had a vision of what was "better," not just for themselves or their organizations, but for all the stakeholders of business, including society at large. Discovering how these virtuous business leaders have come to embrace their concerns is the adventure ahead.

Chapter 2

VIRTUOUS LEADERS: A TRADITION IN AMERICAN BUSINESS

THE AUTHORS OF *Habits of the Heart*[4] have written a landmark description of the development of American society to the present. They report that our national founders believed that the stability and success of our democratic republic rested on the maintenance of virtue among its citizens. Virtue, as noted before, was the quality of citizenship that recognized that the private welfare of each citizen depended on the public welfare of everyone.

The authors of *Habits* also report that over time, as individual citizens, we have increasingly pursued private interests excluding concern for the general welfare. They comment, "with Ronald Reagan's assertion that 'we the people' are 'a special interest group,' our concern for the economy being the only thing that holds us together, we have reached a kind of end of the line. The citizen has been swallowed up in 'economic man.' "[5]

The authors' answer to this problem is the reassertion of a political vision that captures the imagination of citizens and enlists their energies to accomplish necessary change.

The manager in contemporary society as viewed by *Habits* is a technocrat, myopic and partial. The authors' portrayal may seem too generalized, but for the point they are making, it is an appropriate stereotype. However, a large number of business leaders down through the years have stood within the tradition of American civic virtue.

Just as many farmers of antiquity left the corners of their fields unharvested so that the landless needy might share in their bounty, seen as a gift from nature and nature's god, many businesspeople

7

in America have regularly contributed to worthy causes.

From the earliest days of the industrialization of America, generous gifts from the personal fortunes of successful captains of industry—though sometimes given near or in anticipation of death—were dedicated to private efforts to foster the common good. Indeed, the proliferation of private voluntary associations, growing up alongside private business organizations, is an American phenomenon. Libraries, colleges and universities, museums, hospitals, improvement groups, churches, seminaries, settlement houses and even prisons were the early beneficiaries of private philanthropy in the United States. Many remain so today. This is in contrast to other areas of the world where such support normally has come from public funds.

Initially private giving was viewed by many as a religious duty, a function of stewardship. "[Andrew] Carnegie, on the other hand, was one of the first men to argue that philanthropy was not so much a religious duty as a social obligation. Echoing the theories of social Darwinism, he saw his riches—and trusteeship—as having devolved not from Providence but rather from nature which had selected him as one of the fittest in the struggle for survival to amass and redistribute in the public interest,"[6] according to Carl Bakal. Bakal also notes that Carnegie concentrated his benevolences on the able and industrious, and would not support "the slothful, the drunken, the unworthy." In each era of the nation's settlement and development then, new causes were born and responded to by business leaders, often generously, sometimes less so, and sometimes depending upon what group of persons the cause was generated to serve.

In more recent years, the sources of business philanthropy have become increasingly more institutional and less personal. At the same time, perhaps they have become more democratic in the sense that many more causes, covering a wider spectrum of social needs, have been supported. Recent contributions may have been somewhat less dramatic than those made by the early giants of industry, but a substantial increase in the involvement of business people as volunteers has occurred as well. This is not to say that philanthropy and volunteerism have been or are now evenly valued throughout the business community. However, those who declare that "the business of business is business" express a personal opinion unsupported by the fact that many American business leaders historically have responded generously to the social needs of a constantly evolving culture and continue to do so today.

Contemporary virtuous business leaders, of course, are engaged in more than the traditions of philanthropy and volunteerism. Increasingly they have used their business operations as the location of their efforts to improve the human condition. Certainly the passage of laws has forced many of these changes from previous practices. However, some exemplary business leaders have intentionally moved beyond the letter of the law and have voluntarily invested in company-operated efforts to correct perceived deficiencies in the socioeconomic system. Included are child care facilities, remedial learning centers and training programs to employ those previously thought to be unemployable.

These transitional efforts have also included bringing activities previously performed outside the business environment into the business itself. Examples include in-house fitness centers and employee and family counseling services. Some transitional leaders have also been involved in changing management-employee relations from an adversarial process to one of cooperation in resolving differences. This has required greater openness and information sharing about the business by management and an increase in employee responsibility for and involvement in achieving organizational goals.

Still others have comprehensively structured or restructured their organizations to foster individual employee and group self-management and involvement in business decisions about significant issues. Often they have concomitantly included their employees in profit-sharing, bonus and stock-ownership plans. At first glance this intentional structuring to enhance employee personal development, contribution and recognition may not seem dramatic. However, it implies a rebalancing of management power vis-à-vis employees and of employee rights and obligations vis-à-vis the employer. Further it indicates an emerging new relationship between the rights of employees and those of the traditional "owners" of the business, the shareholders.

The point here is that leadership virtue can be manifested in many forms. It also implies that there are more exemplary leaders around than one might suspect, given the eyes to see them. This became clear as I began the task of identifying people to interview. Those who were suggested were from all over the country. Often they were involved in companies with unfamiliar names, quietly performing acts of concern for the common good. Some undoubtedly were known for their deeds locally but few were widely recognized nationally.

EXAMPLES

Take Albert Duval, for instance. The recently retired C.E.O. of Hammermill Paper Company, Al Duval is a modest leader whose solid competence, personal values and dedication to his work seem to have been given appropriate and timely recognition in his field throughout his career. Al Duval's statesmanship was exhibited primarily but not exclusively within the operations of the company. He promoted the decentralized, autonomous management of the Hammermill companies. He sustained the self-respect of employees even when they made mistakes that cost the company money. A participative team leader, he established a company policy that a retiring C.E.O. would also leave the board immediately, permitting the new leader to operate unfettered by the presence of the predecessor.

During his tenure, Hammermill flourished. As chairman of Hammermill's corporate foundation, Duval was able to facilitate generous gifts to causes in the company's home town of Erie, Pennsylvania, and to projects, particularly in higher education, in places where the company had major operations.

Al Duval, a leader of community improvement efforts in Erie, was twice elected president of the American Paper Institute, an unusual honor. Looking back today he says with honesty and some amazement, "I never set out to be C.E.O. of anything." The day he retired from Hammermill in 1985 after 26 years with the company, he left the headquarters building and has never been back. "Not that I don't like the building, I just feel that's the way it ought to be done."

Through four careers, as an educator in a southern university, then an inventor of several optical devices, later a technical manager in an engineering firm and, finally, a redeveloper of residential properties, John T. Ferris of Lexington, Massachusetts, has exhibited some unusual attributes. He has combined his scientific understanding and talents with the qualities of human sensitivity and the patience of a teacher and nurturer of the human spirit. These have been used both within the companies he has worked for and in his community service.

John has given generously of his time and talents to several churches and seminaries. During a major slump in the demand for high-tech products, when unemployed himself, he counseled professional persons traumatized by their resulting unemployment. He has also worked with retired persons seeking to remain productive in society and counseled youth in need of career guidance and assistance.

A midwesterner by birth and raising, John is the son of a minister, a perpetual optimist who has been repeatedly surprised by the good things that have happened to him during his lifetime. Although he has experienced vicissitudes in life, he calls himself an "appreciator," someone who finds essential goodness in everyone he meets. And he is happy for it.

Another example of a virtuous leader is James E. Gallagher. In 1958, Jim Gallagher, a graduate in physics, mathematics and meteorology, with extensive experience as a research program manager, joined five others to found GCA Corporation in Boston, Massachusetts. The mission of GCA was to do contract space and electronics research and to develop industrial applications from new technology.

For the next 25 years, as a vice-president, senior vice-president of operations and senior vice-president of international and government affairs, and a member of the board of directors, Jim helped to steer the growth of this highly successful venture. In addition to his active leadership of professional societies, Jim gave considerable time to his church, to the City Mission Society of Boston as president and chairman, to the Metropolitan Boston Association (Council of Churches) as moderator, and to the Boston Theological

Institute, a consortium of seminaries in the Boston area, as a director.

By the end of 1985, GCA was in serious trouble and Jim was the only founder remaining in the company. Previously he had been removed from the board by the chairman with whom he had clashed over company strategy. The chairman, president and chief financial officer were subsequently terminated by the board. Just at the time he should have been able to retire and take things easier, Jim was asked to assist in saving the company. During 1986 and 1987 Jim Gallagher sold off several business units and realigned the organization to reduce losses and retain as many jobs as possible. Recently, under new ownership and management, Jim Gallagher has returned to the company's board of directors.

Robert Gary, executive vice-president of Texas Utilities Generating Company, is acquainted with adversity. During the Depression he helped his family by providing for most of his expenses by the age of 10. A "walk-on" who became captain of the Texas A & M football team, he earned a degree in mechanical engineering just in time to become a marine during World War II. While working for GE at age 27, he contracted polio and was completely paralyzed. Imaging his muscles back into action, he was completely cured within several years.

Responsible for the operations of all of Texas Utilities' generating capacity with an annual budget of several billion dollars, Bob Gary has been a man with a mission. For the past decade he has focused on the development of people within his company as a number-one priority, to benefit both the company and the individuals. Responsible for originating several successful programs, he has led a pioneering effort in "Whole Brain Development" to enhance employee creativity, to broaden their perspectives and to enrich personal learning and contributions to work, family and society.

A philosopher with ready observations of his own experience he says, "It's what you do when you don't have to do anything, that makes you what you want to be when it's too late to do anything about it." Speaking of his role relative to the employees of his company he has concluded, "I hold a trusteeship for all these people. I want them to have the most fun doing the toughest job there is to do and when it's over to be glad they did it."

Veronica W. Hackett is executive vice-president of Park Tower Realty Corporation. But being a very successful executive and Manhattan real estate developer has not diminished Veronica's concern for others. In addition to being married and being a devoted parent, she gives what little time is left to the Girls Clubs of America as a volunteer following a term on its national board.

Veronica is concerned about the Cinderella myth that still abounds among girls that they will be taken care of someday by a knight on a white horse. In reality, she says, 80 percent of them will have no choice but to work to take care of themselves when they become adults or even before. She knows that girls need special attention and effective role models to change the patterns of teenage pregnancies, substance abuse and dependency that have kept many of them second-class citizens.

From the constant invitations she gets to work for other good causes, she also knows that there are yet insufficient numbers of women in prominent positions in business and in the professions to deal with the needs of society that women uniquely can address.

A host of influences have conspired to produce the values of Jack Meng, president and C.E. O. of Schreiber Foods, Inc., of Green Bay, Wisconsin, the largest privately held cheese company in the world: his fiancée's cancer and extensive surgery just two months before their wedding date; a supportive church family; his in-laws, an eye surgery team who have made several trips as volunteers to treat patients in remote villages of Latin America and southern Asia; the standards set by his predecessors in his company; and the models of virtue he sees in other business leaders in Green Bay.

A graduate of Wabash College with an M.B.A. from Washington University, within Schreiber, Jack is a participative leader, fostering employee self-management, sensitive to those who need space to work out personal/family problems. Within the community he is a leader in the development of a wildlife refuge, a director of several local organizations and an articulate advocate for the support of humane causes. He and his wife recently spent part of their summer vacation as volunteers for Habitat for Humanity helping to construct housing for low-income families and are now involved in a new Habitat project in Green Bay.

By workday Shirley Parris, personnel manager of Managistics, Inc., a BankAmerica Company in Queens, New York, is a forthright but caring overseer of the physical and mental health of Managistics' some 300 employees. But most of her other waking hours including weekends and vacations have been spent as the lay leader of the New York Conference of the United Methodist Church. The conference encompasses some 590 churches, tens of thousands of members and a host of social service organizations.

Shirley has been known both in her company and in her avocation for her competence and uncompromising ethics. As a young woman she moved from her native Barbados to the United States where she was married, bore two children and was divorced. Since then Shirley has seen her children safely through college and out on their own while she has developed a dual career of service to others in industry and in the church.

Eugene B. Shea, president of Eugene B. Shea Associates, is a stubborn, persistent veteran of the ups and downs of the executive employment and placement business. In 1974, deeply in debt, Gene says he prayed that he might repay everyone whom he owed, and if successful in doing that, vowed that he would change his firm into a not-for-profit corporation and "ask Christ to serve as chairman of the board." It took him eight years. Today his not-for-profit outplacement firm specializes in helping executives, managers and professional people to find and get appropriate new positions through professional counseling, marketing materials development, contact development and interview preparation.

Along the way, Gene has volunteered at Cook County (Illinois) Jail teaching mathematics and Bible studies. He initiated a mutual support group called "Failures Anonymous" to help people regain self-respect, self-confidence and through renewed faith to find the strength to resolve their problems. But his biggest project to date has been to write a book, *The Immortal "I."* It is a reweaving of major works of philosophy, psychology and religion, molded and shaped by his unique insights, declaring that we are essentially spiritual in our very nature. Really understanding that, and eliminating our misperception that we are only physical and mental beings, he writes, restores us from alienation to wholeness in ourselves and in all our relationships.

SUMMARY

The preceding business managers are involved in regional, national and international firms all around the United States. They live in small towns, regional centers and large metropolitan areas. Several have been motivated by religious convictions; others have not. Although the principles informing their actions are similar, they have expressed their concern for others in a rich variety of ways.

The common good each has pursued is obviously just a piece of the overall common good. Sometimes it has been pursued within the public arena, other times in the more private context of a business organization, but the context is less significant than the action. Many businesses in the past were hierarchical in structure and authoritarian in operation. Some were callous to the needs of their stakeholders. Others were paternalistic in relationship to their employees. In many cases the arrogance of power was present. This scene has been undergoing many dramatic changes in recent years. Today's virtuous business leaders know that the valid needs of their stakeholders must be satisfied on the stakeholders' terms if the legitimate objectives of their businesses are to be accomplished.

Chapter 3

THE TRADITIONALISTS

TRADITIONAL HERE REFERS to those acts of concern for the common good by virtuous business leaders that have historically occurred most frequently. These are, of course, business and personal philanthropy and the voluntary sharing of personal time and talents for the benefit of worthy causes.

Traditional doesn't mean obsolete. Indeed, the danger is, because some businesses and businesspersons frequently give generously of their treasure, talents and time, that we will take them for granted, accept their generosity and insufficiently appreciate their efforts.

While I was interviewing people for this book, viewing at close hand what has motivated their actions, my respect grew for those business men and women who have quite literally gone far out of their way to serve the needs of their fellows. Regardless of the forms that exemplary business leadership may take in the future, the traditions of philanthropy and volunteerism will remain as evidence that some people, at least, are in business for more than the generation of profits or the accumulation of personal wealth. The basic principles of these traditional leaders, and the concern they have shown for the issues of our common life, will be seen farther on as essential ingredients for the development of a humane society as we emerge from the decline of the industrial era.

Albert Wilson, David Koch and Miles Barber are all chief executive officers of their companies. All are covered neatly by the term *traditional*. But each is forward-looking and has stamped the uniqueness of his own personality both on the company he has led as well as on the contributions he has made to foster the common good.

Albert Wilson's philanthropy and volunteerism are direct

extensions of his vocation. His company provides custom fabricated steel for bridges, buildings and other structures in the Boston and nearby New England area. His avocation is spent building up the cultural and social institutions of the same area.

David Koch was inspired by the model set by the founders of his company and by the example set by other heads of companies in the Twin Cities area. As the result his company has become a leader in its industry and has joined with scores of other firms to make Minneapolis/St. Paul one of the leading areas in the United States for corporate philanthropy.

Miles Barber started out as a fairly conventional entrepreneur despite an unconventional history. He is now involved in a number of unique causes. Getting to know and to be strongly influenced by an unusual California state assemblyman is one of the reasons why Miles is a virtuous business leader today. But the roots of his statesmanship extend quite deeply and predate that relationship.

THE QUINTESSENTIAL
TRADITIONAL VIRTUOUS LEADER

Albert O. Wilson, Jr., Chairman and C.E.O.
A. O. Wilson Structural Company

Now over 70 years old, but with the energy level of a person many years younger, Albert Wilson has begun to think about slowing down someday.

The structural steel fabricating company his father founded in 1923 has always been located in an area north of Concord Avenue in the Alewife section of Cambridge, Massachusetts. When the company opened its doors, the area was still a swamp. Today the swamp is gone and the neighborhood contains shopping centers, office buildings, apartments and condominiums, no place for a steel fabricator.

For the past decade, Al Wilson, Jr., has headed the Alewife Community Development Task Force, planning and overseeing the orderly transition of the neighborhood from industrial to light commercial, research and office buildings. His company, now with 50 employees, will be relocating to a new site, recently a cornfield in northeastern Connecticut.

But Al's immediate concern for Alewife and Cambridge is only the start. Having joined the company in 1939, following his graduation from M.I.T. in civil engineering and one year of training with Bethlehem Steel, he readily accepted his father's high principles of business management. He subsequently embraced the responsibilities of being a businessman, family man, and community and church leader as being one role, all of a piece, and consistent throughout.

His spiritual growth, paralleling his mental and physical maturation, he attributes largely to Dr. Roy Pearson, who was his pastor at Hancock Congregational Church in Lexington when he was beginning his career. Thirty-two years after Dr. Pearson left Hancock Church, Al Wilson could still recall many of his messages. This foundation helped prepare him and his "teammate," Carol, to accept and to deal with the fact that two of their four children had cystic fibrosis and would never survive to full adulthood. "We learned a lot from our children," is the way Al puts it today.

When Al, Sr., died, Al, Jr., who was 39, succeeded him as head of the company. By then Al, Jr., was already a trustee of Andover Newton Theological School, having previously assumed leadership roles at Hancock Church and in Boston-area Congregational Church organizations. Since then he has given generous time and leadership to the state conference of the United Church of Christ and to the national offices of the denomination as well as to the Salvation Army, the Massachusetts Bible Society, the Massachusetts Council of Churches and the City Mission Society of Boston.

Al is also a Rotarian, a member of the Cambridge Chamber of Commerce, on the board of several area corporations and a trustee overseeing the $3 billion invested in the John Hancock Mutual Funds. Along with Carol, Al gives talks to conferences on values and family life and they have long led a highly acclaimed Bible study and spiritual growth class at Hancock Church.

The Wilson family established a charitable foundation some years ago and have since donated over $400,000 to such causes as Andover Newton, Park Street Church in Boston, the Museum of Science in Cambridge, various hospitals and community social service agencies in the Boston area. To help ensure that the available funds go to the most appropriate causes, the foundation board is composed of both family and nonfamily members.

On the political spectrum, Al Wilson, Jr., is a conservative. He believes that the least government is the best government. He doesn't want governmental involvement in social problems "because they don't know how to do it right. This puts a real strain on those who believe as I do," he declares, because somebody has got to be concerned about such problems and do something about them. "To ask our government to do the Christian thing is to ask the impossible," he believes. "We've got to do it ourselves."

"I've never been one of the boys; never have needed acceptance. I'm not one that has been hurt if my peers have not accepted me. If you say you're a Christian, you have to live a life that says it in actions as well as words. I have a responsibility to take care of what God has given me and to use it intelligently."

Al believes most people today are motivated by self-interest and that the sense of stewardship he learned from his father is passing away. However, as he and his brother, Don, have prepared to turn over their company to a new management, all of whom are nonfamily, professional managers, who will run it in its new location, Al says, "We haven't dictated any biblical or any Christian beliefs to them. They have the same concerns we do, but they don't come from the same spiritual foundations. Three are Catholic and one is Presbyterian. I can't guarantee how it will come out," he acknowledges, and he won't try to control the outcome.

* * *

From Al Wilson's religious orientation to life, we now turn to an example from one of America's leading centers of corporate giving.

The 5 Percent Club:
A Twin Cities Phenomenon

David A. Koch, Chairman and C.E.O.
Graco, Inc.

David Koch (pronounced *coach*) is an ardent spokesman for a phenomenon peculiar to the twin cities of Minneapolis and St. Paul,

Minnesota. Known as "The 5 Percent Club," it includes 72 area companies who have pledged to give 5 percent of their profits before taxes to not-for-profit, charitable causes, primarily in the communities in which they operate. Initiated by the joint Minneapolis and St. Paul chambers of commerce, another 35 to 40 companies are committed to giving 2 percent.

The 5 percent figure comes from the amount permitted, since 1935, by the IRS that companies can deduct as a business expense if such funds are donated according to a description of IRS-approved causes. Needless to say, Graco, Inc., is a 5 percent company. (In recent years, the allowed percentage has been increased by the IRS to 10 percent.)

Raised in a rural area near Wayzata, Minnesota, David really wanted to play baseball for the New York Yankees. But, like many "tryouts" before and since, he didn't make it and went on to do other things.

An ROTC officer candidate and business graduate of the College of St. Thomas in 1952, he became a municipal bond broker for Kalman & Company when he left the service. In 1956, he married the daughter of Lee Gray, one of the founders of Graco, a small industrial equipment manufacturing company in Minneapolis with annual sales then of about $5 million.

Lee Gray, without male heirs, convinced David that it was an opportunity for him, and an obligation, to join Graco and assist in the continued growth and success of the company. Within a year of his daughter's marriage, Lee Gray was diagnosed as having cancer, and a year later he died, while still in his early 60s.

In 1961, at age 31, having been responsible for Graco branch office operations for several years, David Koch was named executive vice-president by the company's board, and the following year became president.

"At that time the president of Graco was also the chief executive officer. Annual sales were running about $11 to $12 million." Twenty-five years later, in 1987, Graco's C.E.O. was still David Koch and its annual sales volume was in excess of $239 million, over twice what David had expected he would see during his years with the company. Also, now Graco is a recognized leader internationally in fluid handling technology, "specializing in systems and equipment to move, control, deliver, dispense and apply fluid materials," according to a recent Graco annual report.

That report went on to read:

> Graco's basic business mission is to serve people through profitable growth. The Company has identified four specific "stakeholder" groups—customers, employees, shareholders and communities. It strives to serve the needs of these groups in a thoughtful, equitable, and balanced manner, assuring that all stakeholders share in the Company's successes. Graco management is committed to meeting the needs of customers through a strong emphasis on quality and innovation in products and systems. The Company seeks to provide rewarding work and growth opportunities for all of its 2,000 employees.
>
> Graco is dedicated to enhancing the resources entrusted to it by shareholders through the sustained profitable growth of the Company. Finally, Graco is a good neighbor and member of the communities in which it is located and feels an obligation to help those communities solve their problems.

From the beginning of his tenure as the leader of Graco, David Koch felt a keen responsibility to develop the company in a sound manner because he knew how hard its founders had worked to get it on its feet. But it is David's sense of responsibility in another area that makes his leadership truly exemplary. David believes strongly in the concept that businesses operate at the pleasure of the public, that businesses have a public mandate that has been given to them and that can be taken away if businesses do not acknowledge their responsibilities to be concerned about the quality of the common life of their communities.

"I don't want to suggest a simplistic solution that says that if in fact all businesses would be 5 percent contributors the business system would be saved. But a lot of wonderful and profound things would happen in all the communities of this country if that were the case."

David speaks to the fact that most companies give little to community causes:

I am embarrassed and ashamed as a businessman that 50 years later [since 1935] most companies give nothing. I think that is an indictment of the business leadership of this country. Then we complain when the government gets involved! We are not going to let people starve in a democracy like this and with the wealth of this country. We are not going to let people live in inadequate housing. The voters are not going to stand for it. But, if we in the private sector don't respond better than we've responded thus far, there's no choice.

We in business have done a lousy job of doing our share. Business has a lot of resources; we have a lot of products and services; we have a lot of management skills; and we have a fair amount of money. We can share that very efficiently with the community, if we aren't greedy, if we don't just sit back.

Long years back I decided that companies exist to serve people, that management and employees can't get very enthused about just growing for the sake of growing. That's not a very exciting mission. But, if in fact we can equate it with being of service to people, all of us inherently want to be of service to people, we do that by operating a business successfully.

We have something over 2,000 employees, so we equate what that means to them. We paid them $83 million last year. Why? Because a little company started in a service station in downtown Minneapolis 60 years ago and today provides jobs for 2,000 people around the world. It provides retirement benefits, holiday pay, health and accident programs and career opportunities. So that's why it's important to those people that we exist and grow.

In 1987 we did $239 million worth of business. We think we were of service to our customers. These are people who had problems handling fluids, or semifluids, or some material that had to be moved and applied somehow. We think we really helped those people, otherwise they wouldn't have bought our products.

We've got about 2,500 shareholders who have invested their money in the company and what do they want? Well, they'd like to have some dividends. They get a modest dividend from Graco from a percentage standpoint, so they want appreciation. These are real live human beings as well. Some of them are pension plans. A lot of our employees are shareholders and a lot of people in the community own Graco stock. We have a responsibility to them, not just to exist but to grow. And not just to grow but to grow profitably.

And finally, we have the various governments within which we exist. We paid about $12.5 million worth of taxes last year to different governments, primarily the U.S. government. If we hadn't paid that, somebody else would have had to. And so, we think that government wants us to be profitable and wants us to grow and go from a few employees to a lot of employees and go from lower earnings to higher earnings.

Therefore, it comes down to profits, which the public really doesn't understand. Profits are bad news to a lot of people, and I'm saying profits are good news for everybody! There isn't anybody who should be against profits because of all the wonderful people that we help when we operate profitably and successfully.

In short, David Koch sees the 5 percent corporate contribution system as a profit-sharing plan for the community. It is a way that a company can share its success with the communities that support it and with the citizens who continue to provide it with its franchise to operate because it is important to them that it is there and doing well.

* * *

Corporate concerns for the welfare of their communities, of course, can be expressed in a variety of ways. One way, perhaps more the norm for socially sensitive individual firms and entrepreneurs around the country, is how Miles Barber has proceeded.

AN UNCONVENTIONAL TRADITIONALIST

Miles Barber, Chairman and C.E.O.
The Allied Companies

Now surrounded by the material signs of obvious success in his attractive new office building in Santa Clara, California, Miles Barber seems to be enjoying it in real contrast to his puritan upbringing.

Born in 1939, the youngest of five children and the only one to go to college, Miles Barber grew up on a small orchard farm in Yakima, Washington. He graduated from Cascade College in Portland, Oregon, in 1961, then took three years of seminary training at Western Evangelical Seminary in Portland. "I had a desire to impact my world somehow in terms of making things better," he now recalls.

One of the things that became very clear to me about halfway through seminary was that my original vision regarding working in the church probably wasn't going to work. That is, I did not see my particular church or *the* church [in general] having the kind of impact in changing people's lives and making a difference at the velocity or the level that it was capable of doing. I found that very frustrating. Part of it was that there was as much pretension in the church as there was outside the church. For all the rhetoric, there were still the egos and the empires and the politics that got in the way of doing the job.

I'll share an experience that I had in seminary which I think was a turning point in my life. I was in the chapel one day, by myself, kneeling, praying and asking God to give me the gift of the Holy Spirit. As I was kneeling there and praying, I heard a voice just like you and I are talking here. It said, "Miles, you have got all you are going to get. There isn't any more." I opened my eyes and I looked around and there was no one there. It just got me. I stood up and I replayed that, "You've got all you are going to get. There isn't any more." It dawned on me, like a real revelation: There is no further gift. You have got it. Now do something with it. I walked out and I closed the door and I have never been back. At that point, I nearly left the seminary, but a dear friend who was one of my professors, Bob Bennett, convinced me that it would be a good thing to finish out my education, complete my thesis and then make some determinations. So, I did that.

Miles had married in 1958 while he was a junior in college. By the time he left seminary, he had two daughters. To feed his family while he was in school, he began selling insurance. Following seminary he returned to Cascade College for several years as associate dean of admissions, a job he truly loved. But the school ran out of funds in 1965 and was not able to meet its payrolls. He was soon back selling insurance in Portland. He then became an agency manager and opened a new office in Santa Clara in 1969. With 128 offices in the company nationwide, his office when opened ranked 128. Within 18 months it was ranked seventh. He had hired, trained and licensed 72 salespeople in that period who, in turn, produced those results.

After giving considerable thought to his future, Miles decided he still really wanted to make an impact in this world and to do so he would have to generate some wealth. He determined, however, that wealth was a product of performing some function particularly well. So he quit the company he was working for and started his own firm, Allied Associates, specializing in packaging employee group insurance programs for smaller insurance brokerage firms. Such firms had neither the staff nor the expertise to develop appropriate programs for their clients. Eventually Miles designed a new multiple-employer product and established a company to administer all aspects of this group insurance program. The organization did $300,000 in premiums in 1977. Ten years later its premiums were running about $32 million annually.

Along the way, Miles added a travel agency and a commercial real estate development and management operation to his group of companies. He was able to do so, he knows, because of the committed people who had joined him in growing his businesses. They, in turn, have helped Miles develop new ventures as opportunities presented themselves. The Allied Companies now also include a computer software company, a spinoff of an internal operation established to design software for the administration company. They have also become part owners of a liquor store-delicatessen-catering business and have purchased the Santa Clara weekly newspaper with circulation of 45,000.

Once sole owner of the Allied Companies, Miles has established an employee stock-ownership plan, funded by profit sharing. It now includes 35 employee stockholder participants.

True to his desire to positively affect the world, while building his business, Miles also volunteered his time to various established community causes. But several years ago, he decided to do something bigger. He began an annual golf tournament to raise funds to send underprivileged kids to summer camp. The first year 40 kids benefitted from the tournament. In 1988, 185 kids were able to attend after the tournament raised $20,000, having attracted 160 golfers. The Santa Clara YMCA has now joined the project supplying the counselors and the camping facilities. Miles now serves on the "Y" board of directors.

Since 1979 when he was president-elect of the Santa Clara Chamber of Commerce, Miles has been a friend, supporter and collaborator of California Assemblyman John Vasconcellos. Miles became treasurer of Californians Preventing Violence, a not-for-profit organization that Vasconcellos initiated to learn about the causes of violence in society. Among its many findings is the fact that 75 to 80 percent of all felons in California were abused as children. The organization has focused on educational and remedial programs in high-crime target areas attempting to determine how violence can be reduced.

The Allied Companies and another major local corporation have also been involved in an experimental program for the benefit of their employees and their employees' children. The program provides counseling in conjunction with the Bill Wilson Center in Santa Clara for teenagers and their families because of the home problems that can develop and become acute at this period of human growth. The center operates a home for runaways which is constantly full to overflowing.

Miles, the ex-evangelical, ex-seminarian, believes that life needs to be balanced between freedom and responsibility, between enjoying life and being concerned for others. "My focus is to personally represent what I perceive to be a balance, to bring a degree of sanity back to the application of faith in action in my little world. I think what I do is comparatively pretty small, meaningful only perhaps to me. But my focus will continue to be on the application of what I personally sense to be of value in my community."

SUMMARY

The foundations for the actions of Albert Wilson, David Koch and Miles Barber may well have been similar. All three grew up in situations where religious teaching was taken seriously. Likewise, all have been inspired over time to accept a stewardship role along with the responsibilities of managing their businesses.

Wilson mentioned a pastor who influenced his actions. For David Koch it was the experience of inheriting the privilege and responsibility of leadership from the hardworking founders of his company. The climate of community support engendered by other business leaders in the Twin Cities undoubtedly reinforced this predisposition. For Miles Barber the more recent influence of new relationships may have enhanced his earlier concerns for the welfare of society.

Traditional philanthropy and volunteerism, of course, are discretionary actions. There is no guarantee that a traditional virtuous leader who is head of a company will be succeeded over time by other virtuous leaders. In fact, Wilson, Koch and Barber have relied on establishing models of behavior rather than dictating how others should behave. Interest in philanthropy and volunteerism then is not "built into" the organizations they lead. For them personally, however, philanthropy and volunteerism are not discretionary.

On the one hand, the discretionary dimension could be seen as a fatal flaw in this traditional approach. On the other hand, when it occurs, it reflects a central strength and purpose of our democratic republic, a prime virtue: active and voluntary acknowledgment that our private welfare depends upon the adequacy of the general welfare of society.

Chapter 4

THE TRANSITIONALISTS

AS IT HAS been defined here, the traditional focus of virtuous business leadership has been on the needs of persons outside the business organization, that is, on the community or on society in general. Nothing stays the same for very long, however. New conditions constantly arise in human society that demand new responses.

The reality is that most virtuous business leaders could well be called Transitional because of the dynamic circumstances of our contemporary culture. For our purposes here, however, the term *Transitional* will cover those leaders who have specifically focused on emerging issues and have developed unusual responses, which have sometimes involved their organizations as well as themselves. Many new responses "take root" eventually and become part of a growing body of traditional responses. Others remain unique because of the peculiar circumstances of a particular place, time and need or because they involve ideas whose time has not yet arrived.

Examples of several of these Transitional variables are seen in the statesmanship profiles of Margaret Hansson, Dan May, Norbert Berg and Carol Green.

Margaret Hansson has discovered through her personal experience and by close involvement with efforts to encourage entrepreneurship that small business development can be personally satisfying and sometimes financially rewarding. She is also convinced that small business development is absolutely essential to the maintenance and growth of our national economy. She is particularly interested in products that improve the environment.

Dan May was the last C.E.O. of Republic Airlines before it was sold to Northwest Airlines. Republic Airlines avoided what most other major U.S. air carriers experienced while reducing costs in order to stay competitive in the wake of deregulation. How they did it required a major change in the practice of industrial relations. It is the Dan May story. Its lessons have apparently not yet been widely learned by management or labor in many industries.

Norbert Berg has been a key player in the development of the uniqueness of Control Data for almost three decades. As a "right hand" for William Norris, the company's founder and long-time chairman, Berg oversaw the institution of many progressive employment practices. These earned Control Data the reputation of being one of the best companies in the country to work for, especially for women.[7] But perhaps most significant were its multiple responses to employing the disadvantaged, responses which, to date, have not been widely replicated by other U.S. firms.

Carol Green echoes Margaret Hansson's business development experience. Along with Margaret, Carol provides a model for women to observe, and to understand what it takes to achieve personal business success, and in return, to contribute to society.

From this sample, as one might suppose, Transitional business leaders as a group have pursued a wide variety of issues. Each has been successful both in traditional business leadership and in modeling a broader concern for people and society. Their efforts have produced more than personal results, however. All have led the development of exemplary organizations.

ENTREPRENEURIAL BIRTHING

Margaret S. Hansson, President
M. S. Hansson, Inc.

If scenic vistas inspire the imagination and motivate actions in response, the cause of Margaret Hansson's achievements is clear. From her home, and place of business, a panorama of the east face of the Rockies is visible, stretching north and south of Boulder, Colorado, for as many miles as a clear day will permit.

But more than scenic vistas have produced Meg Hansson. Some lives are lived in almost predictable continuity with their past. Hers has been a life of some apparent discontinuity until all the parts are viewed at one time. Knowing her pattern of thinking helps you to understand how things have turned out the way they have for her.

Margaret Hansson is a liberal in the true sense that the word implied before its pejoration. She has always viewed things widely before deciding. Why else would this native of West Virginia have ended up in Colorado; or this graduate of a fashionable eastern prep school, whose mother went to Vassar, have gone to Antioch College; or this granddaughter of a Republican senator now find herself at periodic odds with the party of her ancestry?

Although she is not a particularly religious person, Margaret has a strong set of convictions about justice borne of her personal experiences. And not that she eschews tradition, but just because something is old or repetitive has not made it right in Meg Hansson's mind. Knowing these few facts about her then, it is no surprise that she has followed three discernible paths almost simultaneously, interweaving them throughout her adult life, at least to date.

Her "family path" perhaps predates the others. She is married to Pete Hansson, also an Antioch graduate. Three of their four children were born while they continued to live in Yellow Springs, Ohio, after graduation while Pete began his career in radio/television news and sports broadcasting in Springfield and Dayton. For some years then, even after they moved to Boulder, Margaret focused primarily on getting each of her children off to a promising start. All are now grown and are graduates of Antioch.

Once the children were all in school, Margaret started down a second path, following in her mother's footsteps as a business woman. Although she majored in literature at Antioch, thanks to the school's requirements to take a broad range of subjects she also had physics, geology, biology, and astronomy as well as philosophy and English, providing her a broad view of the world. Margaret soon began doing a little advertising layout work and producing mai-order catalogs for Gerry Cunningham. Also an Antioch graduate, Gerry and his wife had settled near Boulder where he had started a small business, Gerry Mountaineering, producing lightweight mountain hiking and camping equipment.

As her work for Gerry increased, she started a separate company which she called Gerry Designs. In addition to advertising work, she began to research new materials and product sources to fill out and upgrade the Gerry Mountaineering line. One of the items that emerged from their research and collaboration caused Margaret, with Gerry's help, to form Gerico, Inc., to produce back carriers for babies. This required the development of a market broader than one composed of mountaineering equipment enthusiasts. Along the way, they also started Highlander Publishing Company to inform people about mountaineering and mountaineering equipment and to promote that activity to an increasingly recreation-minded public.

Throughout the 1970s, Gerico, of which Margaret was president and C.E.O., grew rapidly, topping out at about 350 employees. "I wanted to own a company that was excellent for all the people that worked there and to incorporate the best ideas there were since they were mostly women. I wanted to be clear that they had the opportunity to share working hours and that we had places to care for their children. The other thing was to make an absolutely true blue product. I felt really good about our product. The corporate culture got very famous. We were well known for being a good place to work."

It was a piecework, needle-trades operation. Gerico management cooperated closely with its workers to make productivity improvements and yet protect employee earnings. Employees were consulted and often made the decisions regarding policies and practices that affected their lives at work.

When Gerico became a very successful and financially attractive company, late in the decade, Meg had the opportunity to merge Gerico with a large company and to diversify her investments. Because of her dedication to helping fledgling ventures get started, however, most of that diversification has not yet led to founding a "new Gerico."

An example is PureCycle, one of the companies she invested in when it was just being organized. The PureCycle concept seemed to be a winner. Take a tank full of household water, euphemistically called "black water" (yes, containing *everything*), run it through a process of five to eight steps, depending on which iteration of the device is being considered, and end up with very clean, pure water in a tank at the other end.

Unfortunately it turned out to be economically unfeasible to produce a system applicable for a single-family home. Although 40 units were eventually manufactured, a gigantic operating loss was generated in perfecting the product. The venture attracted many investors when it first began, most of whom have remained remarkably loyal to PureCycle. By the time things had really gone sour, Margaret had become chairman of the board of the company and remains so today.

She refers to the PureCycle experience as one where, holding on to a rope attached to a balloon, she didn't let go in time. Having not yet let go, she has had an interesting ride. Now under new technical and operational management, a reorganized PureCycle is successfully using its extremely important technology to produce water treatment products for a variety of commercial and industrial applications.

Anatel, a company making instrumentation for measuring contaminants in water, is another company Margaret has an interest in. A spinoff from PureCycle, it also appears to have considerable promise.

In the past several years, she has worked with a former Israeli Air Force pilot on perfecting and establishing the commercial feasibility of a new method of suturing that does away with the necessity of tying off. Also, two inventors of an interesting plastic material with many possible applications have sought her help in focusing on specific applications and securing financing to produce and market the product. Finally, Meg has designed a line of lightweight containers to hold oxygen or other gases or liquids in a novel way.

In short, through her company, Margaret acts as a sort of midwife for would-be entrepreneurships, helping them to focus their efforts, to do marketing studies, to develop business plans, to secure capital and, if necessary, to secure the people who will be required to launch the venture successfully. She is interested both in seeing new businesses get started and in investing in those of promise that require outside investment that can use her knowledge and expertise.

As the result of the success of Gerico, Margaret was appointed by President Carter to be one of the commissioners for the White

House Conference for Small Business in 1980. She credits that conference with initiating studies and actions which for the first time produced hard data regarding the importance of small business to the U.S. economy. For example, 80 percent of new jobs in this country are now generated by small businesses.

Since that conference, and as a result of it, a major increase in the sophistication of small business people has also occurred. This has provided them with the tools to engage in more effective lobbying to have their points of view understood in the state and national legislatures regarding such matters as the tax structure, the insurance crisis and tort reform.

Most individual states have now developed a governor's council on small business and assigned a continuing arm of the executive branch to work on small business development including annual conferences. In Colorado, Margaret is a member of the Governor's Small Business Council, which has been actively studying the impact of small business on the state and discovering the needs of small businesses. The purpose is to assist entrepreneurs in developing business plans, identifying appropriate counsel and securing financing.

Her own success and acumen have also brought Margaret other interesting opportunities. For two years she was a member of Northwestern Mutual Life Insurance Company's Policy Owners Examining Committee. The committee was established over 70 years ago to provide policyholders, who in mutual companies are the legal owners of the business, an opportunity to look into any matter they wished to regarding the management of the business. Margaret was also a member of the board of ISI, a mutual fund located in San Francisco, until it was purchased in 1986 by the Sigma Group in Wilmington, Delaware. She is now a board member of another mutual fund, the Midwest Group of Funds, with headquarters in Cincinnati. Beginning as a member of the board of the United Bank of Boulder, she later joined the board of its parent, a 43-bank holding company in Denver, and is a member of the board of Wright & McGill, makers of Eagle Claw fishing tackle.

Finally, the third path Margaret has followed during her adult years has been her concern for issues of justice and equity in society. When she was a child in West Virginia, her family continually employed black servants. She recalls reading the daily newspaper to their illiterate cook on many occasions: " 'Read me the paper, Bumsy,' she would say while she got our dinner." Another black servant, an attractive mother of two small boys, knew French and Latin: "I was taking them in the ninth grade and she made sure I was doing well in both." The fact that these talented people were treated differently, that they came and went by the back door, was not lost on Margaret.

Later, as residents of a major university community, Margaret and her family successively had four minority students living with them during their law school years. Two were black and two were Hispanic. Three of the four are now lawyers and the fourth works for Pacific Bell. Their presence in the Hansson household ensured that discussions of racial issues abounded during the years the children were growing up.

Margaret's other concern for social justice and equity has focused on the development of women as leaders in society. She has done this by participating on the Committee of 200, the National Association of Women Business Owners and the Colorado and International Women's Forums. These organizations meet regularly to provide a network of contacts and support for those seeking to increase the influence of women in leading our major institutions.

Although she might well have considered retiring now that she is in her 60s, Margaret Hansson reflects that she has been gathering information and developing her credentials up until now and is looking for an opportunity to give back some of what she has gained by supporting a cause of a more global nature. What that might be is not yet clear, but using her method of first scanning the horizon broadly, her choice will likely be forthcoming soon. She has been working on projects in Argentina and in China and is continuing to focus on PureCycle and its program for producing clean water, making potable water available around the world.

* * *

For another view of Transitional leadership, we now turn to an industry undergoing major changes.

SEEKING A BETTER WAY

Daniel F. May, Chairman (Retired)
Republic Airlines, Inc.

The average U.S. citizen, let alone the traveling public, knows that the airline industry has gone through some wild gyrations since deregulation. Initially deregulation spawned a host of new lower-cost carriers, pressuring the traditional standard-bearers of the industry into concessionary bargaining, downsizing and, in some cases, bankruptcy. Of late the result has been a round of mergers, acquisitions and consolidations. Republic Airlines of Minneapolis was no exception to these dynamics, although the sequence was somewhat turned about.

Republic was really the continuation of a regional carrier, North Central Airlines, after North Central merged with two other regional carriers, Southern Airlines and Hughes Air West, in 1980. In the case of Republic its financial troubles began after it became a small national carrier, subjecting it to competitive pressures on a broad front.

Between 1980 and 1983 it was increasingly questionable, particularly to outside observers, whether Republic would survive the competitive wars. Revenue enhancement programs and cost reductions were required in every area of the business, especially in the largest area of cost, employee compensation. But Republic did survive and its survival is a tribute particularly to one man, Dan May.

Dan May, a veteran then of 24 years of service with North Central Airlines, served as chief financial officer for 10 years prior to these acquisitions. In early 1980, Dan was elected executive vice-president of Republic and became president and C.E.O. late the same year. Dan credits his rise through the organization to the fact that his predecessor in each job he had was his boss, always the same person, Bud Sweet, from whom he learned much about the management of people.

Dan May grew up in Portland, Oregon, the somewhat rebellious son of strict evangelical Christians. His parents decided when he was 18 years old that he should go to a Bible school rather than to college. Although Dan had wanted to go to a university to study electrical engineering, his parents had their way. After a year there he found that it wasn't as bad as he thought it would be and he stayed another two.

Then at 21, he began a ministry in a small mission church in the mountains of Idaho. The rural community there was composed mostly of miners, sawmill workers and lumberjacks and their families. Dan learned to relate to the population and over the next five years provided for their spiritual needs. Securing some appropriate skills along the way, Dan did accounting on the side to earn enough to provide for himself and, now married, for his wife and small children.

As his children approached school age, Dan considered whether he should stay in the community, which had only a two-room school, or go elsewhere. He also wondered whether he should stay in the ministry or, because he liked accounting, get an education in business. In 1956, he opted for the latter and went to the Twin Cities to attend the University of Minnesota where he eventually received a degree in finance and accounting. After he passed the C.P.A. exam he went on to study by correspondence course to get a law degree as well.

During the time he was going to school, Dan had to work to maintain his family, so he became an accountant for North Central Airlines, fundamentally the same organization from which he would retire 30 years hence. The company was then only eight years old, employing around 500 or 600 people.

Dan credits his conservative background and his personal difficulties as a teenager and as a young adult—trying to determine who he was—as being formative of his subsequent perspective and actions as a manager and leader.

> I'm conservative in the way I think about things. I'm conservative politically. But also I think I have a liberal's heart for the disenfranchised. I'm on the board of Young Life. I'm very much interested in youth, in how we move our youth in the right direction through those difficult years. The liberal side of me says there's a place in this world for everybody. We ought to find the right places for people.

I've often seen in the organization where we had square people in round jobs. Rather than fire them, our job as management is to find the right spots for them, because everybody has certain abilities. The main thing is to get them in the right place.

Generally, I have felt that people ought to like where they work. They should like to come to work in the morning. If you have happy people, then they'll work harder for you. My style has always been one of leadership, getting people to work for me because they wanted to work for me, not stand behind them to kick them in the rear end to get the job done. That's been my main philosophy, a sort of participatory management style, seeking input, working as a team.

Although Dan thinks he might have appeared autocratic at times, he has always believed in communicating, letting people know why he made often unpopular decisions. "Credibility has always been very important to me. I've always tried to deal honestly with our people."

Back in the 1970s, representatives of the various unions representing Republic's (then North Central's) employees began meeting periodically to coordinate their actions within the company and to insure that they would avoid jurisdictional disputes. After a time they decided that they wanted to include a management representative as well. They asked the then-president, Bud Sweet, if this would be all right and specifically requested that Dan May be the management representative. "That worked out and I started working with the union leadership. We worked out our problems rather than going through the normal grievance procedure. That gave me a chance to build my credibility with the unions."

Having gone from the bottom to the top of the company certainly contributed to Dan's success in dealing with the employees. He knew many of them personally and they knew he was honest and fair with people.

I think dealing with people with integrity is a very important part of business ethics. A person has to believe internally that he must be honest. He has to have that kind of background. You don't make an honest person out of a dishonest person. In your mind you have to believe in fairness and honesty. I think being ethical also goes along with that. That's what ethics is, that you are a fair person.

Every time I dealt with a person, I tried to deal fairly whether the issue involved a termination or some other form of discipline. Quite often employees would come to me following some disciplinary action. I'd always listen to them. If I didn't think they'd been treated fairly, I would go back to our people and ask them to look at it again. I'd never reverse another person's decision without that person having a chance to think it through after talking to me. I built a reputation for fairness and I didn't always give them what they wanted.

Several other procedures built into the company served to enhance its positive relationship with its employees:

One is that we used to do psychological testing of our management group. We were always looking for "people" people. If you find people who like people, they tend to make good supervisors. We were interested in hiring supervisors that basically had people at heart. The other thing I did was to set up a program, a sort of participatory situation, where people who had ideas or questions or anything would have an open channel upward so they knew that we were concerned about them. It eventually became the Presidential Action Committee. I took people out of the union to run this. It had a hot line as well as a "write-in." We had Quality Circles in a lot of our cities and they would send their input in. We gave them almost immediate feedback. That worked very well for us.

Dan May's reputation and relationship with Republic's employees and its unions became invaluable in the darkest days of the company's history in the early 1980s. For its survival, it became imperative that the company secure pay reductions of 15 percent from all of its employees, union and nonunion. Unlike various other airlines, Republic was able to accomplish this without incurring serious acrimony or having hostile confrontations.

During those days, on a regular basis, often once or twice a week, May met with the union representatives and periodically with groups of employees to keep them closely advised as to what was happening to the company. "I would tell the people what was happening, what we needed, and when we needed it and often have the union leadership support me. Obviously the employees had to vote eventually and make the decision. We worked together through that period of difficulty to sell the people on the program, the concessions, to reduce costs to save the airline and not go the way that Braniff and Continental went." Braniff and Continental had both been forced to declare bankruptcy.

During the worst of Republic's troubles, Dan May was both chief operating officer and chief executive officer. It was difficult then to attract anyone to the organization to share the burden of corporate leadership and it was determined that there was no one in the company to do so.

Dan began a series of Wednesday morning breakfast meetings of the key officers of the company so they could keep each other informed of what was going on and act in mutual support. Several of the company officers had known Dan's background and also knew that he continued to be active in church affairs. They suggested that the Wednesday breakfast meetings include a time for devotions and a short word of prayer.

> They said that it might be helpful for us to do this. I said, "OK, let's do it. The only problem I have with it is that I don't want anyone to feel like I am forcing my beliefs on them. I believe what I believe because I think that it's true, but I am not trying to evangelize the world." They said they thought it could be meaningful. I said, "All right. Let's get together. Three or four of us will get together and see how it goes. If it works, we will ask others if they want to attend." So we met for a while—the four of us. Well, we didn't want the others to feel like we were a clique. So, I said, "Let's tell the other officers what we are doing, invite

them if they want to come, but make it very clear that it is not necessary. I'd like you to share with them what's been going on."

I introduced the subject and the other officers that were there talked about what we were doing. I told them that you were not expected to come just because you were management. However, if you are interested, you are welcome. As it turned out, most of them came. [To get things started they read and discussed one of Dr. Robert Schuller's books.]

Most of the people that attended, I would say probably all of them to some degree, were church people. A lot of them were Catholics. That was no problem, coming from various church backgrounds. They all really participated. I think together we learned a lot about how you live your life. We'd talk about that and how we should treat our people in that situation [during Republic's troubles]. We always wanted to treat our people in a fair and ethical way. And obviously, scriptures have a lot to say about that. And it made us think about how you give people hope.

That was part of what we were trying to do. If management is down, the rest of the company is going to be down. Those Wednesday morning meetings really helped to keep our spirits up. The thing that we were concerned about was that we didn't want the employees to feel that we were just getting together to try to pray ourselves out of trouble. When you do things like that, it is often taken wrong. We tried to play it down. I would never talk about it to the press because I didn't want our employees to feel that we were trying to pray our way out of trouble instead of trying to manage our way out of trouble.

A lot of my executives [who participated] at that time would come to me and say, "That was really important to me and I learned a lot." It was a real time of sharing.

By the spring of 1984, Republic had secured most of the concessions it needed and the future was beginning to look brighter. The company was then able to attract Steve Wolfe to the organization as executive vice-president. A short time later he was made president and chief operating officer. Dan May then became C.E.O. and chairman of the board. Steve had grown up in management at American Airlines, had then been at Pan Am and later was president of Continental prior to its bankruptcy. Currently, he is C.E.O. of UAL, Inc., the parent of United Airlines.

Over the next two years, however, it became increasingly clear to Republic management that the airline industry was in a period of consolidation and that only a few national carriers would remain. Smaller carriers were being acquired by or merged with other carriers at a rapid rate. The Republic board decided that picking its purchaser would insure that a greater number of its employees would retain employment. For reasons of headquarters location and route synergy, Republic picked Northwest Airlines.

By 1986, its recovery completed, Republic was well on its way to making $150 million profit for the year, probably twice what Northwest would make in the same period. But Northwest's total assets were many times greater than Republic's and the three-year contractual period of pay concessions made by Republic employees was quickly coming to an end.

Northwest had been considering several airlines for acquisition, Republic among them. Republic had a strong domestic system; it served many of the major cities that Northwest served; and the chairman and president of Republic, May and Wolfe, were willing to step aside. Republic and Northwest both had their main base of operations and maintenance facilities in Minneapolis.

Dan May believed that most of Republic's rank and file personnel would be absorbed by Northwest. In order to maintain and operate the Republic fleet, all the flying crews, flight attendants and mechanics would be needed. Cabin cleaners, ground servicing crews and passenger service agents could be more adversely affected, however, especially in cities where both carriers had operated beforehand. And, of course, fewer middle managers and department heads would be needed.

The income lost owing to concessions made by Republic personnel was virtually recovered through the combination of profit sharing and the purchase by Northwest of preferred stock which Republic had given to its employees.

If there was a negative side to the acquisition, it was the difference in management style between the two carriers. According to Dan May, "My philosophy, as well as my predecessor's, was that we are in a service business. The problem with the confrontative type approach is that the unions always keep their people stirred up. They are always mad at management. Unions do that fairly effectively. How can you run a good service business when your people are always mad at you? So our plan was that if we could keep our unions happy, we could keep our people happy, and they were going to keep our customers happy. That is why we always tried to have good labor relations."

During the years that Dan May was advancing through the ranks at North Central, and then Republic Airlines, he continued serving the church and church-related organizations. He has also been involved with the Minnesota Association of Commerce and Industry and the YMCA; he has been on the board of Minnesota Public Radio, nationally known for the Garrison Keillor show, "Prairie Home Companion"; and he serves on the boards of five corporations.

Like David Koch of Graco, Dan May has engaged in business-church dialogues, primarily coordinated by Wilfred Bockelman, a Twin Cities clergyman.

Quite often the church is critical of business and our ethics, of how we treat people. Do we have a concern for the poor? Probably as business people we often misjudge the church, too. We need to have more dialogue. A lot of pastors are out of touch with reality in what's going on in business. Having been a pastor, I see both sides of it. I can see where pastors are coming from, but I don't think they understand where we come from a lot of times. It is easy to be critical of us. But people need to have jobs, and I am a true believer in the free enterprise system. This system has given us the jobs and wealth that we have in this country. Many church leaders would love to tear it all apart. There needs to be more dialogue in this area. I am sure they feel that we don't understand them either, but I know they don't understand us.

* * *

Quite literally just down the street and across the expressway from Dan May's old office, another Twin Cities example of exemplary leadership has been in action for the past three decades. We now turn to the story of Norbert Berg and his work at Control Data.

THE OTHER SIDE OF THE TWIN CITIES

Norbert R. Berg, Vice-Chairman of the Board
Control Data Corporation

Ironically, with over $3.5 billion in sales, 1985 was in many ways the lowest point in Control Data's history. In that year its losses, following several decades of rapid, profitable growth, exceeded $500 million.

In early 1986, Control Data's founder and C.E.O. for 28 years, William C. Norris, turned the reins over to the company's president, Robert M. Price, who became chairman and chief executive officer. Norbert Berg, who had been deputy chairman under Norris, retained that position when Robert Price took over.

Norb Berg was born in 1932 in Edgar, Wisconsin, where his parents raised their eight children. The values of a small town "where everybody knew everybody and everybody cared about everybody and their problems" formed the foundation stones of his youth and subsequent career. The Franciscan nuns at the local parochial grade school added their mortar to firm up these footings.

He left Edgar during his teens to attend a boys' prep school, St. John's, in nearby Minnesota, staying on in this Benedictine community for his college years as well. He received a bachelor's degree with a major in business in 1955. His college years were interrupted by the conflict in Korea, where he served as an infantry officer. Returning home, he received a master's in industrial relations from the University of Minnesota in 1957.

Upon graduation, Norb married Marilyn, a University of Minnesota journalism graduate. During the next two years they lived in New Jersey, where the first of their four sons was born. Berg reflected that his wife provided a secure and supportive home for himself and for their family over the years, which was especially important during the early years when Norb traveled extensively and there were three boys in diapers simultaneously.

In 1959, the Bergs, expecting their second child, returned to Minnesota where Norb joined Control Data Corporation (CDC) as a personnel supervisor. The company was then two years old and employed 180 people.

> I came in and started doing their recruiting and setting up some of their human resource practices. After a couple of years, I became the director of administration for the corporation. I set up virtually all the administrative functions of the company except accounting and finance. I grew up with these functions. Eventually it got to the point where I was assistant to the chief executive in addition to doing the overall administration. In 1977, I was appointed to the board of directors and in 1980 became deputy chairman of the board. It was about that time I began to pass various administrative responsibilities on to other executives so I could be free to become an almost full-time trouble shooter for the company. We found it worked out very well with a person to do that. My priority of the day, here, every day, has been the crisis of the day. I have been a part of every major organizational decision, strategic decision, for the past 27 years.

Because of his close association with Bill Norris, through the years Norb was able to influence what CDC did in developing its internal culture. He was also involved in determining how the company would respond to the needs of society with which it was confronted. More often those needs were sought out as opportunities both to serve society and to extend its computer business.

Many critics of the company have claimed that it was Control Data's "social programs" that contributed substantially to its recent financial problems. Norb denies this allegation, however, citing that the costs of the social responses of Control Data have been grossly overestimated and have in fact helped attract many very able personnel to the organization and opened opportunities for new business as well.

Unlike its neighboring companies in the Twin Cities area, Control Data is neither a 5 percent nor a 2 percent company. As Robert Price put it in his "Letter from the Chairman" in the 1985 annual report in answer to the question "What is going to happen to Control Data's social programs?":

> One of Control Data's commitments is to apply its technologies where they can profitably and productively address unmet needs. Some, but certainly not all, unmet needs represent major opportunities for the Corporation's technology and products. As with all our businesses, we discriminate as to time frame, the level of investment required and the degree of potential among these opportunities. Most important, we operate business ventures not "social programs." We will be selective in those businesses that we pursue.

Since 1985, Control Data's financial fortunes have improved through a restructuring of its operations and investments. In 1986 the loss was cut approximately in half and in 1987 the company showed a profit of over $19 million.

Control Data has historically been known as a socially responsive organization. But it truly has approached the subject uniquely both inside and outside the organization. For example, Berg stated, "Internally, we were the first major corporation in the United States to go to flexible hours. Flexible hours allow an employee to set his or her own hours within a standard core hour period with supervisor approval. I heard about flexible hours in Germany and said, 'It's a good idea. Let's do it.' It's turned out to be a godsend for a lot of our parents. You could go to the dentist or doctor and didn't have to worry about coming in late. It has worked very well for us."

Additionally, Control Data started the first employee assistance program (EAP) in this country. Initiated by Berg, who was convinced many years ago that employees have a large number of personal and family problems that can negatively affect their work performance, Control Data sells the EAP it has developed to other companies as well. In addition to CDC's employees, 250,000 employees from 155 firms are currently covered by the CDC program.

This program generates more than $3 million in annual revenue for the company. "About half of the cases are employment or job related and the other half are personal. The numbers are staggering. We've had our EAP in place for a dozen years. The number of people we have touched is a beautiful thing. Today it is hard to realize why some companies don't have one."

An important part of the employee assistance program is the peer review system, which is the last step in the grievance process. It is not visible to the public, but the peer review system is important to setting the cultural tone of the company. This system provides for a panel of two of an employee's peer group and one manager chosen by random selection to serve as the final arbiters of a grievance the employee may have with the company.

The company has no unions representing any of its over 40,000 employees. Berg hastens to add, "We have always had the posture that we were pro-employee, not antiunion, and never will be antiunion."

In the area of employee health and fitness, Control Data has also been a pioneer. It has dispensed with sick leave. In its place they have put "well days." Those that are not used become vacation days. Additionally, their "Stay Well Program" is sold to other companies. It includes classes on nutrition, diet, life-style development and fitness and no-smoking and weight control clinics.

Another simple but creative Berg idea has been the 900-plus garden patches that employees have cultivated on an undeveloped piece of property visible from Berg's corporate tower window. The "Golden Hoe" award has become a highly prized annual recognition of champion gardeners.

In the late 1960s, with riots occurring in cities across the country, companies were urged to get involved in the problems of race and poverty. "We sat down at that time, Bill Norris and I, and we sent some people out in the streets. They came back and said people want jobs. They don't want more training programs. We had tried. We had run a bus from the inner city out to our suburban plants that ring the city along the beltline. We tried to bring inner-city residents out to our plants without much success. We had the Urban League and the NAACP out, over the years, in order to try to get more minority employees."

Seeking a more successful route, CDC decided to open a plant on the north side of Minneapolis, in the heart of the inner city. During those days of overt hostility toward almost any actions taken by white-run organizations, the company proceeded with this plan despite a series of confrontations. "But we did it and we learned a lot of things in trying to do it right."

They had to throw out their traditional employment application forms, which scared people off. When absenteeism, tardiness and turnover were seriously hampering their efforts, they began an employee counseling process that led to the later development of the corporate employee assistance program. "We started out doing financial counseling with people who were getting garnished all the time. Landlord problems. We got our law firm to put a lawyer in there one day a week just to work on landlord and similar problems. We did chemical dependency counseling because we had alcohol and drug abuse problems. I kept sending some of our young managers down there in the late 1960s and early 1970s as resources, just to solve problems. One of them is now a vice-president. And, it worked."

From day one, the company's approach was to build a new plant in the ghetto and put a product in it, a computer controller, that was critical to its business so that the community would recognize that it wasn't an experiment, that they were there to stay. "Pretty soon we had a stable work force. We also took the attitude that our productivity and quality standards would be the same there as anywhere else. This was not to be looked upon as charity. It was a very successful operation."

Control Data also joined with other firms to open a day care center near the plant in order to minimize absenteeism and turnover. It was programmed to provide more than custodial care and it was large enough for other companies to use as well. In 1986 it was turned over to Catholic Charities to operate for the community.

Norb recalls that in those days of racial unrest the need for jobs in the inner city was clear. As the company was growing very rapidly, jobs were one thing Control Data could readily supply. In 1969, Control Data opened a second ghetto plant, this time in Washington, D.C. By 1986 it still had a 96 percent black work force and the plant was sold to a black entrepreneur.

CDC's third inner-city plant was built in St. Paul to employ persons unable to work a full workday. It was initially planned that the plant would assemble wiring harnesses for computers. The plant started in an old bowling alley. By the time the new building was ready, changes in the high-tech business situation made production of the harness unnecessary. Fifty positions had been promised the community and hundreds of people had applied to work part-time in these positions. Berg held a staff meeting regarding the dilemma and one of his young managers suggested that they use the facility and personnel as a central location to bind, stitch, punch, drill, staple and collate the manuals and customer publications the company produced. It continues to do so today for CDC and 40 to 50 outside customers.

When the building was completed nearly 18 years ago, it was the first new building in that area of St. Paul in the last 75 years. It now employs several hundred people, many of them minority mothers who can only work the four or five hours while their children are in school. Black high school and trade school students, only able to work a few hours after school each day, are also employed there as are a large number of Southeast Asians in addition to some mentally retarded personnel. "It's not earth-shaking work, but it's not minimum wage work either. It has to run as a business. Their charges to the rest of the company get challenged regularly versus what it would cost if we were to do it outside."

During that same period, Bill Norris suggested to Norb that they should try a plant in Appalachia. A small team of managers was sent out to identify an appropriate location. They were steered in the direction of a community that looked like a "can't lose" situation, so they turned it down, asking to see a town that was really impoverished. They ended up locating in east central Kentucky, in Campton. The town is in the center of the second poorest county in the United States, home to less than 500 people. Moving into a new building being built by the local Chevrolet dealer, Control Data employed several hundred people there until 1985 when they sold the operation to one of CDC's former executives. The plant was an unquestionable success. The employees beat the work standards very quickly and not even snowstorms, which made driving impossible, kept them from work.

In the early 1970s, Governor Wendell Anderson of Minnesota asked Berg to chair a committee to select an ombudsperson for the state of Minnesota for people in the corrections system, both inmates and staff. The person selected soon ran into some difficulties coping with the volume and intensity of the work. His dilemma was identified by J. P. Morgan, a lifer, who was a member of the ombudsperson selection committee. Norb found a CDC executive who was willing and made him available to spend six months helping set up the ombudsperson program. In this way, Control Data began to learn about the prison systems in America.

The company was also asked by the commissioner of corrections to review the prison industries program, which was then in some disarray. A group of six manufacturing executives from the company performed a systems audit on the prison industry operations just as they would for one of CDC's plants. At the end of the study they recommended a number of changes, including the establishment of a steering group, a kind of board of directors to oversee the industry's operations, and a general overseer to work full-time with prison officials for a year or two to get everything running effectively. The company supplied the overseer for two years from its executive group and several company managers became members of the steering group. In so doing, the company's knowledge of prison operations and needs accumulated rapidly.

J. P. Morgan, the lifer previously mentioned, enlisted Berg's help in establishing an in-prison program where inmates, after doing their normal daily work, could take college courses and get degrees from the University of Minnesota. Control Data helped initially by supplying funds and computer terminals to get the program going. By 1986, the program was largely self-supporting. The inmates had developed a telemarketing business, doing around $30,000 a month in revenues, the profits from which are used to pay for inmate tuition, books and so on. The last word was that J. P. and the board he established to run the program were working on an extension process, beyond the walls, a kind of halfway mechanism for those ex-inmates who hadn't finished their degrees while in prison. The program enables them to continue to do the telemarketing work and to go back inside the walls after hours to complete their college classwork.

As the result of all this experience, CDC has marketed computer terminals in 80 prisons throughout the United States where, among other things, they are delivering basic skills remediation course work and employment preparation courses. The content of the courses came out of Control Data's experience in running inner-city plants.

Speaking of Bill Norris, Berg says, "He's like a Johnny Appleseed on the jobs subject. Before Hubert Humphrey died Norris used to see him and talk about jobs and job creation. If you look at the problems in society that have to be addressed, many of them stem from unemployment. Alcoholism, drug abuse, wife beating, child abuse, suicide, health problems and a host of crimes are all statistically related to unemployment."

From his involvement with the White House Task Force on Small Business, Norris learned that 80 percent of the new jobs created in the United States come from businesses of under 20 employees and 90 percent from businesses of under 100 employees. Using this and other information, Bill Norris decided CDC should get involved in small business development through a job creation network. The network has attracted would-be entrepreneurs throughout the United States and helped them develop business plans, secure capital and supportive services and technical assistance from volunteers employed by companies in their areas. Through this effort, for those involved in it, the usual statistics—an 80 percent failure rate during the first five years—have been reversed, to a 20 percent failure rate over that period of time.

CDC has also been involved in using its computers and other technical services to help provide resources for welfare recipients in California, to keep track of the educational progress of the children of migrant workers, who move frequently and must constantly be re-enrolled in new schools, and to match up and reunite Southeast Asian refugee families who have been split up with members being sent to different camps. In another case, homebound partially able persons are taught via computer by a teacher who is an inmate in Stillwater (Minnesota) Prison. Some of these learning applications have turned into longer-term profitable ventures for the company. Others have not.

Personally, Berg was responsible for establishing an organization in the Twin Cities called "Twelve Baskets." It stemmed from a television show he saw several years ago about a woman in New York City who collected surplus food and took it to soup kitchens to feed the poor and homeless. With a grant of $25,000 from Control Data, Berg organized an operation that collects food left over at restaurants, at banquets, from caterers and from other large gatherings and distributes the food to shelters and food kitchens for the needy. Today, run by volunteers, the operation collects several thousand pounds of food per day for this purpose. The food is put into containers designed for this specific purpose, approved by the state health department. Those who donate the food receive a tax credit for the cost of their donation.

Besides developing new business opportunities for the company, Berg truly believes that Control Data's approach to meeting the needs of society has attracted a very high caliber of personnel to the company. "We know that we have one of the most successful college recruiting programs in the United States. We know that by virtue of the fact that everyone pays roughly the same. We know what our acceptance rates are. We also know that kids flock to sign up with our interviewers. They tell us that they feel good working here. They accept our offers."

Asked specifically about the sources of his personal social sensitivity, Norb replied, "Obviously the Benedictine priests and the Franciscan nuns have influenced my value system." But his parents, he recalls, also contributed a strong sense of sharing, of taking care of people less fortunate, of being your brother's keeper. Berg is a little impatient with some people who have a "when did you quit beating your wife" attitude about business people and who, he feels, have done less to meet society's needs than businesses have in many cases. "I don't find that Catholics, Protestants, Jews or Moslem people have a corner on sharing. I find that some people have a dissatisfaction with the status quo, an inability to just sit back and say there's nothing that can be done about it. I'm always amazed that a lot of people will help if it gets organized. 'Twelve Baskets' is an example. A lot of these things are really easy to do, they just are. It is providing an environment in which people can take a risk and share their ideas. A critical part of the environment is what you reward and what you recognize."

On June 30, 1988, Norb Berg retired from active daily service to Control Data to pursue a variety of personal interests. He remained on CDC's board and as its vice-chairman. In addition he chairs the Capital Fund for St. Paul Seminary and the National Board of Pheasants Forever. He also is a member of the Minnesota Racing Commission and is on the boards of the *Catholic Digest*, the First Trust National Association, and the H. B. Fuller Company.

Upon Berg's retirement, Robert M. Price, Control Data's C.E.O., stated this about him:

> In the areas of human resources and public affairs, he earned a national reputation as a pioneer in creative, caring and progressive programs. Many of the new human resource practices that are now accepted as standards through the United States and in some cases, throughout the world, were started at Control Data under his direction. The list of the programs begun under his direction [is] virtually endless and provide[s] the basis for Control Data being cited in the book [*The 100 Best Companies to Work for in America*] and Control Data's recognition as an opportune workplace for minorities and females.

Bill Norris also reflected on Berg's years of service to the company:

> Norb Berg was uniquely vital to the building and growth of Control Data. Among the many important contributions that he has made perhaps the most important was his ability to resolve and reconcile differences among a large and diverse management group. That ability came about because of his creativity, dedication, integrity, and caring for others. A real tribute to his effectiveness in that role is the fact that this contribution was largely unseen and he sought very little credit for it.

53

BREAKING DOWN BARRIERS

Carol B. Green, President
Carwell Franchise Corporation

Another member of the Committee of 200 and of the National Association of Women Business Owners, Carol Green will tell you there were three factors that influenced her life so profoundly that she credits them with causing her achievements to date.

One was attending public schools in New York City, where she grew up. Quite fortunately while she was in high school, an experimental class was established for students with I.Q.'s above 132. "In evaluating it, I could say that there were pluses and there were negatives. But in my own personal life, it was filled with positives because I was able to understand that I was intelligent, that being intelligent meant something." The program permitted her to take physics and trigonometry and calculus and other subjects not readily available in the usual high school program. It also got her thinking about attending college, which introduces the second factor, namely her father.

Although a college graduate and owner of a small business, Carol's father did not believe girls should go to college. They were supposed to get married and have children and rely upon their husbands. Carol prevailed, however, and is not the first person to have been repeatedly challenged to achieve continually greater things in order to prove a parent wrong.

Her father's influence prevailed for a time, however, as she began college. Carol wanted to major in economics, but he talked her out of it. Initially she majored in education at Queens College. A two-year contemporary civilization course, heavy on history and philosophy, opened up a whole new world to Carol. "I was able to broaden my horizons and think about the things I should value and what is important and what is not important."

She soon married, however, and was the mother of two children by age 22. Still living in New York at that time, having left Queens College, she attended classes at Hunter College two nights a week. This required taking a bus and three subway trains in order to get there.

When her husband took a new job, the family moved to Newark, Delaware, and Carol started attending classes at the University of Delaware. It was there that the third major factor influencing her ultimate success was introduced. She began to volunteer, first as a reader in a preschool center. "It was extremely rewarding in every way that you can measure, because not only did I get an opportunity to get directly involved, I eventually went on the board of directors. Here I was, basically an insecure person, without any social skills and I got a lot of warm fuzzies, a lot of positive feedback. So volunteerism helped me grow, helped me become more articulate, more visible, besides rewarding me for feeling very good about things that I was involved in."

Her second volunteer effort involved joining Weight Watchers. There she helped people to lose weight after she had lost a large amount of weight herself. She soon became a group leader. "It was the first time in my life I was actually influential over the outcome where I could motivate, educate and inspire people to make changes in their lives." She amazed herself in her ability to speak in front of large groups. Her classes were very popular, with people sitting on the floor to listen when all the seats were taken.

She had two classes. One was composed of faculty and staff members at the University of Delaware. The second was held in a union hall in Elsmere, a blue-collar suburb of Wilmington.

> I had been fat all my life so I had always looked at myself as an ugly duckling and now my own self-esteem and my self-confidence were growing. I continued to get lots of positive feedback.
>
> What I am saying is that part of my volunteerism has helped me to grow as a person, that it was not all self-sacrifice. In fact, I am convinced that the more I have given, the more I have gotten in my life; that I have been rewarded far more than what I have given. I have had an extraordinary life as the result of the giving in my life.

Eventually, the family moved to Denver, where Carol had secured the Weight Watchers franchise for an area which included all or part of four states: Colorado, Wyoming, western Nebraska and western South Dakota. Over the period of the next decade, essentially the 1970s, she developed it into one of the largest Weight Watchers franchises in the country, with approximately 100 outlets in the four-state area.

In 1975, in her living room, Carol Green, along with several others, initiated the Women's Bank of Denver. Opening in 1978, it was in the black within two weeks and recouped start-up expenses within 10 months. Prior to founding the bank she had observed at close hand how slowly institutions change so she felt it was time to do something about it. A bank credit-card operation had previously turned her down for a credit card without her husband's signature even though she was president of her own company at the time and was earning a six-figure income.

Also in Denver, working under the auspices of a professor at the University of Denver, while running a business, Carol was able to get her college degree through the University-without-Walls program of Loretto Heights College. It took her 21 years overall because so much of it was on a part-time basis. And her final major was economics!

Several years ago, when the corporate unit of Weight Watchers became a division of a major company, the operation was changed somewhat in its relationship to its franchisees. Carol decided the time had arrived for her to do something else. She developed a plan to establish a new kind of organization, a business consulting firm specializing in franchising, and sold the Weight Watchers franchise. The new firm was called Franchise Services of America, Inc. "We took a company with a concept through all the franchising stages in order for it to become a full-fledged franchisor. Then we had a wholly owned subsidiary called Franchise Network U.S.A. It did nothing but market franchises."

Unlike traditional franchise marketing where a franchisor markets its own franchises, Carol's organization had 12 offices in major cities, primarily in the western and southwestern states, with each office representing about 40 companies interested in establishing franchises.

We ran it like an executive search firm. Prospective franchisees came in to find an appropriate business, one that they could afford, a business that they had the skills for, a business that they would enjoy and one that was available in the market. Some markets were oversaturated with certain kinds of businesses so we wouldn't recommend opening it in that particular market. We went through this procedure. It's like selling a house. The sellers pay you for it but you have to find a house to please the buyer. The franchisor paid us a fee for finding a suitable franchisee.

Franchise Services represented companies that covered a whole range of products and services including hotels and motels, fast food restaurants, specialty restaurants, delicatessens, transmission shops, lube shops, automotive detailing, carpet cleaning and dyeing, vinyl repair, weight control, maid services, a retail pet center and shipping and packaging stores.

"Franchise brokering has had a terrible reputation. We felt idealistically that we could come in and establish a credible company, that we could set ourselves apart from the pack." Each of Franchise Services' 12 area offices was a franchise itself.

Carol owned a little less than 50 percent of Franchise Services, a public corporation with approximately 400 stockholders. In addition, all of her employees owned stock in the company.

Recently Franchise Network U.S.A. was sold to a group of franchisees, and Carol was negotiating the sale of her interest in Franchise Services in order to accept a new challenge, to become president of Carwell Franchise Corporation. This new franchisor of auto rustproofing and auto fabric protection centers has a successful product line developed by a Canadian firm and will be located in the Denver area.

Carol obviously believes in franchising. She also continues to believe in volunteerism. She has worked for the local Boy Scouts organization for many years, chairing the Explorer Program, composed of approximately 50 percent boys and 50 percent girls, for three years. She sees it as a great opportunity for young people to learn what particular vocations are like before making choices about careers themselves. Carol has also been a member of the local executive board of the Boy Scouts in Denver and the only woman serving on the regional board. She recently established an endowment fund for the Explorer Program.

Carol has been involved in other aspects of education as a college board member, a position which she regrettably was forced to give up because of too many obligations. For two years she was on an area advisory board on career education as well.

A staunch believer in the free enterprise system, Carol has been on the board of the Denver Area Chamber of Commerce for four years and has been vice-chairman of the Colorado Association of Commerce and Industry. As a member of the Colorado Small Business Council she has chaired the Committee on Women and Minorities in Business. A delegate to and national committee member of the most recent White House Conference on Small Business, she chaired the Colorado delegation on tort reform and product liability.

Although she has no personal political ambitions, she has actively campaigned for several candidates. At this point, she believes some area of public service might appeal to her someday, perhaps appointment to a senior position in the Department of Commerce. She is afraid that as a nation we have made some very big mistakes. She believes that giving opportunity to the people on the periphery is essential as a matter of public policy. "Look at communism. You set up opportunities for communism and radicalism when you exclude people from power." Carol believes in a pluralistic society. She's unhappy with the wave of fundamentalism that she sees in America today. "I believe in pluralism. I think it has been very healthy for the United States."

Carol was raised in a nonobservant Jewish family. They tried very hard to assimilate into American society. "I was brought up with ethical values. My father was adamant about truth, about honesty, about dealing with people. A handshake was your word. I am still that way."

A blind uncle who refused to accept his blindness as a handicap and who achieved a variety of successes in his life has been an inspiration to Carol. She believes that accepting personal responsibility for herself and what has happened to her in life has been important to her success.

When I sorted that out, the power was in my own

hands. I could not pass the buck. I was not overweight because I was overfed by my parents. I was then overweight because I was overfeeding myself. That gave me power. Everyone is responsible for their own feelings, actions and behavior.

It also has given me power as a boss, because in business a lot of women have fallen down because they have taken a maternal position in terms of their employees. And maybe some men, too. I take the position that I work with adults and I expect people to act like adults and be responsible for themselves. I introduced a participatory business environment long before it was the "in" thing to do. Instinctively, I believe in allowing people to work without someone standing over their shoulder, to be responsible for their quality and the timeliness of the work.

It is very important to Carol that people know that she has "come up through the ranks" to get where she has gotten. She wants others to know, especially women, that they can do it as well. "There is great opportunity. It is there. You have to risk. It is not luck. You have to be willing to take risks, make choices and do things. And you may get hurt. When I started the Women's Bank, I was willing to take the risk because I could afford the risk more than other people. I would be hurt less. It turned out to be very rewarding."

As the result of her work, her achievements and her risk taking, she has been asked to participate in community groups with other successful risk takers. "What I've found out is that really successful people are giving people. They are not people who take. You read about the scandals; they are out there. But, for the most part, I think the true community leaders are people who give generously of themselves and reap the benefits of a richer, better life."

Contributing time to the community through various organizations is no extra burden for Carol.

It makes me feel good. I feel like I am doing something. I am very thankful to live in this country. I am very thankful for the life I live, for the opportunities that I have had. It hasn't been easy to go to four colleges and graduate. But the sense of satisfaction, of accomplishment, is great.

I am not a person to dwell on the negative. I dwell on the positive. I think that sometimes in life things go wrong, but they can have positive outcomes. I am not a person to point out negatives. I have to try to reconstruct them into positives and see what I can gain. I've tried to teach that to my children. Out of adversity, strong people emerge. If you don't have any friction and difficulty, there is no way to test and grow and stretch.

My philosophy is that everybody has difficulty in their lives and successful people handle it differently than unsuccessful people. Some people spend all of their lives blaming those things for their failure and other people use those things and suffer the pain. When I switched from housewife to businesswoman ahead of the movement, I suffered great pain because I thought my friends were rejecting me. What was happening was that I was a different person and they didn't know who I was and I didn't quite know who I was. So, sometimes understanding what's happening takes time and you can only gain an understanding looking back. I try, when I am going through something difficult, to be philosophical about it and realize that is part of my growth, my becoming stronger, becoming healthier, becoming better. That all has to do with what you are looking for. What is the philosophy that makes those of us go, that makes those of us succeed and do what we do? It's how I get through adversity and I do get through adversity. I am very strong. I am extremely strong, but it didn't start that way. I had to grow to become strong. I am self-actualized even when I am swimming upstream. I have confidence in myself. On that note, you have my inner self. You know more about me than most people know about me.

SUMMARY

When reviewing the motivational influences behind the actions of these Transitional leaders, a wide variety is evident compared to the Traditionalists. A liberal-arts-and-sciences education and becoming a successful woman entrepreneur, combined with her predisposition to be a caring and nurturing person, seem to have energized Margaret Hansson through a succession of experiences. Her linking of social purpose and business objectives is evident in virtually everything she has undertaken.

Dan May developed a sense of responsibility for others early in life because of family and religious influences. He credits Bud Sweet with helping him ground those principles in the practical dimensions of managing the people of Republic Airlines. When times got tough, the trust the employees had in his leadership generated the cooperation necessary to save the company and thousands of jobs.

The context of his upbringing including the ethics of his family, the influence of religious instruction and the supportive community from which he came produced an unusual level of social consciousness in Norbert Berg. It is little wonder that he would be attracted to work for William Norris when Control Data was barely a company. The synergy developed in their relationship undoubtedly accounts for much of what ensued.

Carol Green's motivation seems to have come from a combination of a bright mind and high energy subjected to negative reinforcement but just enough opportunity at the right time for her to break out and show what she could accomplish. Observation of her blind uncle who refused to let himself be handicapped undoubtedly had its early effects as well. In recent years, the supportive relationship of other successful business leaders, many of them women, should not be underestimated.

Upon reflection, it is clear from these profiles that these people have accomplished what they have accomplished on their own. It is also clear that they couldn't have done so without the inspiration of many other persons and a supportive sociopolitical context.

The great amount of freedom our unique American system provides is easy to take for granted. Transitional business statespersons have used that freedom to be creative in identifying and responding to a variety of human needs. Their efforts have benefitted society as well as their organizations and themselves. Absent that freedom, private citizens and organizations could not respond to the needs of society. This is the often hidden side of the coin of free enterprise. Though frequently touted as being a system that only serves the capitalist, without identifying and serving human needs businesses cannot sustain themselves.

The virtuous dimension, of course, comes into play when perceptive and socially alert business leaders identify human/social needs that other business leaders ignore or judge to be inappropriate subjects for their attention. Virtue comes into play when, as Carol Green would say, problems are seen as opportunities. Such perception and creativity, often abandoning outmoded assumptions and applying new principles, are also characteristic of the virtuous leaders we next encounter.

Chapter 5

TRANSFORMING THE AMERICAN ENTERPRISE: A HUMANIST, A CHEERLEADER AND A REGENERATOR

CONCERN FOR THE human/social dimension is not discretionary in Transformational organizations. It is their central attribute. Transformational business leaders are participants in a quiet revolution. The potential of their efforts is slowly becoming apparent. One observer, projecting the consequences, declared that companies undergoing social transformation in the economic arena may well be heralding the fulfillment of the American Revolution.

Each of the next nine profiles, in three chapters, portrays the unique history of a person who has developed, or attempted to develop, a Transformational business organization, one that is different from the traditional hierarchically structured enterprise. No two are alike. The backgrounds of these virtuous leaders vary significantly. Some have approached their work pragmatically. Others have been consciously religious or philosophic in charting a course for the development of their organizations. Some have clearly based their efforts on the principles of democracy.

Despite the various paths taken the intended and, for most, the achieved results are very close in terms of the values reinforced and the organizational attributes generated. In all cases it has meant sharing power and authority with those who traditionally have had neither or little in the management of a business. In most cases, it has also meant sharing the success of the business with those employees who have contributed to that success, through profit-sharing and/or stock-ownership plans. Universally it is also recognized by these leaders that the management methods consciously employed in these transformational organizations are intended to serve the best interests of all parties involved with the enterprise, a happy coincidence of doing good in order to be able to do well.

Each story was selected for inclusion in these chapters because of a particular message that the story has for us.

At 3Com, Bill Krause and his team designed their organization carefully and pragmatically. Working from scratch in 1980 they have attracted an unusually committed group of overachievers who have propelled the company to recognized leadership in their industry.

Billye Ericksen at CAPSCO bought the company and has maintained its family feeling. She introduced characteristics in its management once thought to be feminine but increasingly seen as appropriate to enlightened leadership anywhere.

Hal Bolton also bought the company, Dahlstrom Manufacturing. He has found that good intentions and traditional problem-solving are necessary but insufficient in the face of a tradition of labor-management mistrust that has pervaded his company and his community.

Together these Transformational leaders are involved in a broad spectrum of American businesses: from heavy industry to electronics, from manufacturing to distribution, from construction to insurance and other services. Their experiences indicate that no area of American business is beyond transformation, given the appropriate environment and committed leadership.

A GRATEFUL, COMPETITIVE, PRAGMATIC HUMANIST

L. William Krause, President and C.E.O.
3Com Corporation

Among us mortals, successful leaders are sometimes the most complex of people, and seemingly not always consistent. One part of Bill Krause, self-portrayed, and affirmed by his associates, is a highly disciplined, competitive, results-oriented pragmatist. Another part, observable to outsiders, is a gracious, fun-loving, value-centered student of life. And there may be other parts equally as enigmatic.

The words *fortunate, right place, right time, growth, learning,* and *fulfillment* all loom large in his vocabulary.

A superior product of a military school of engineering, the U.S. Army and an on-the-job management education, he has developed a life plan which is now only in the second of three phases and has already produced a model corporation for the next generation of companies to emulate.

History

Bill Krause, C.E.O., and Bob Metcalfe, one of the founders of 3Com Corporation, may tell you that the company's rapid growth and financial success have been due to a lot of people besides themselves. But it all started with them.

The 3Com name and its product concept, PC workgroup computing systems, date from 1979, when Bob Metcalfe, the inventor of Xerox's Ethernet, left Xerox ostensibly to start his own consulting business. A year and a half later, with the help of venture capitalists, Bob linked up with Bill Krause, a veteran Hewlett Packard PC marketeer, and the new company was really under way.

Sales in 1981 were around $500,000. In fiscal 1987 they were $155,856,000 with an after-tax net income exceeding 10 percent of sales. (These figures include Bridge Communications results. Late in calendar 1987 the company merged with Bridge Communications, with the 3Com name surviving.) For fiscal 1988, sales increased to $251,948,000, net income to $22,547,000, and return on equity was a high 19.3 percent.

Fast as its growth may seem, 3Com and its unique value system did not emerge automatically as the result of some high-tech wizardry. The unique history of Bill Krause played a significant role in the company's cultural development.

Son of a professional army officer, Bill and his family moved frequently in the years before he went to college. He started kindergarten and attended the early grades in Japan and graduated from high school in Germany. In between, he went to parochial schools in several locations in the States.

The negative side of the experience, he recalls, was that he never had a neighborhood that he grew up in. The positives were developing the ability to adapt readily to new people and new situations and to appreciate the world's variety of cultures and languages.

His college years were spent at the Citadel, where he was on a partial athletic scholarship and majored in electrical engineering. While he was in Charleston (S.C.) he determined that the 45 or so years between then and retirement would consist of three phases of approximately 15 years each. The first phase would be his learning phase, learning about business and all its basics. The second phase would be spent building and running his own company. The third phase would be a "serving phase" wherein he would give something back to society through some form of public service. Explaining how he arrived at this life's plan, particularly the third phase, Bill confided, "I've lived in some places in the world where there was a lot of poverty and where people didn't have a lot of material things. So, I saw myself being lucky because of my parents and what they had done, and just society in general, by providing schools that you could get into if you extended the effort. As it turned out I was a pretty bright guy, so I just felt as though I should repay that in some way. I felt very fortunate to be in a society where all those things were happening."

Bill's brightness permitted him to skip several grades in precollege years. By age 21 he was a second lieutenant in the army, in charge of millions of dollars worth of high-tech electronic missile equipment. His unit was responsible for training the air defense corps in the manning, maintenance and use of air defense missiles. His staff consisted of technical noncommissioned officers, between 35 and 50 years of age, who had learned about electronics through experience, not through education. As a 21-year-old who was supposed to lead this unit, Bill observed, "I very quickly learned that there was a lot of followship in leadership and that perhaps the best thing that I could do was to create an environment where I could get out of the way and make sure I didn't prevent the troops from getting done what needed to be done. That was a very useful learning experience.

"It also taught me what I didn't think life should be. I really found the army stifling because of its bureaucracy and hierarchy and its excessive structure."

After two years in the army, Bill joined General Electric Company and was put into a fast-track manufacturing management training program. He was soon made a shop floor supervisor, managing union laborers who again were in the 40- to 50-year age range. This was in the middle of the 1960s, when the adversarial relationship between management and labor was the accepted situation throughout American industry. Bill readily concluded that approach was fundamentally wrong for everyone concerned.

In 1967, Bill Krause made the most fortuitous move of his career, joining Hewlett Packard (HP) just as they entered the personal, then called desktop, computer business. He had concluded that he didn't want to be an engineer in industry nor to be in manufacturing or operations management. The next logical choice was sales and marketing, which is where he went when he joined HP.

HP had achieved an annual sales volume of about $200 million by the time he joined it. Ten years later it was to be 10 times that size. At Hewlett Packard, because of the values of its founders, Bill learned how to run a business from a humanistic point of view as opposed to an adversarial approach to employee relations. He learned to organize people and help them to plan their objectives and then lead them to achieve those objectives; what an operating statement and a balance sheet were; what a mission was and what marketing, product and business strategies were; and, furthermore, how they all related.

Applying these tools, Bill Krause was very successful at HP, staying some 14 years and becoming general manager of the personal computer division by 1980.

> I wound up staying at HP much longer than I thought I would, for several reasons. One is because I'd expressed an interest in building my own business. That was to be the second phase of my career. As I got up into management at HP, they oriented me toward assignments where I was starting new businesses for them. I found that absolutely exhilarating, thrilling and fun. The second reason was that it was such a fabulous place to work. Leaving it was hard in the sense that I didn't want to leave and find myself competing with my paternalistic parents, if you will. So it was hard.

A friend from HP, Gib Meyers, who had left to become a venture capitalist, knew of Bill's interest in running his own business. Having made contact with Bob Metcalfe, he arranged for the two to meet. Both had known of each other and of their respective achievements before they met, so great mutual respect preceded their meeting.

Although Bob was deeply involved in the scientific aspects of developing electronics technology, Bill had long since lost his engineering bent and was a combination marketing-oriented business pragmatist and, by his own admission, an amateur social psychologist. But underneath, their values were consistent and their talents agreeably complemented each other.

In his amateur social psychologist's role, Bill had concluded that the social circumstances of Americans were changing, and that although the HP operating environment was completely appropriate for the post-depression, post–World War II era, when employees sought security, a new working environment was now required. Hewlett Packard had instituted a policy of no layoffs, of lifetime employment, of worker participation in decision making through quality circles and so on, before ever hearing about such things coming to us from Japan.

What Bill saw in 1980 to 1981 were people who wanted to satisfy those needs that were on the upper end of psychologist Abraham Maslow's hierarchy of needs. They sought self-actualization. Bill readily translated that into entrepreneurship, the desire to take risks, to build a business, to be responsible for planning and executing their own work, to be responsible for the results and to participate in the rewards.

> So we came up with a concept at 3Com called "Confederated Entrepreneurship." It is sort of a blending of the old with the new. These are two fancy-sounding words, but if you look at their definitions, it's really quite simple: *Confederated* means a group of people who share a common goal. That is what HP has done so well. They put together a group of people who had this common set of goals. *Entrepreneurship* is a person or a group of persons who are willing to take the risks of starting a business for the sake

of profits. What I felt was really a tremendous opportunity in starting a business, beyond just its economic importance, was the societal importance of creating a new form of business, a new form of company, a new kind of culture. This kind of culture would be what I would call the "Hewlett Packard" of the decades just before we move into the 21st century. I believe as we move forward, further and further away from world wars and depressions, people are looking to gain self-fulfillment.

Bill experienced the interest in employer paternalism waning, being replaced by the "me" generation, but moving through that to a desire for self-actualization.

Another thing that guided me was a phrase that a friend of mine taught me. Whenever I got upset with somebody, he would remind me, "Do you really think that person has a stamp on their forehead that says, 'What can I do to make your day miserable today?'" It helped to bring out to me that (a) people really don't have an aim in life to make your life miserable. And (b) the other thing that guided me was what were all the things that I liked and didn't like about business and work? I assumed that if I liked them or didn't like them then other people felt a similar way. In other words, if I felt that I was being over-managed or undermanaged, then other people felt that way, too.

Philosophy

Behind the concept of Confederated Entrepreneurship was Bill's understanding that as C.E.O. of 3Com he was responsible for creating the proper environment. Actually, he admits the full clarity of his role and what needed to be accomplished in building the organization consciously occurred to him only after the fact, after it already was well on its way. After being with the company for five years, he took a sabbatical.

I began asking myself, I am president of this company

and it has been successful: What does it really mean? So I defined what a company is. It is a single-sentence definition: A company is nothing more than a group of people who have developed a process for generating results. The emphasis is on people, process and results. So that said to me I can influence the people, I can influence the processes and I can use the results as the feedback mechanism. It said to me that we had to have an environment, or a set of processes, whereby people could act toward common goals but with a great deal of independence, autonomy and freedom.

In its early stages of development, a visiting professor of organization behavior at Stanford, Don Yates, assisted the 3Com management team in clarifying its objectives, defining its goals, identifying its core values and developing its framework for decision making. Interestingly, Don Yates was brought into 3Com by its venture capital group, Mayfield Fund, which emphasized the importance of the human and organizational aspects of new ventures. Bill relates:

> We actually created this framework in our company using an acronym called MOST. M stands for mission, O stands for objectives, S stands for strategy and T stands for tactics. Through the use of that acronym and by defining what each of those words meant, then by creating an actual statement of what our mission is and statements of what our objectives are, that really provided the framework for people to act toward common goals with a great deal of independence and freedom.

Rather than stating its mission, objectives and strategy in sterile abstraction, 3Com uses them continually in its working life in both spoken and written form. These excerpts from its 1986 annual report are a case in point:

> The computer industry is entering a new growth era, which we call the third computing millennium. Customers have a growing need to network their stand-alone PCs at

the workgroup level to create fully integrated business and office productivity systems. This new market for PC-based workgroup computing is projected to have a compound annual growth of 49 percent per year, from $291 million in 1985 to $2.15 billion in 1990. Over the next three to four years, 3Com plans to maintain pace with this rapidly developing market and grow to $250 million in sales primarily through internal product developments.

The two cornerstones of 3Com's marketing strategy are to achieve customer satisfaction second to none and to market its products through leveraged channels of distribution.

3Com is a team of people who have developed a process for generating results. The Company's number-one critical success factor is its ability to attract and retain capable and motivated people.

We are fortunate to have exceptional people who have a fierce sense of pride and who are dedicated to customer satisfaction second to none.

We have five primary objectives for fiscal 1987: (1) enhance customer satisfaction, (2) exceed $100 million in orders, (3) develop new markets, (4) manage our financial basics and (5) keep 3Com a great place to be.

With a sound understanding of our market and a strong team of capable and motivated people, we look forward with enthusiasm to the opportunities ahead. Thank you for your continued interest and support.

The mission of 3Com deserves further exploration. As Bill says,

Most businesses have a mission to create some product or service that adds value for some set of customers to provide returns to shareholders. I got to thinking about that and I said, Wait a second. People come here and they have fun and they laugh and they talk and they are energetic. The reason is that here people want to be known in life for having participated in the creation of a great company, a company that truly adds value and dimensions other than just financial. We created a new way of doing business where people, in fact, can act as entrepreneurs toward common goals, can get personal satisfaction, in fact, develop as human beings, become better human beings in life because they work at this company.

In elaborating on 3Com's culture, Howard Charney, a senior vice-president, indicated that, to begin with, the company attracts people who have a high need to achieve. Charney himself is such an example. An M.I.T. graduate in mechanical engineering, he also has graduate business and law degrees. He joined 3Com in its infancy following several years at IBM and at Memorex where it was hard to see what impact he was having on their results. With minimum internal politics, Charney says, you get promoted at 3Com because of what you contribute.

Charney believes 3Com's value system is its essence. Total integrity in all relationships is its core value, with courteous treatment of and open communications with its employees central. Charney defines the "fun" Bill Krause sees 3Com people having as their wanting to and their experiencing winning. "It's a funny kind of fun. It's where they're contributing, where they're solving problems."

According to Debra Engel, 3Com's vice-president of human resources since 1983, the company goes to extraordinary lengths in interviewing job candidates. They want candidates to know about the company's values, but also its absolute requirement that they contribute and perform, before accepting a position. Those who are hired tend to stay. Turnover at 3Com is half the rate of other Silicon Valley companies.

Regarding 3Com's objectives Bill Krause says,

By choosing the results we wish to achieve, it is also a statement of our principles and values. You can ask virtually anybody in our company what our objectives are and they will tell you the following four statements: Our number-one objective is to achieve customer satisfaction second to none; two, build a quality organization of capable and motivated people; three, manage for profits sufficient to fund our long-term growth; and, four, earn market leadership and grow faster than our competitors. They are not written on signs or posters. Whenever we write some document we frequently refer to them. But people know them. They hear them all the time. We live it and our actions reinforce it.

Kathryn Petry, a 3Com sales promotion specialist, proved Bill right. She knows the company's four objectives well, readily putting them in her own words. Kathryn lasted 16 to 20 months in each of several previous companies in Silicon Valley, but after being at 3Com several years, she said she had no intention of leaving. She's observed that the company is conservative in conducting its financial affairs and in adding head count or facilities only when the sales are consistently there.

Another 3Com concept is what Bill calls Management-by-Priorities. At intervals appropriate to each supervisor-employee relationship, each person writes down what his or her priorities will be for the next period of time and exchanges them, reconciles them, and then each is able to proceed with optimal autonomy for that period without having to be concerned about what the other person is doing. It is an alignment process that insures, throughout the organization, that the right things are being worked on at any one point in time, and reinforces the entrepreneurial dimension.

3Com products are designed to satisfy the needs of what Bill describes as the third computer millennium:

> When I go through this prattle about the three millenniums I usually give the enabling technology and the social driving force of the era. In the mainframe era, the social driving force was that of the fatherly figure of paternalism and "the organization man." [Management information] all went to the centralized authority. That was to fit the social need of the day which was "I'm putting my faith in the organization and in Dwight D. Eisenhower, etc."
>
> Then we went through an era where we wanted to make ourselves more competitive so we distributed our computing into departmental computers, where we about

put a computer into every building. That was the era that I grew up in at HP. The hero of the day was Jack Kennedy and that was laying the groundwork for doing social good, etc. When all that got destroyed, it paved the way for the "me" generation which then, in fact, paved the way for the personal computer, which was a backlash against the organization and all the centralization. It was sort of taking it all the way to the extreme, to the individual. And that was actually too far. They went too far. They didn't realize that individuals don't work as stand-alone individuals in corporations, that all departments are collections of work groups which are collections of individuals who work together on common projects with common supervisors. So, we are leaving this second millennium of the time-shared computers with departmental applications and entering the third millennium where the enabling technology is networks of PCs and work group computing applications. In symmetry you can see corporate, department, work groups. From a technical imperative point of view, you can see batch processing mainframes, time-shared minis, network PCs, etc. It really presents a rather compelling historical perspective.

A 3Com network is the result of PC users, value-added resellers and 3Com sales and technical representatives working together to tailor 3Com hardware and software necessary to link PCs for specific purposes. It requires knowledgeable, conscientious and hardworking 3Com people. Bill says that working at 3Com is more than a job. The company expects the best from all of its people all of the time. Unlike the paternalism of HP, at 3Com it is performance that counts.

If you can't perform, we just don't have a role for you here. If you are trying hard and you have a sufficient skill set and it's just a matter of learning or getting up to speed, there is tolerance to that degree. Our principal civic duty has been to provide an environment where people have more than just a job, where they are contributing to their company. They feel part of the company and they believe that they themselves as human beings are growing and developing. It is a company that has principles relative to things like substance abuse. We have a real simple policy on substance abuse. You abuse substances, you're fired. We, the management, don't do the firing; the people [employees] do it. It's their company, they are responsible for maintaining the credibility of the company. We don't have a person who is in charge of quality. It is everybody's job to perform in a manner that produces quality.

New ideas at 3Com come from anywhere in the company. A person with an idea puts it into the electronic mail system and it either grows or dies there as others support it and add to it or ignore it.

I am really fortunate in the sense that there is a tremendous amount of peer pressure in our company to perform. Our incentive systems are structured that way. By perform, remember what we are performing against—our values—customer satisfaction second to none, and building a quality organization. The simplest way of defining what that means to us is the three kinds of work we expect—smart work, team work and hard work. All three are necessary. When we talk about performance, we talk about performance against our values. Managing for profit: it is incredible to me how people pinch pennies around here, sometimes to excess. Gosh, I find someone at work on a Saturday doing something. "Why are you doing this?" "Well, I could save $10.00 if I did this myself."

Kathryn Petry agrees that working smart is important at 3Com. "When Bill Krause walks down the hall, he'll ask you what you're working on. He's tough. When he asks you questions he wants straight answers. He doesn't want a wishy-washy response or for you to agree with him. He wants to know that you have thought a question through."

Bill's emphasis on thinking things through pervades 3Com.

Debra Engel says the company believes every action is important. "With even the smallest decision you are sending a message. Therefore, everyone learns to be very conscious about what they're doing and why they are doing it."

The entire operation at 3Com is covered with incentives. Every employee has individual goals and there are corporate goals as well. For achieving or contributing to each, there are incentive awards. Overall there is a profit incentive bonus. Profits above a minimum level based on return on equity are divided 50-50 between employees and shareholders. The shareholder portion goes to the bottom line as added return on equity and earnings per share; the employee portion is divided 50-50 again. The first portion (now 25 percent of the total) is paid out to every employee as a percentage of his or her annual pay. The second portion is paid out based on unit performance against certain revenue, profit and/or quality goals.

The percentage paid to shareholders also benefits 3Com employees because every 3Com employee can easily become a shareholder. When the company was organized, its venture capital supporters were astounded by Bill's and Bob's insistence that every employee be offered stock options. The company now also has a stock purchase plan and is looking into a way to give new employees shares when they are first employed.

Bill is a strong believer in employee stock ownership even for production employees.

You want production people behaving as owners. You want them to be pinching pennies. Every person can make a difference. As soon as you stop saying that every person can and will make a difference, they won't.

One of the small things that I have been able to contribute is what I call the concept of self-fulfilling prophecy. I think we have had the ability to actually cause people to think they were bigger and better than they actually were for some short period of time until they actually became that big. We believed in them and counted on them to perform at those levels.

We communicate widely throughout our company,

our mission, our objectives and our strategies. Strategy has to do with decisions about how you better serve your customers. That is the most important part. The second part is that it is all relative to the competitive alternatives, so we make visible to our people who our competitors are and what their strengths and weaknesses are so they can do something about it.

Bill says that all of this, of course, creates pressures on 3Com people. He also recognizes that life is not fair and that there were never any guarantees that it would be. It is just full, he says, and how full is up to each of us to determine. Business is very competitive, and it does an injustice to employees not to keep them closely involved in and informed about those competitive dimensions. He cites the incredulity of Ford and GM workers when their California plants were closed.

They would say, "I have worked at this plant for 19 years. Every day I'd come to work and work my heart out. I did everything I was asked. How come I lost? Where did I go wrong?" Point of fact is that the worker didn't do anything wrong. He was never asked or never made aware of what wasn't being done or what the competitive environment was. I mean the worker didn't have a stamp on his forehead that said, "What can I do to build cars that don't have quality in them? Nobody ever asked me to build a car with more quality in it or where the quality problems were." It is so simple.

It is clear, on talking with Bill, that he is and has been the company cheerleader. At a gathering in 1982 when a major new product release was announced and awards were presented to contributors to the product, Bill was presented pom-pons in recognition of his cheerleading the project. The pom-pons still grace his office area today. His office, by the way, is formed by area dividers and there is no door at its entrance.

Asked what has inspired him and sustained his efforts over the years, Bill easily mentioned a list of people who have been of great help to him. His wife of 20 years, an assistant principal in a middle school whose career specialization has been in counseling and guidance, topped the list as a sounding board, a questioner stimulating new thinking.

Others mentioned were, not surprisingly, David Packard and Bill Hewlett. He met Bill Hewlett at lunch in the HP cafeteria the first day he began working there, December 11, 1967.

> Honest, my first day there I am sitting next to Bill Hewlett at lunch. We got to talking about what I was going to be working on, what area of the company. So I told him that I had joined the marketing department selling the new desktop computers. He wound up spending two hours, an hour at lunch and an hour after lunch, where he personally took me to the laboratories and introduced me to the people who were working on the desktop computer project. Then afterward I would get periodic calls from him. He was doing his own market research on how the marketing of the product was going. Periodically he would call me and ask me if I wouldn't mind going with him on a sales call to visit one of his friends to show him the product.
>
> It really made a profound statement to me. So now I have my own company. So what that said to me is that I should do the same for the people in my own company. Little things, like I will go and spend a day working in manufacturing, assembling products in blue jeans and shirt sleeves, right alongside the people assembling products. Why? Just to show that I care, for number one. And for number two, I learn a tremendous amount every time I do that.

Later at HP, Bill got close to David Packard. Bill describes him as someone you always felt was treating you as a peer, never talking down to you, a person of profound principles and style.

As a student of military history, Bill admired General Patton because of his aggressiveness and athletic prowess—a winner. Viewed from afar, from John Kennedy he learned the importance of intellect and the use of humor to defuse tense situations. At one

Halloween party for the company, Bill dressed up as a Teddy Ruxpin bear with a string attached to him, which, when pulled, recited the litany of the four company objectives in a mock mechanical voice.

Bill says he has learned much from Bob Metcalfe, as well, reinforcing his own belief in the importance of ethics, integrity, moral conviction and commitment as these relate to business leadership as well as life in general.

Also, Bill credits the other members of his management team, his "peers in running the business," with having provided him with much learning and great support in his leadership role and as a growing person.

Coming back to his life plan, Bill asked, "How will I know when I'm done with this phase?" Speaking for himself and for Bob Metcalfe, "Both of us look at it much the same way. I will know when the company has adopted and embraced the principles so well that I am no longer needed to preach them. We will have created an organization of people who have a process that follows our principles and allows them to generate results without us needing to be around."

At its current rapid growth rate, 3Com is still very much in the stage of being created. It will be a while yet before Bill and Bob are no longer needed.

* * *

Still within Silicon Valley, Billye Ericksen, the subject of the next leadership profile, has experienced life very differently than Bill Krause. Yet they share many convictions regarding the need of employees to grow and to be responsible for the management of their efforts.

FROM CHEERLEADER TO LEADER

Billye Ericksen, President and C.E.O.
CAPSCO Sales, Inc.

Periodically during the process of conducting interviews for this book, the fact emerged that one deeply felt conviction seemed to energize these people in such a way that it became the vehicle that empowered them to achieve great things.

For Billye Ericksen that deeply felt conviction is that many women are poorly treated in our society because they are economically dependent. Hence, her entire adult life has been devoted to becoming economically independent and to helping others achieve the same goal.

She's bigger than life and yet only five-and-a-half feet tall. She has more energy than two average people put together, a mind of her own, but with the patience to listen and to learn from others. She owns a successful electronic-component supply company lock, stock and barrel and she wants to sell it to a group of her employees as soon as they are able to run it without her. No wonder the large companies she's worked for in the past were too small to contain her. She says, "I've never had a mediocre idea in my life. I have *great* ideas!" and you soon learn she's just telling you the truth.

History

The chic, confident, commanding presence of Billye Ericksen today would have been tough to predict 40, 30, maybe even 20 years ago. Billye, the second of four daughters, got off to a shaky start, with her parents divorced when she was a sophomore in high school. Her father was a building painter and her mother drove a city bus and worked in a meat packing company in Spokane, Washington.

A cheerleader then (and now) Billye married a high school football hero and over the next several years became the mother of three. By age 23, Billye and her husband were also divorced and she found herself on her own. "There was a lot of pressure to stay married, but at the time, I realized 'This isn't right. The two of us shouldn't be together.' We were growing apart."

Wishing to put the past experience of living under constricting conditions in Spokane behind her, Billye moved herself and her three children, two of them still in diapers, to California.

The family's circumstance at the time is best described by a story she tells.

One time, my children and I were at my sister's in Petaluma, California, at Christmas. I was working at Lockheed. The children were quite small. I called a neighbor to see if there was any mail. She was watching our dog. She said, "What do you want me to do with this food?" and I said, "This food? I don't know what you are talking about." And she said, "The Lockheed 'Buck of the Month Club' has brought you a turkey and candy canes for the children and beans." At first I was just horrified. I thought how do they know that I am so poor? But all they had to do was go through their rosters to see here is a divorced woman with three children working as a clerk-typist. You know it didn't take much to figure it out. At first I was upset about it and then I thought it was kind of funny. Then I wondered what they were giving for Easter because we needed it.

As I was raising the children, I don't know how many times we declared that this was the last supper. There was nothing else that we had to eat. That was it. And I'd cook it all because I thought something is going to happen, and something always did. We were all healthy, none of us starved to death.

This was also the case as I would be working at a job some place and I'd think, "This is really not a good job for me. I am so unhappy." I would quit the job and go home and announce to three children that we weren't working anymore. We were going to look for something else because that wasn't a good job for us. And everybody would say, "Yeah, that's fine." I look back now, what in the world was I thinking about? But I had such confidence that I would get something else.

How did that confidence come about?

I think there were a lot of times when I was totally defeated. I can remember telling the kids that what is inside these four walls is what we can control. We have to be very good friends. We have to be very supportive of each other because outside there we can't control what is happening to us. I was a child growing up. I was a child raising children, if you think about it. I was so young and had such a little bit of exposure. But at times I was devastated by what happened.

I felt that at least I was in control of where I was going to work. There seemed to be a lot of positions, so I was able to change jobs. I felt I had some control in my life and I was so relieved to be out of Spokane because I had very little control there.

I think some of my strength came from my father. At times I was really quite disturbed by his role in my life because he had decided a long time ago that I was his son. "Bill's my boy," he would say. And later I realized that he was emphasizing my ability to take care of myself, in fact, take care of others. Even when I was very little, I was the one who was supposed to defend my three sisters. I think that's where I learned to negotiate so well.

I was in a position where if my sisters would get into some kind of tiff in the neighborhood, I was the one who was supposed to go straighten everything out. My father was a proponent of fighting. He had to go and do battle. I never lifted a finger to anyone, but I can remember standing nose-to-nose with different people and insisting that things were a certain way. Maybe when I fool the people I meet, I fool myself as well because I was scared to death and yet my father had decided that I had the power. As I went through a divorce and raising children, I would think about who gave me this strength and I think my father had a lot to do with it. My mother was absolutely intimidated by my father and I could see that wasn't the right situation. As I would see women or men who were in subservient positions, usually women, I felt a tremendous need to help them be set free.

In 1959 Billye began her career at Lockheed.

I used to think, somehow or other I have to get this little team through life. I realized very shortly that my education was going to be a tremendous shortcoming to me. So I started going to school in the evenings. I took 10 lessons in shorthand and I could do 80 words per minute because I picked that up very quickly. I was highly motivated, that's the thing—self-motivation—I was highly motivated to do that. Class by class I started taking programs in the evening. Sometimes I would either take my children or work them in by having them somewhere in the school while I was in class. This was before they had any day care or child care for parents. And I would work a lot of evening jobs because I had to support my family.

As the result of accompanying her to evening jobs, her children never saw her career as something that took her away from them because they were always involved in it.

Leaving Lockheed, Billye went to Philco-Ford (now Ford Aerospace and Communications). There she observed that her fellow clerical workers knew a lot about how their departments operated, acted as buffers for their bosses and really could be administrative assistants if they only had the opportunity to upgrade their skills a little. She called to see the head of the industrial relations department and told him that she would like to put on a noon presentation to tell the clerical women in the company about a certified professional secretary program that she thought they would all be very interested in.

"He said, 'Well, most of our women like to shop during lunchtime,' and I thought, 'OK, I don't care, I'll just talk to a few of them.' There was nothing he could do to dissuade me from this thing. He said, 'Don't feel too bad if no one shows up.' "

Billye had some charts made up by the graphics group down the hall from where she worked, reserved space in a company auditorium and sent out memos announcing the meeting.

When the day and hour arrived, so did a standing-room-only crowd of women. The head of industrial relations gave her an "I don't know what happened" shrug as Billye arrived. She was astounded. Surprise turned to momentary mindless shock and then to elation. It was her first speaking engagement and it turned out to be to a large group of women, something she has done many times since.

With such an evident need, Billye decided to teach the program herself. She got the adult education organization in Los Altos, California, to authorize the program and, taking a class at a time herself, a chapter ahead of her students, she taught typing, short-hand, introduction to law, introduction to economics, accounting for nonaccountants and so on. Her class size grew as she went along because it exposed her students to areas of learning they had never known before.

"One of my students came up one night and she said, 'I'm going to have to quit.' I said, 'You're a wonderful student, why are you leaving?' And she said, 'You know, when I go home and tell my husband what composes the gross national product, he is so threatened that it's ruining our marriage.' " Not married herself, Billye hadn't anticipated such a response. She could understand it intellectually, but it was confusing to her why it had to be that way.

Now, as president of her own company, she is asked to sit on the boards of many area community organizations. And now she realizes that there are very few others like her in top management positions or on the boards of either large or even small companies. "I think there are more women in middle management but they haven't made the big breakthrough. I'm talking about the break-through from middle management into top management posi-tions. It hasn't happened yet."

Several years ago Billye was asked to return to Lockheed to speak to Lockheed's women on Lockheed Women in Business Day. "It was fun to look back; it was like a class reunion." She told the assembled women, "If there are no women ahead of you and you've been there for a couple of years, quit, because you are not going to make it. It's just not going to happen. It's set up that way."

After hearing her first presentation to the women at Philco-Ford, the head of industrial relations had her transferred to his department. Two years later Billye went to RCA as a clerical employee in industrial relations. The head of the group soon promoted her to a peer management position level with himself. From then on, he managed the employment function and Billye ran personnel relations. Over the next few years, remaining in industrial relations work, she went on to management positions at Control Data and at Singer.

As she moved up the ladder her understanding of organizations, and of women's opportunities within them, increased.

> As I would run into a competitive situation, usually with a woman in the office, and she would be upset that I got promoted or that I was trying for a better position, I would take the person aside, usually to lunch, and make the comment that my success is your success and yours is mine. What we have to do is realize that you and I aren't the enemy. The enemy is out there and we have to work very hard to come together on this. So what I did over time is participate in education programs, encouraging other people to go to school. Just take a class, any class, just take a class. Take one at a time.
>
> Probably one of the best things that happened to me is the first letter I got from someone whom I really encouraged to quit work and go back to school. That person got her degree and wrote to me and thanked me for that influence and she asked what could she do for me? My response was, "Do that for someone else. That would be the greatest payment." I became almost a fanatic on the way "out" is through education and *out* meant independence.

At one company, Billye learned the tough side of personnel relations when the company went through a drastic reduction in operations and, thus, employment. Billye acted as a kind of pressure relief valve as laid-off employees came in to pick up applications for food stamps and would tell her about their fights with spouses, imminent auto repossessions and so on. But she also discovered there that an industrial relations job was not a power position in the company. When budgets were cut, her programs were eliminated regardless of the need for them. As the result, Billye began to take courses in accounting and financial management.

With this new interest in the financial side of business, Billye left that company and began working in a small company as the accounting manager, with industrial relations under her as well. In fact, she was with three small companies, the last one for four years, before joining CAPSCO. That company, Integrated Microsystems, Inc., was her first real exposure to electronics. She began as a bookkeeper and left as treasurer. She also began there to sense a personal responsibility to serve the community. As a woman business executive, she was sought out to serve on the boards of several community agencies, the United Way and Umbrella House among them. Umbrella House was a support organization for women in life transitions (e.g., returning to work, going through a divorce, victims of wife battering). Through that experience, Billye began accepting speaking engagements where she could address working women, encouraging them to see that they were important role models for others who had not yet declared their independence from intolerable situations. "The concept of empowering women to free themselves was very exciting to me and any time I had an opportunity to speak to women, about their own lot and about what they had to prepare themselves to confront, I did that."

Continuing on her new career path in finance, Billye joined CAPSCO Sales, Inc., in 1977 as its controller. Originally organized as Capacitor Sales Company in 1962, by 1977 its annual sales volume was $3.8 million. Following a series of cost analyses of products and reports which Billye prepared on how to improve revenues and profitability, she was promoted to manager of distribution. In 1979, sales increased to $6 million and in 1980 to $8.6 million annually.

In 1980, Billye was named vice-president and general manager of CAPSCO and in 1981, having learned how to put together a leveraged buyout by working on the sale of a sister company of CAPSCO, Billye arranged a $1.2 million purchase of CAPSCO from its previous owner.

Sales of CAPSCO moderated during the recession years of 1981 through 1983 to the $6.5–$7.0 million annual level. They rebounded to $10.2 million in 1984, and declined to $9.1 million in 1985 and $7.5 million in 1986 and 1987 as the electronics industry again fell on hard times. The target for fiscal 1988 was $8.7 million.

Today CAPSCO is the largest passive component (capacitors, resistors, etc.) distributor on the West Coast, and the number-one passive component distributor in the United States for companies such as Murata-Erie, Panasonic, Cornell Dubilier and Unitrode. CAPSCO also does some value-added, light assembly work in its 20,000-square-foot facility in Sunnyvale, California, employing approximately 40 people overall.

Among those employees, until recently, were the three original members of Billye's "little team": Kathy Ericksen, CAPSCO's vice-president of operations until she returned to school early in 1987, Ken Ericksen and Kirk Ericksen, who are, respectively, sales manager and operations manager.

Philosophy

The real story of CAPSCO is found in its employee spirit and culture. The company's line card, identifying the products it carries and the manufacturers it represents, tells a lot. The cover shows six human figures, three women and three men, in Olympic sweatsuits, with gold medals around their necks, giving the victory sign, against a backdrop of representations of historical breakthroughs, including elements of space technology. In the center is Billye's illustration of her RIM Management philosophy and above the entire scene it says, "When the right people get together, Great Things Happen." Below the figures it reads, "CAPSCO—Expect Great Things."

On the inside, the "Cover Story" reads,

> When the right people get together, great things happen. Creativity, perseverance and cooperation balanced with a spirit of good will are powerful elements of humankind.
>
> The world is always moved to a new and better place when those people who recognize their role in making things happen come together for the benefit of others as well as themselves.
>
> Expect great things from the CAPSCO team.

On the following page all 40 CAPSCO employees are pictured.

RIM Management is Billye's graphic description of how CAPSCO operates. Instead of a pyramidal hierarchy of authority, CAPSCO people are all positioned on a circle, a rim. Everyone is potentially responsible for anything that may arise in the company. They are not responsible to do everything, but they are responsible, if contacted, for example, by someone outside the company, to see that that person is put into contact with the right department or that a question they have gets answered and a problem resolved. As Billye describes it, "If somebody calls and I get the message and it happens to be for someone else, then I also have a responsibility to see that the thing 'closes.' It takes a little more time, but what it does, it calls on everyone to participate, to be here, to be involved in what's happening in this company."

To go along with RIM Management, Billye developed a slogan, "Let the marginal employee work across the street." Both RIM Management and the slogan she developed are Billye's way of dealing with the problem of deadwood in organizations, and the bureaucracy and parochialism of large companies that encourage employees to say, "That isn't my department; that isn't my job."

Billye insists on employee competence and performance. One corridor wall is covered with charts signaling key factor progress of each department against predetermined objectives. It is in full view of anyone visiting the company, suppliers and customers, as well as employees. But she also cares when employees are off from work because of illness. Those absent for more than one day can expect a personal inquiry from her to see how they're doing.

Every employee participating, getting involved in understanding and seeing that the work of the company is done to the satisfaction of each customer, every time, requires teamwork. Team building sessions are a way of life at CAPSCO. CAPSCO note pads, developed during one team building session, exemplify the company's culture. They contain a series of slogans.

CAPSCO Honors Professionalism—

- Exhibits Flexibility and a
  Positive Attitude
- Self Motivation and a
  Positive Attitude
- Continued Learning and a
  Positive Attitude
- Good Communications and a
  Positive Attitude
- Keeps Commitments and a
  Positive Attitude

As Billye says, "This becomes the standard by which we judge each other." Additionally, the company has developed a set of operating principles.

AT CAPSCO, WE ARE COMMITTED TO THE
FOLLOWING PRINCIPLES:

Excellent customer service starts the minute we receive an order and continues through collection.

Maintenance of a work environment conducive to open communications, risk taking and problem solving.

Hiring, developing and retaining superior employees who share the rewards of superior effort.

Growth only if it is profitable growth.

WE BELIEVE IN THESE PRINCIPLES BECAUSE:

They are good for our employees.

They are good for our customers.

And, because these principles are needed to keep CAPSCO the superior company it is.

Recently, following input from employees, a CAPSCO Mission Statement was developed.

CAPSCO MISSION STATEMENT

CAPSCO is dedicated to being a leading authorized distributor specializing in stocking passive components. Our mission is to provide excellent service to our customers, at a fair profit, while providing a workplace committed to extensive employee involvement. Our community, and our reputation of ethical responsibility, are important to us.

OUR AIM is to be the top distributor for each of our factories, maintaining correct inventory levels, and assuring profitable sales of that inventory through aggressive turn rates. Computerized Inventory Control methods and regular monitoring will assure the wellbeing of our major asset (inventory). Our partnership with our factories and rep firms will be based on mutual trust and effectiveness.

CAPSCO is dedicated to being a better place to work by setting high standards for employee performance, and then providing the opportunity for all employees to participate in both technical and personal training. We recognize that people are the key to our success and that the individual is always the critical contributor.

CAPSCO is dedicated to providing excellent service to our customers through better understanding their needs. We devote ourselves to satisfying those needs by getting to know our customers both personally and professionally.

When there is a disagreement between people at CAPSCO, Billye won't listen to one side of the story without having the other person(s) present. When the issue is not readily resolved, she has both parties go into a conference room and wrestle with the problem jointly until the right answer is worked out.

At CAPSCO, Billye claims every three employees do the work that five would do in any other company. With universal profit sharing in the company, the three can get paid what five would receive elsewhere as well. But as Billye says, "It's not money that keeps people at companies; it's involvement; it's commitment."

Each major unit of the company works in an open area without walls, partitions or dividers so that communications can be direct and immediate. Billye's office, until recently, had walls but they were entirely of glass so nothing was hidden from the view of employees and her office door remained continuously open. She recently moved her office to another part of the building to allow her sons to occupy her previous office and one across the hall in order to assume greater responsibility for running the business on a daily basis.

As Ard Sealy, CAPSCO's vice-president of finance and administration, has noted, CAPSCO is different from other companies he's worked for. "The management decisions are made the same way, but there is more concern for people here." For example, new mothers or fathers who are employees at CAPSCO are allowed to bring their babies to work the first six months after they are born, to establish the bonding Billye feels is necessary between parents and their offspring. That concern for people includes those who are in need outside the company as well as a concern for employee welfare. The company has adopted three South American children through the Foster Parents program. Pictures of the children and letters about them are prominently displayed on the bulletin board in the employee kitchen-lunchroom area along with pictures of employees involved in community service activities.

Billye is always interested in ways to personalize business relationships. Late in 1986, a companywide effort was undertaken to gather recipes from employees, spouses, suppliers, customers and others for a company cookbook to be published and sent out to the extended CAPSCO family for Christmas.

Several years ago, Billye heard Tom Peters speak at a national seminar of the United Way.

He was speaking about the value of the individual in the company to a point where when he finished I thought I should get on the plane right now and go home because I've got to get this message to everybody real quick. I bought the cassette immediately. Then I thought I've got to do something special with this cassette, it's got to be presented in a "Tom Peters" way. If I just tell one person at a time, they won't get the feel from each other.

So I rented a hotel suite at the Sheraton. I wanted dinner served and I directed that no flowers be on the tables. I wanted absolutely white napkins, white plates, as plain as possible. I asked them to take down the wall decorations, and they did. The room was stripped, completely bare of decorations. Then I bought some posters. One was a poster of a hundred different kinds of beer. Another was a poster of eggs as far as you could see and three eggs in front broken open. One had a blue yolk, one a red yolk and one a green yolk. Another was a poster of rows of naked women, but one had on a corsage and lipstick. Another was a poster of four or five babies at a table and they were obviously making decisions. They were participating.

I put these posters around and everybody came in thinking, "Something's going on here." I explained to them that first we were going to listen to this fellow and then we were going to talk about how to apply it to us. I had a cassette player and we all got around theater-style and I popped in the Tom Peters tape and he took the ceiling off our little conference room. Then we talked about how special each of us is and that's what each poster represents. This is us, these babies making decisions are us and these eggs, although we're like all eggs, we're the eggs with the red, green and blue yolks. It was one of the best meetings we've had and Tom Peters was there in spirit because we were what he was talking about. We're just like Hewlett Packard, we just don't have as many zeros in our annual sales figure. It was an exciting time.

CAPSCO's personnel policies and practices are developed by its personnel committee comprised of nonmanagement representatives from each department of the company. Recently the committee wrestled with what the company's stance should be regarding employee use of drugs and drug testing.

When depressed conditions hit the electronics business, a reduction in payroll costs was required at CAPSCO. The entire work force was called together. Out of the meeting came the decision to reduce company paid holidays by two to resolve the problem. Company general meetings always involve all employees. The value-added department is comprised largely of people from Southeast Asia. At a recent meeting, so that this group of people could better understand their opportunities and where the company was going in the future, Billye brought in an interpreter who could speak their language.

She is also interested in seeing her employees advance. For example, her administrative assistant for three years, Diane Huber, has moved into a product management position with the company. A company ex-receptionist, Valerie Deeny, has become a successful field saleswoman for CAPSCO.

Several years ago, Billye decided to paint a picture of the company's future for her employees to use as career planning information. She showed how at $6 million annual sales, she was really the only person needed in management to run the company. At $10 million it was a different story however. She credits her daughter, Kathy, with being very instrumental in their achieving that level, along with a controller who has since left the company.

Mindful that her three children could appear to be blocking any chances for the real promotion of others in the company, Billye identified 14 important leadership positions that would need to be filled as the company reached $20 million annual sales. Further, she announced, when that occurred, she would be gone.

She is developing her key managers to take over the management and the ownership of the company within the next several years. The plan is for a group of some five people involved in the company to buy her out sometime after the annual sales volume grows to exceed $20 million. She has announced her plans to everyone who needs to know—including the employees, her banker, attorney, accountant, customers and suppliers.

To assist in the management development process, Billye has established a board of directors comprised of three outsiders, respected business professionals with other Silicon Valley companies. They are William Flanagan, vice-president of manufacturing, Amdahl Corporation; John De Santis, vice-president of manufacturing, Zentec; and Jan Blakslee, vice-president of human resources,

Spectra-Physics. The CAPSCO team being developed has been spending a series of six-week periods assigned to each of the organizations of the three outside directors, learning about sales and marketing, finance, operations, personnel and organization management. In addition to director's fees while the development process unfolds, the three outsiders will receive shares in CAPSCO when the new team purchases the company from Billye. In the meantime, she has been making liberal use of the board's talents, meeting with at least one member of the board weekly regarding a particular issue.

And what does Billye do after the buyout? She has served on the boards of the San Jose–Cleveland Ballet, the San Jose Repertoire Theater and the Euphrat Art Gallery for personal enjoyment and education. She is involved in a program called "Californians Preventing Violence," one aspect of a more comprehensive effort titled "Toward a Healthier State," launched by California Assemblyman John Vasconcellos. Billye is drawn to this latter type of activity because, as she says, it is less self-oriented than some other community efforts, and she believes she can have a greater impact using her talents in that type of endeavor.

And she's still mindful of the fact that women haven't yet "made it." "Women have had the vote for 75 years and only 9 percent of all elected positions in the whole country are filled by women. You see, they are not ready to vote for each other yet. You've heard about 'divide and conquer.' Women have been divided and conquered for a long time." The issue of controlling her own destiny and of freeing other women and empowering them to control theirs remains a driving force for Billye Ericksen.

* * *

The contrast in terms of philosophical foundation between Billye Ericksen and Hal Bolton appears to be extreme. But is the "real" distance between them actually as great as the mileage between California and New York State?

A TRANSFORMATION IN PROGRESS

Harold Bolton, Chairman and C.E.O.
Dahlstrom Manufacturing Co., Inc.

Transformational leaders, as they say, aren't born, they're made. Hal Bolton has been consciously about the task of making himself Transformational throughout his life.

Adding grist to the mill, he has become Transformational while also trying to develop new products and new markets within an old company that has a work force of skilled craftsmen and a history of traditional industrial relations.

Hal's belief structure and philosophy of life are surely unusual. But the challenges he has faced at Dahlstrom are similar to those faced by many other business leaders today who would like to transform their organizations into highly motivated, self-managing operations.

Dahlstrom

Tucked into the southwesternmost corner of New York State at the foot of Chautauqua Lake, Jamestown is a rust-belt industrial community with an illustrious past and a questionable future. The town was once the home of many well-known and highly respected manufacturing firms, most of which have now moved, gone out of business or been bought out. Its in-town industrial landscape contains many acres of vacant or partially occupied multistory manufacturing facilities. Not that new firms haven't come into the Jamestown area recently or that newer facilities haven't been built there. But those buildings that remain unoccupied, or only partially so, are grim reminders of past failures, primarily in traditionally conducted, adversarially based industrial relations.

The adversarial approach, founded on mutual distrust between management and labor, reached its destructive zenith in Jamestown in the late 1960s. Spurred by an obvious decline in the economic health of the community, under the leadership of the then-mayor, Stan Lundine, a Labor Management Committee was established to begin the long process of building trust between the warring factions. In their initial sessions, representatives of companies and of their unions angrily traded stories of betrayal of each by the other until it was obvious that something had to change. Aided by academic consultants, including Tavistock pioneer Eric Trist, a new attitude of mutual responsibility and cooperation began to grow slowly in the community. Much of the credit for the improvement belonged to Joe Mason, a union official, labor co-chair of the committee, who caught the vision and worked diligently to open the minds of managers and laborers alike to new possibilities. Unfortunately, several years ago Joe Mason died of a heart attack while still in his early 50s.

Another effective leader in this change effort, as management co-chairman, then and now, was Harold Bolton, chairman and C.E.O. of Dahlstrom Manufacturing Company.

The Dahlstrom Company is older than Hal Bolton by a score of years, having been established originally as a manufacturer of architectural metal products, metal doors and building facades of the type rarely seen today. By 1972, Dahlstrom was a six-division company, with virtually no "winners" among the divisions. Hal Bolton was its chief operating officer.

History

A 1954 graduate in mechanical engineering from Ohio University, Hal received his master's in industrial administration from Carnegie Tech after spending several years as an army officer. After beginning his career at the Louis Allis Company in Milwaukee, Hal was introduced to the metal fabrication business at Allsteel Equipment in Aurora, Illinois. Some years later, he joined Art Metal Products Company in the Jamestown area with the challenge of turning the company around. Art Metal, an old-line manufacturer of metal office furniture, during the 1960s had decided to replace its multistoried facilities in Jamestown proper with a new modern one-story plant of some 930,000 square feet in Lakewood, an adjacent community. In the process of building the new facility, the company's sales declined, its market share dropped, and the new investment proved to be too large to swallow. Art Metal was forced into bankruptcy and liquidation. It was then that Hal Bolton joined Dahlstrom.

Dahlstrom was no prize either as it was then constituted. Hal got several divisions turned around, but the Jamestown division continued to lose money. In 1973, he left the company, put together a leveraged buyout and purchased the Jamestown operation, continuing the name Dahlstrom Manufacturing Company.

Since 1973, Dahlstrom's product line has undergone major changes. In fact, as Hal says, "We have no product of our own. The only products we have are the skills and services we offer. We are really people oriented in what we sell. It's relatively precision, skilled craft-oriented work; labor intensive, not capital intensive; competitive."

The Dahlstrom Manufacturing Company fabricates precision-engineered metal cabinetry, structures and enclosures for computers, business, medical and communications equipment and so on. Every item they make is competitively bid and nonproprietary.

After buying the company, Hal experimented with doing a joint venture with the union to change how business would be conducted. "We even had a productivity sharing plan in here for about six weeks and the union voted it out. We mismanaged it. Some of our people started leveraging it, using it to pick out low performers rather than using it for rewards. So we lost that."

About the same time that Hal acquired Dahlstrom, Cummins Engine Company acquired the new, then-vacant, Art Metal Products plant. After several years of start-up work, Cummins began to machine parts and assemble diesel engines there. Talking to Cummins personnel, particularly a friend, Craig Colburn, about the unique approach to organizational management being instituted by Cummins in the Jamestown facility, Hal learned about other options to traditional methods of industrial management. He was already conscious of the fact that the ability to make any changes in how management and labor related to each other depended on the trust that each had in the other. Without actively developing mutual trust there could be no foundation upon which improvements could be built.

Philosophy

The work of building trust proceeded over the next several years at Dahlstrom. A company philosophy was then delineated and written principles of operation developed with some union participation. The wholehearted participation of union personnel was sought, but both the leadership and membership held back from becoming fully involved. As Hal puts it, his desire was to build a common belief structure that the company would attempt to live by, for everyone at least to understand if not to subscribe to.

"We walked the union executive committee through the whole thing. It [the company statement] talks about trust, respect, security, responsibility, authority, safety—those basic issues."

The Dahlstrom belief structure document is a lengthy one, composed of 21 principles, introduced by a statement of conditions that the company feels need to be changed in order to improve the way business is conducted today. As C.E.O. of Dahlstrom, Hal Bolton has put the stamp of his business perspective on the introduction to the document. That perspective stems from his view that there no longer is a cohesive economy in the United States.

At one time the whole U.S. economy tended to go together. When automotive and housing were going, everything else flowed behind it because they were such a drawing, such a dominant force, that they really ran the rest of the economy. That isn't true anymore. The economy is split off into all kinds of segments and subsegments. Even in the computer business, micros will take off where large systems aren't going anywhere or big systems will be selling and the micros won't be. There are no general statements that you can make.

I like Naisbitt's observation, and some from others, that we are really in a paradigm change. And a paradigm change is like a trapeze artist who has let go over here and he has not yet found the hand that grips his. We are in between trapezes and nobody knows what the rules are going to be when we get to that new trapeze. They are trying to apply the old rules, but they don't apply anymore. Until we get the new rules defined, we are going to be running around in this environment of change and not understanding.

For a review of excerpts from the Dahlstrom belief structure, see Figure 1.

Figure 1

INTRODUCTION

OUR WORLD IS DRAMATICALLY CHANGING

1. The standards of performance demanded by our customers have increased dramatically in the last 5 years. That change will continue in the future.
2. Competition has increased dramatically and will continue to be a significantly higher threat in the future.
3. The capacity of workforces has increased dramatically.

"We've always done it this way" IS NO LONGER VALID

The dramatic changes in customer expectations, competition, and the workforce demand dramatic changes in the way Dahlstrom does business.

SURVIVAL DEPENDS UPON ADAPTING TO THE NEW WORLD

The customer ultimately decides who will survive. All competitors have the same technology available. Therefore, success will ultimately come down to who manages their people resources the best and applies the technology the best.

Many of our competitors are beginning to make major strides so we must begin soon to avoid being hopelessly behind.

MANAGEMENT DIRECTION— NEW STANDARDS OF EXCELLENCE

Realizing the above view of the world is true, and recognizing that adaptation to the new world is a management problem, we recognize our responsibility to lead the process of change and have spent considerable time determining what Dahlstrom's must do to survive. It is our hope that sharing these philosophies and beliefs openly with every employee will help us all to aim for a common purpose—achieving new standards of excellence for our company and for each individual employee.

Following the Introduction are a preamble and statement of company philosophy (Figure 2).

Figure 2

PREAMBLE

Maximizing results of our enterprise depends on unleashing the creative talent and energy of every employee and focusing it toward Company objectives.

Anything less will result in failure in a world where our competitors are increasingly recognizing this reality.

Survival now depends on people aligned around a vision of excellence.

We must be the most capable, caring and aligned people.

PHILOSOPHY

Dahlstrom is an organization of people working together to achieve excellence and leadership in our field.

- Providing customers with the highest quality products and services at lowest cost and at a competitive price.
- Maintaining continuous improvement.
- Maintaining profitability.
- Creating for one another an environment of trust, mutual respect and support within which everyone has the opportunity to develop his/her full potential.

The 21 principles are listed, and elaborated on, each on a separate page, with the fundamental beliefs and operational implications of each principle described.

These principles are shown in summary form in Figure 3.

Figure 3

PRINCIPLES

By following these principles, the Dahlstrom philosophy will be practiced.

1. Employees are trusted and accorded respect as important human beings.
2. All employees expect themselves and each other to behave responsibly and in accordance with the highest ethical and moral standards.
3. Provisions are made for economic and employment security, as well as wellness of employees and their immediate families.
4. Employees participate in recognizing opportunities, preventing and solving problems and in appropriate goal setting and decision making.
5. Full understanding and satisfaction of customers' needs are paramount in the thinking and practice of all employees.
6. Excellence, with respect to people, is performing to the maximum of one's ability. The organization is responsible for making a fit between an employee's capabilities and the work that needs to get done.
7. A work atmosphere is created and maintained within which cooperation, creativity, experimentation and innovation are encouraged. Mistakes are used as learning opportunities.
8. Free, open and effective communication regarding all aspects of the business is the rule. (Employees' rights to privacy are honored. Any withholding of information is fully and fairly explained.)
9. Safe, clean, healthy, efficient and attractive physical facilities are provided.
10. Profits are the fruits of excellence and are used to perpetuate the business, benefit employees, stockholders, and the community.
11. Compensation is such as to attract and retain top quality employees throughout the organization.
12. The union maintains the integrity of the contract and provides leadership in achieving vision and promoting philosophy-principles.
13. Authority and responsibility for processes are delegated to employees accountable for those processes.
14. Goals are important and must be clearly established, understood and committed to.

15. Encouragement is provided to support continual learning, skills development and the realization of full human potential of all employees.
16. Individuals and groups are recognized and honored for exceptional achievement.
17. Every effort is made to familiarize all employees with our business process to enable people to better understand their roles in it.
18. New technology is constantly being searched for—
    * to combine efficiency and uniform precision
    * to eliminate boring, repetitive, dirty and dangerous work for people
    * to support thinking, fast, effective communication
    * to support continual improvement.
19. Employees are encouraged to balance their lives between work, family, and civic/religious/recreational activities. Excessive business claims are not made that infringe upon these other commitments.
20. Systems continually support the most effective ways of getting work done and are understood and followed.
21. Responsibility for the well-being of the entire organization as embodied by these principles is felt by all employees.

Despite this invitation to participate, and then being involved in presentations to enhance their trust relationship, the union decided to hold onto its traditional, adversarial, contractual relationship with the company. "We are continuing to live by our belief structure, insisting that we model the behavior that the structure says that we ought to be modeling and sooner or later we think that it might begin to penetrate their consciousness."

Informing Hal Bolton's overall perspective is what he calls his personal "belief structure," which is close to theosophy in its fundamental content.

In our philosophy of human evolution, the whole evolution that goes from animal to man, which is from the physical to the emotional to the mental-concrete to the mental-abstract on up to a higher spiritual state, it takes a long time for man to progress up through these levels of consciousness. Predominantly humanity is probably still in the emotional phase particularly in our country and in a lot of the more industrialized countries, polarized at that level. That doesn't mean that people don't think or don't have spiritual aspirations, but predominantly they are active at the emotional level. That's why football games and those kinds of things are exciting to people because of the whole charged feeling in them.

To me that's where most people are. You have a group of people who are in the mental realm now, and then you find a few who are a little spiritual and beginning to apply spiritual values.

I'm involved in the Theosophical Society. I sit on the Theosophical Investment Trust that manages the funds that help support the Society. But I am concerned about any one society like that, because, like the churches, they tend to become anthropomorphized in their beliefs. They have an image and that's the only image that applies and I don't believe that. I think there are all sorts of things that are as viable and contribute as much to spiritual growth as what the Theosophists have to offer.

Hal's belief structure is rooted in a search he has conducted throughout his adult years for abiding values. At one time he had thought of going into the ministry, then decided that was just an idealistic impulse based on his desire to satisfy a feeling that he couldn't quite grasp. "I have been a member of about every church you could imagine, trying to find one that had the answers. Of course, for me none of the churches do."

Hal has concluded that the biggest problem with religion, or with a philosophy such as his, is getting beyond trying to understand it and applying it to everything you do. He believes Christianity is a fantastic religion.

It's a shame that people haven't tried it yet because the principles of it are nothing different than what we talk about. If you separate Christianity from the church, I have no problem with it. It's when you begin to protect the institution rather than teach the belief structure that I have the problem. That is why I am now no longer involved in a standardized formal religion, although I support a church in the sense of making a donation to a church because I still feel a lot of people need what the church has to offer.

My belief structure says that human beings are polarized at a level of consciousness depending upon the number of evolutions, of incarnations, they have gone through. We are not equal and one reason is we have not all been around the same number of times. There is neither good nor bad. There is no judgment involved in the whole system. Those that have been around more are probably going to have a higher level of consciousness and those who haven't have a lower level of consciousness. But the higher level of consciousness you have the more responsibility you have also, and, therefore, you ought to apply that responsibility in all endeavors, not just go to a study session once a week or church once a week, but make it a part of what you do every day.

How you get people to open their minds to a higher level of consciousness is a very difficult thing. There is no answer to that. All we can do is to provide windows and concepts that embrace higher thoughts and hopefully some will accept them in their subconsciousness perhaps and begin to grow and begin to accept the fact that there are some different ways of doing things.

Hal does not impose his beliefs on the organization by insisting that others believe as he does. His managers cover the normal spectrum of religious affiliation. He believes that whatever happens in life was meant to happen. His response to events, then, is primarily acceptance of what has happened. He believes there is a flow of energy to life and that you must learn to live with that flow of energy. Things work out when they are meant to and don't when they are not meant to. Hal met his wife, who is from Finland, on a beach in Spain. "We just somehow managed to get to the same beach at the same time. I got there because I was lost; I went to the wrong beach. Actually I don't think anything like that happens accidentally."

The Boltons share beliefs with a small group of people in the

Jamestown area that is part of a broader network, really international in scope, though not formally organized. Periodically a teacher, foreign or domestic, comes to Jamestown and the Boltons and the others they are involved with are exposed to new dimensions of their belief structure, which have raised their levels of human consciousness.

They gave up drinking alcoholic beverages many years ago and now are also vegetarians. They know that these new ways have made some of their business and community friends somewhat uncomfortable, but they try never to impose their beliefs on anyone else. It would be counter to their beliefs to do so.

How he is viewed in the community is really of no concern to Hal. "People can believe about me any way they want. Nobody can affect my thinking unless I want them to or my feelings unless I wish to feel that way. If I wish to feel badly because somebody says something about me, that's my problem. External beliefs about me are not particularly important to me."

When Hal bought Dahlstrom's he also purchased a small tool-and-die business in Jamestown, a kind of vertical integration move. His business strategy has been to develop regional fabrication facilities close to customers as opportunities develop. With that in mind, in 1980 a Florida plant was purchased and in 1985 another was opened in Ireland to service United Kingdom clients.

The Irish plant was designed to operate according to Dahlstrom's principles from day one.

> We set that up on a skill-based compensation system, with recognition and participation and information flows and open communications. I spent a lot of time on the initial design of that, working with the folks over there. Our folks over there say, "We don't know what is different about this place, but we like it." We don't have time clocks. We believe in trust, and we say, "Hey, if you guys are going to violate the principle that we trust you to get to work on time, we may be forced to put time clocks back in. We are telling you we trust you. We expect you then to work, with respect back, with us, so that we can continue to work this way together."

Several years ago, Craig Colburn left the Cummins Jamestown (Lakewood) organization to become president and operating head of Dahlstrom–Jamestown and to lead the daily effort to change the way the company involved its employees in the management of the business. Recent focus has been on educating the lower levels of Dahlstrom management in the principles the company espouses, showing them how those principles, once in place, will create a more productive and growthful operation for everyone involved. By no one's admission is the effort yet successful. But Hal and Craig have persisted because they know it is in the right direction. And it has only been underway for a few years. The dilemma is the same one that for years has plagued businesses wishing to develop more people-oriented methods for internal operations. The managers and supervisors they have relied upon at Dahlstrom to establish the new methods are frequently technically skilled in the mechanical aspects of the work performed but less skilled in human relations. To maintain business efficiency they are essential, but from a human effectiveness standpoint, they are not inclined to relinquish old patterns of behavior very easily.

As Craig learned the business, Hal increasingly has been able to focus on the units located outside of Jamestown, on company financial operations and on real estate matters. The company has 600,000 square feet of multistoried plant in Jamestown and has been trying to lease out or sell about two-thirds of it for other uses.

Hal has accepted his share of community responsibilities in Jamestown, true to his belief structure. In addition to co-chairing the labor management committee and serving on the Theosophic Investment Trust, he is past president of the United Way and of the local manufacturers' association, and has been on those and other local community boards. He also is president of the Jamestown Community College Foundation.

The board of directors at Dahlstrom is composed of six members, three insiders and three outsiders, despite the fact that the company is privately owned. "We have kept it balanced. There is no vested interest here. There are no selfish decisions. It is run with a lot of logic behind everything we do. We have fun doing it."

When Hal hired Craig, he did so with the idea that Craig would succeed him. They developed a buy/sell agreement so if Hal decided to go off and do something different someday, Craig could buy him out. About doing something different, Hal says, "I have said that when I'm supposed to do that, I will know what it is. I have been keeping my senses open and looking and seeing what might happen."

Where Hal is philosophical in his approach to life and business, Craig is pragmatic. Both, however, believe strongly in the Dahlstrom principles and share the vision of what Dahlstrom is to become.

However, asked how he felt about turning the company he has nurtured and owned over to someone philosophically different from himself, Hal replied virtually without pausing, "If that's what happens, then that's probably what's supposed to happen anyway. When it was in my care I tried the best to take care of it. When it's in somebody else's care then they have to take care of it according to their way of taking care of it. Whatever I move on to, I will apply my principles to. I don't have any ownership here you see; I mean ego. That makes it easy."

Chapter 6

Transforming the American Enterprise: With Understatement, Excitement and Lightning

KEN IVERSON AT Nucor and Bill O'Brien at Hanover Insurance each head now successful companies which once required intensive care to survive. These are models of lean organizations that know why they are in business. Both recognize that people are their most valuable assets even though one business is capital intensive and the other is labor intensive.

The Bruce Copeland story provides many lessons. His experience attests to the fact that sometimes virtue must be its own reward and that even in failure there can be success of a higher order.

* * *

A variety of given conditions and circumstances face every business leader. Some leaders are dealt more favorable or more promising hands than others. However, it is rare when a combination of conditions and circumstances integrate well and at the right time with the personal experiences and talents of a leader so that a real long-term success can emerge from the prospects of failure. The story of Ken Iverson provides us with such an example.

An Understatement in Corporate Effectiveness

F. Kenneth Iverson, Chairman and C.E.O.
Nucor Corporation

In the story of Nucor Corporation, of how it arose phoenixlike from the ashes of its predecessor, the process appears to have been deceivingly simple. To the outsider, Nucor today seems to be a well-oiled machine purring its way from one success to the next.

But, on closer inspection, it is clear that many parts make up its complex system and that each part has been well polished by the experiences of the past two decades and by a highly committed management team and work force.

The wonder is that a company immersed in traditional heavy industry should perform so well. Its secret, of course, is that it has always taken the human/organizational factor very seriously.

Nucor

Nucor Corporation's 1987 annual report is an excellent representation of the company itself. It has a deceptively plain cover, green in color, with a block of white lines overlaying the plain background. Upon a closer look, the white lines become names, some 4,600 of them. It is a listing of all the employees of the company.

The opening paragraph of the letter to stockholders sets the tone for the report:

Nucor's record sales of $851,000,000 for 1987 were 13 percent higher than the year earlier figure of $755,200,000. Net earnings of $50,500,000, equal to $2.39 per share, were 10 percent higher than the $46,400,000, or $2.17 per share, in 1986. In 1987, the company had a 13 percent return on average equity, the same as 1986.

Further on, the letter reads:

With strong feelings of responsibility and loyalty to its employees, the Company has not closed a single plant or laid off a single employee for lack of work for many years. All Nucor employees have part of their compensation based on their productivity or the success of the Company. Productivity is high and employee relations are good. In 1987, the Company generated $189,000 of sales per employee.

The letter ends:

The success of your Company is due to the efforts and loyalty of employees and the support of customers, suppliers and stockholders.

The remainder of the report of this mini-mill steel maker and steel products manufacturer is a factual review of business activities and financial results expressed without superlatives. In short, it is a model of understatement.

Going back to the 1987 cover, a very close look at the list of names of employees reveals, between Alice Isom and Patricia Ivey, the name F. Kenneth Iverson, chairman and C.E.O. of Nucor and chief architect of its unique method of operation.

To the visitor seeking to learn about the company and its chairman, trying to find Nucor's corporate office is a curious experience. Expecting some hint of grandeur or at least a nameplate on the exterior of the building housing Nucor's headquarters, one soon learns that only a small corner on one floor of that building in Charlotte, North Carolina, is required for the 16 people who compose the total corporate office group. The rest of the building is occupied by a wide variety of other enterprises. The office decor is as understated as the format of the annual report.

There are no privileges of rank evident at Nucor—no company planes, no company cars, no reserved parking, no executive dining rooms or lavatories, no hunting or fishing lodges, no first-class tickets for flying on company business.

There are also no differences in hard-hat colors in plant areas. Everyone wears green except maintenance people, who need to be spotted easily in cases of emergency. They wear yellow. And there are no retirement or pension plans. Everyone in the company is

111

covered by the same company-paid health and dental insurance.

The work force at Nucor is entirely nonunion and is supervised by a minimum number of management employees. They compose four levels—foremen, department heads, vice-president/general managers and president/chairman. Ken Iverson considers that Hugh D. Aycock, president and C.O.O., and he are on the same level and share the responsibility of overseeing the total company.

But, for all the things the company does not have, it is not a cheap employer. Average production employee pay is $30,000 a year with melters able to earn over $40,000. Additionally employees of the company regularly receive 10 percent of the company's annual profits before taxes, which is put into a deferred payout trust plan for each employee based on his or her total pay. In the time it takes an employee to be vested in the plan (nine years), a production worker can accumulate over $100,000.

The heart of Nucor's productivity system is its production group incentive plan. It was first introduced into the company through the acquisition of a joist plant in 1962. Now in a more refined form, the system is in operation throughout Nucor's steel making and steel products manufacturing units, where natural workgroups of approximately 30 persons work against prescribed standards measuring their daily performance. It is normal at Nucor to expect groups to produce twice what the daily standard has called for. Bonuses are paid weekly for the previous week's results.

Rules regarding bonus participation are strict, however. A person missing work for one day or who is late more than a half hour receives no bonus for the entire week. A tardy worker loses bonus for that day. Four "forgiveness" days are allowed each employee every year, however, to cover excusable unexpected emergencies or unavoidable absences.

Nucor has located its mini-mills and fabricating plants in small towns in rural areas where it believes the hardest-working employees are located. Nucor's incentive system doesn't appeal to everyone. When they start up a new operation, initial employee turnover is high. Gradually the workers who can't adjust to the pace leave and the turnover rate reduces practically to zero. A few years ago, eight or nine people were needed to be added to the Darlington, South Carolina, plant. A small ad in the local paper brought 1,200 applicants to the plant gate on a Saturday morning. Even the local highway patrol headquarters couldn't help with the traffic problem. Three of their people were in the line to apply!

Nucor keeps its people, and keeps them employed. They haven't had a layoff for lack of work for over 15 years. The reason for this is the company belief that you can't get good people if you lay them off during slow times and try to hire them back again. Second, in most Nucor plant situations, it is the largest, sometimes the only, employer in town. Hence, Nucor feels it's their social responsibility to keep workers employed. They have nowhere else to go to earn their living. When a slow economic period comes along, Nucor reduces the work week to four days. In some cases, they have even operated only three days for several weeks. "We call it a 'share the pain program,' " Ken says, because the four management levels, each paid an increasingly larger share of total compensation from incentive bonuses as you go up the ladder, are even more heavily affected than the production work force.

> The average hourly employee will have his compensation during this period drop 20–25 percent because he drops from five to four days. The department head's compensation drops 35–40 percent, and the total compensation of the officers drops 60–70 percent. So, we never get any questions from employees about, "Why isn't my pay better" or something like that. All they ask is, "When do we get back on five days?" I'm a great believer in that because I think that management's pay should drop more because they have more responsibility for the decisions that mean success or failure of the company, obviously.

> The group production incentive system is self-policing.

> If somebody comes into a group who doesn't perform at the group's level, and accordingly threatens the compensation of the group, they either take their own methods of training him to bring him up to level or they get rid of him eventually.

Another characteristic about it is that they [groups]

have been responsible for many of the developments in processes and productivity that the company has had because they benefit, of course, from the added productivity. So, over the years, they'll make suggestions as to how to do it better or how to change it so that productivity will increase. Now, if we're going to keep our integrity with that employee, it requires that we accept that. So basically, we never change these standards; they remain the same regardless of how much bonus they might make. There is one very strong exception to this. That is, if we make a capital expenditure of one million dollars or more, we then will go to the group and say, "Look, we're making this capital expenditure and we've got to get our return on that investment and so, we'll share the added productivity that comes from that investment."

The grievance procedure at Nucor is simple and clear.

If somebody doesn't like a decision that's been made by the foreman, he then goes to the department head. If he doesn't like the decision from the department head, he then goes to the general manager, supposedly in writing. It's seldom that way really in fact. And if he doesn't like that, he is supposed to write to me. Eighty percent of them never write. They pick up the phone and say that we've got a problem and I understand maybe you can help us. We probably end up between Dave Aycock, the president, and myself, with at least one, probably two, of these a month.

Open and frequent communications with employees is a way of life at Nucor. "Every general manager is required to have at least one dinner a year with every employee in his organization in groups of no more than 50. If the mill has 500 employees, that means 10 dinners a year and generally they do it twice a year, so they have 20 dinners."

The general manager is limited to 20 minutes to discuss business conditions and anything new affecting the plant. Then the rest of the meeting is the employees' with three ground rules.

1. Whatever is brought up must be relevant to the business.
2. Personalities are not discussed.
3. An employee can say anything about his or her job or the company even if it's derogatory and by the next day it's forgotten. Guaranteed.

In new plant situations, the employees ask about the insurance program and profit sharing, obvious things to discuss. They soon realize the company is serious about this, however, and bring up a whole range of other issues that are bothering them.

The company also conducts a periodic survey asking what the employees like about the company, what they don't like and what they would change if they could. Survey results repeatedly focus on one issue, Ken says. " 'I want more communications from my foreman.' It seems as though they're almost insatiable about this. 'I want to know what my job opportunities are. I want to know what's happening to the company, where it's going, how it expects to get there.' That's just something, no matter how much training you do, always crops up." To improve this situation, foremen at Nucor are trained and retrained in how to be better communicators. But, Ken indicates, all the training in the world never seems to be enough.

I'm a strong believer, first of all, in the purpose of business. You can look at it like this: The blood in your veins is not the reason you exist, but you can't do very well unless you have healthy blood in your veins. Well, the same thing is true about profit. You can't grow and you can't create opportunities for people if you don't have earnings in the company, but it's not really the reason why the corporation exists. Over a long period of time I've come to believe a corporation exists for its survival and for its propagation so that it can continue to create opportunities for people and, in some cases, their children and grandchildren, long after the people who presently operate the company may be gone. I am also a strong believer that charity begins at home. I get very concerned when I see companies who don't pay their employees very well when they could, but they spend vast amounts of money on arts or in the community, I guess, for the aggrandizement of the executives of the company, and I think that's wrong. They ought first of all to look after their own employees, create opportunities for them, and make sure they are taken care of.

Many Nucor employees are also stockholders, taking advantage of the company's plan, purchasing stock at a 10 percent discount from market with Nucor paying the brokerage fee.

The company is also known for being a responsive, reliable and ethical supplier in the marketplace. Its sales force is instructed that if they are ever in the presence of competitors at an industry meeting and the subject of prices comes up, they are to turn their drink glasses upside down and leave the meeting immediately. "That's not to be obstreperous," Ken says, "but people will remember the incident; that's the reason for it."

One unusual benefit offered to all Nucor employee families is its scholarship plan providing $1,500 a year for four years to the children of employees to help pay for post–high school education or vocational training. It began as the result of a 1974 accident in a Nucor plant in which four employees were killed. The management met to consider what it might do to assist the families over time. "We had good insurance programs, so there wasn't a problem with day-to-day living. But we thought, there were a bunch of children involved, 12, 14, something like that, and when they got ready to go to college, that's when the financial strain would develop."

The managers decided to establish a scholarship fund for each of the children involved. Then someone said that some scholarships should be available in the company for the children of current employees as well, giving out four or five to each division every year. That led to a comment from one general manager who said that they couldn't do that. It was their philosophy that if something were done for one employee, it had to be done for or be available to all employees. Upon investigation they discovered that the demographics, plotted out, made it a very feasible proposition to cover all employees. Since its inception some dozen years ago, over 2,000 children of employees have used the program. In one recent year, 260 children of employees were attending 120 different learning institutions throughout the country on Nucor scholarships.

History

Now how did all of the above come about at Nucor, and what was the background of its leader that it should develop in this manner?

One could speculate that Ken Iverson must have received a classical education in the liberal arts and sciences and was exposed to the pioneering theorists in organization behavior at a well-known graduate school of business as a foundation for the unique development of Nucor.

In truth, Ken Iverson went into a U.S. Navy V-12 program after graduating from high school in Downers Grove, Illinois, in 1943. After two semesters at Northwestern University the navy sent him to Cornell University, where he graduated several years later as an aeronautical engineer. After completing his tour of duty, Ken returned to the Midwest and to Purdue where he received his master's in metallurgy in 1947, not yet 22 years old.

For the next five years, he was a research physicist at International Harvester, becoming assistant chief research physicist before leaving in 1952 to become chief engineer for a small foundry owned by Burgess Battery in Freeport, Illinois. When the foundry was sold two years later, Ken joined Indiana Steel Products in Valparaiso, Indiana, as assistant to the vice-president of manufacturing. Indiana Steel hired him to set up a laboratory to do spectrographic analysis. When that was accomplished they had no real job for him, so he resigned and joined Cannon Muskegon Corporation as chief metallurgist. At Cannon he was involved in vacuum metallurgy, oversaw the production of the first uranium ingot to power the *Nautilus* submarine, became production head of vacuum metallurgy and then sales manager of this company which was in the forefront of alloy metals technology particular for aircraft applications.

In 1960, at age 35, Ken moved to Little Ferry, New Jersey, to become executive vice-president of a company called Coast Metals, also in the aircraft alloys and metals business. After two years there, with the president of the company unwilling to permit Ken any stock ownership in the company, he left to do some consulting for another firm interested in buying metals companies. That firm was called Nuclear Corporation of America.

Those familiar with the folklore of executive search, at this point, might wish to acknowledge that Ken's job history thus far was a poor predictor of his subsequent tenure with Nucor.

Shortly thereafter he recommended that Nuclear Corporation purchase a successful joist plant in Florence, South Carolina, that was for sale because of the death of the founder and owner. The Nuclear management, knowing little about the metal fabrication business, said they would buy it if Ken agreed to join the company and run it. Ken did agree, becoming vice-president and general manager of the joist manufacturing operations of Nuclear. The South Carolina facilities were expanded and a second plant added a year later in Nebraska. In another year, Ken moved to corporate headquarters in Phoenix and became a group vice-president in charge of joist operations, a rare metals plant and a contracting company, all owned by Nuclear.

Nuclear Corporation of America was a miniconglomerate of some eight heterogeneous operations doing about $20 million in total annual sales. It was formed as a spinoff from Reo Motors when the assets of that company were purchased by White Consolidated. The one continuing division, which constituted Nuclear Corporation initially, made nuclear instruments including radiation counters and detectors. The added operations included a design graphics business, a diode business, a leasing business and the contracting, rare metals and joist manufacturing operations. The company was losing $300,000 a year by 1965 when it defaulted on the repayment of $2 million in loans to two banks. The president of Nuclear resigned and Ken Iverson, now managing the company's only profitable operations, was elected president. The remainder of the year was spent getting out of the diode, design graphics, leasing and construction businesses through sale and liquidation. The company's name was changed to Nucor Corporation in 1972.

"Since that time, since 1965, the company has never had a loss quarter. It's made money every single quarter since then," Ken relates with a hint of pride.

"In 1967 we bought a very small, I think we paid $125,000 for it, business that was practically in bankruptcy making joists in Fort Payne, Alabama. We then started construction of another joist plant in Texas. Meanwhile, always in the back of our minds was the fact that 58 percent of our sales dollar was the cost of steel. We were buying almost all of our steel offshore at that time. We knew that we needed to do something to have an economical supply of raw material and the only way to do that would be to build a steel mill."

So, Ken and two associates went to Europe for two weeks, touring a dozen steel mills and talking to steel mill suppliers. They determined that they could build a steel mill and produce steel as efficiently and as cheaply in the United States as foreign producers could supply it here. Initiating that action, Ken recalls, also began their "bet the company" phase, a period that Ken believes occurs at least once in the life of most, if not all, successful corporations. "That's what we did. We leveraged the company up absolutely as far as we could. At one time or another during this period we were probably close to 50 percent debt to capital."

The first mill Nucor built was in Darlington, South Carolina. They never poured an ingot. They went into 100 percent continuous casting from the beginning. "I won't go into all the problems we had in starting up that first mill because, again, we were kind of on the leading edge." For raw material they used scrap, again saving energy and reducing production cost.

Since building that first mill in 1969, Nucor has built six new mills in Nebraska, Texas, South Carolina and Utah. They have also built several new joist plants and expanded their steel products manufacturing operations while broadening their offering of mill products. Thus the marriage of technological innovation and of a productivity-oriented organizational culture has produced an enviable record of both financial and human resource results.

Philosophy

Ken Iverson declines to take personal credit for the innovations that Nucor has achieved. For example, when asked where the company's personnel system came from, he replied, "From the managers as a group. We meet three times a year. One of these meetings, generally it's the midyear meeting in May, is entirely devoted to personnel policies, personnel practices, pay considerations. It works as a group. They make the decisions in this group, over many years now; they determine the policies and practices of the company. I'm a great believer that they have to be comfortable with it, they have to believe in it or it's not going to work. Just that I believe in it isn't enough."

Issues of ethics, of fairness, of what is the right thing to do come up at each officer's meeting and are often intensely debated before a consensus is reached.

However, in asking Ken whether the present Nucor culture began with his assuming the presidency of the company his reply was, "Yes, no question about that." Then he added in his typical sharing manner: "Here we had a $20 million business that was all torn asunder and we had a great opportunity to build a company in the management style that we felt would be successful and a management style that we all felt comfortable with."

Those involved had obviously read a lot about innovative and productive ways of organizing plant work forces. Ken acknowledges that it would be impossible to determine the true sources of many of the ideas incorporated in the Nucor system.

The first meeting of the management to rebuild the company the way they wanted it to be was held in early 1966 in a motel near O'Hare Field in the Chicago area. However, the way the company is organized and operates today did not spring full-blown from that meeting. Rather it evolved because of the conditions of openness and participation that Ken Iverson established early on and the management group has maintained at Nucor since then.

I never had any inspiration to be an enlightened leader. I didn't originate a lot of these [ideas]. They originated from the group working together. I guess I got the idea of organizing the company that way primarily from my experience in industry before and what I thought would be a good way to have it operate. It gradually developed by itself because these general managers wanted a big voice in what the company philosophies were going to be and then they, in turn, were encouraged to give their people a big voice. It went through a whole developing process, I guess.

During a visit in late 1987 to Nucor's Vulcraft Division and Nucor steel plants in Norfolk, Nebraska, the words of Ken Iverson gained substance. At both plants employee turnover is virtually nonexistent. At Vulcraft, one opening in 1986 attracted 250 appli-cants. Dan Nielsen, a production line supervisor, started with Vulcraft as a rigger in 1967. Within three months he became a lead man. Such a thing is unheard of today. In 1988 all of Dan's crew had been with the company 10 years or more.

Ron Nielsen, no relation to Dan, one of those at Vulcraft with 10 years of service in 1988, isn't too worried about the resulting lack of advancement. "We have our jobs to do. There aren't any places in Norfolk that pay as well as this. We've never laid anybody off. When it's slow we go to 32 hours. That's still better than anybody else makes in this area."

Dave Aycock started Vulcraft Norfolk after being at the Florence, South Carolina, plant. In 1977 he became head of the Darlington, South Carolina, steel mill where he stayed for several years before becoming president. Dave's successor in Norfolk as vice-president and general manager is Don Holloway, also a hands-on operating manager. Don tours the plant daily to observe what's happening and to be accessible to anyone who wants to speak with him.

Over at the Nucor–Norfolk steel mill, the attitude about the company is the same. By 1987 Don Morrow had been there nine years, having started on the construction crew building the second steel mill. He runs a cut-off machine, but fills in wherever else he's needed. "The way our pay is set up it pays for us to help each other out." Don likes the fact that he's responsible for his work and is left on his own to do it. But he knows his supervisor is available when he needs him. "Here you are more on a personal basis with your management."

Mike Hart is a transplanted easterner. He also had been at Nucor–Norfolk for nine years in 1987. A maintenance supervisor, Mike joined Nucor, he says, in part because of unions. Where he worked before he felt he had no control over what would happen. "It seemed like we spent more time figuring out whose job it was than doing it." At Nucor, he says, there is more cooperation between workers and managers. And, he affirms, "I don't have to ask my boss every time I want to get involved in something."

After 17 years at Inland Steel, Hank Collins joined Nucor as manager of the Norfolk rolling mill in 1985. He says he left the best of the big to join the best of the small. He appreciates Nucor because decisions are made right at the plant by line people regarding changes or additions as long as they are within the limits of the capital budget. "The accountability is here. We know this is our company. It is a 'we' thing. There is very little discussion that 'the company' is doing this or that. There is very little that is withheld, if any, from this work force. All the costs, all the data that's important to the running of this division is available to this work force as it is to me. And it should be. They should know what is going on in this company."

One cannot help but be impressed by both the dedication and the intelligence of the Nucor work force. Those observed in Norfolk are solid, down-to-earth people with no ego protection obvious. This absence of pretense is certainly modeled by John Doherty, the designer of Nucor's Norfolk mills and the only person ever to be the vice-president and general manager there. In 1986, production facilities expansion required that a new office building be built on the property. In 1987, it housed the 25 people, including John, who provided accounting, employment and sales in support of the plant population of 500 production workers. Like everyone at Nucor, John abhors anything that isn't productive and accountable. He says that the leaders of many companies have brought on the problems they have today because they've forgotten what they were there for. At Nucor, he says, the order of attention is to employees, then to customers, then to suppliers, then to the community. And if you do that right the stockholders will do okay. In many companies, he feels, attention to the stockholders unfortunately comes first.

John's comfortable but utilitarian office and conference room appeared to be well used. His conference room table was strewn with the materials needed to do his work—much of that involving ways to increase the productive use of space and equipment. His door was literally always open and he was accessible to any employee at any reasonable time.

As a corporate citizen of Norfolk, the Nucor plants have contributed generously to area needs and Nucor personnel are visibly involved in a wide range of civic activities.

The lessons to be gained by studying Nucor are many. All of its pieces seem to fit one another and operate to reinforce each other.

It is obviously a technically efficient organization. But unlike closely controlled efficient organizations of the past, it achieves these results through optimum openness in communications with employee groups. These groups are significantly involved in running the business and do so in a highly self-disciplined manner, under leadership that readily lets others share in the responsibility and fun of management. It still sounds deceivingly simple.

* * *

Transformational leadership, as we have now seen, is not confined to any one industry. It certainly has not been commonly observed previously in traditionally capital-intensive "smoke stack" businesses. And the recent growth in people-intensive service industries has presented new and different challenges to their leadership. Our next profile describes how Bill O'Brien and his predecessor, Jack Adam, of Hanover Insurance have met those challenges.

Excitement in a Mundane Business

William J. O'Brien, President and C.E.O.
The Hanover Insurance Companies

Uniformly, the business leaders interviewed for this book have been thoughtful, articulate persons of conviction. They have all believed in the "rightness" of what they have been doing.

Furthermore, most have arrived at that state of confidence and certainty through the experience of trial and error, supplemented by self-generated study, as opposed to prior formal training in the behavioral sciences or through management education.

Bill O'Brien epitomizes this in his work with the people of the Hanover Insurance Companies. Together they are growing a humane enterprise, a never-completed task. The focus of the people of Hanover is on the development of every Hanover employee. The results as indicated in this profile are impressive.

Hanover

Perhaps John Cooper put it most eloquently. John is a commercial multiperil analyst in the Hanover Chicago branch office. "I've worked for three insurance companies," he said. "Everywhere I've worked, I've kept a special file in my desk. I've put things in it to cover myself in case I'm ever challenged about an underwriting decision I've made. The difference is here at Hanover my file is empty." John's file is empty because Hanover tries to run on trust, not on fear. To begin with, Hanover has a clearly stated purpose for being in business. That purpose is to provide property and liability insurance to as many Americans as it can at a price they are willing to pay; to provide an environment within the organization so all employees can grow to fulfill their potential; and to earn a profit for future growth and to reward its investors.

Hanover is also a vision-led company. Each accountable organizational unit in the company is encouraged to develop a vision to guide its operations. A vision portrays how a unit wants to be seen, what it wants to be. At Hanover visioning is an ongoing process involving every unit, department or branch.

In addition to a vision, each unit participatively establishes its annual goals in an iterative process in conjunction with other units with which it is interdependent or to which it is responsible. Discussing a recent goal-setting and budgeting process, John remarked, "In the other companies I was never involved in a process like this. Here we get a feel for what we have to do, whether we have options, what kind of input we have. So when we finally set our goals, it is no surprise. We are involved in the process while the goals are being set. In one company I worked for I would never have known anything about the budget, unless my boss said sometime during the year that we were over budget and told me what the budget was."

John's special file is also empty because Hanover is a value-guided company. The values are specific. John is very familiar with three of them.

The first of these values is *merit*. Merit means that Hanover people consciously focus on making every decision based on what best achieves Hanover's vision and is consistent with its values. Concern for the assumed desires of persons in authority or other political pressures play no part in such a process.

Besides applying merit to the decisions he makes, merit is visible to John in how he sees Hanover managers treating their employees. "Recognition here is done on a consistent basis. There is a logic to how you are recognized. People who are known as star performers here are star performers because they produce, not because someone favored them."

A second value is *openness*. At Hanover, data about the company's operations are available to all employees. John was skeptical about the reality of this value when he started with the company. But it turned out to be true. Shortly after he arrived a report from the Chicago commercial manager to the branch vice-president, with a copy to the corporate vice-president of underwriting, was routed to John. He thought it was a mistake that he got the report. He soon learned that such routings were routine to everyone in his area.

A third value is *localness*. Localness means that a decision is made or an action taken at the lowest level of an organization that is competent to do it. Interventions by higher levels are inappropriate and demoralizing according to this Hanover value. For John, localness means that what he experienced as rules or directives from upper management in other companies are at most guidelines at Hanover. Guidelines give him much more freedom as well as responsibility to do his work. Also, if an employee wishes to transfer or qualify for a promotion in another branch, he or she must be interviewed and accepted by that branch. In his previous experiences, people were moved around from office to office as mandated by managers at the company headquarters with no local input requested or allowed.

Do merit, openness and localness really pay off at Hanover? Yes, says Joe Rovito, one of the Chicago branch's newer managers. Joe is head of the claims department and has been in the insurance industry for almost 20 years. Like John Cooper, he was with two organizations before joining Hanover in 1985.

Immediately before coming to Hanover, Joe was vice-president and claims manager for a small insurance company in Chicago. "What was nice about that company was that it gave me an opportunity to try to create a claims department of my own, of what I thought a claims department was supposed to be. It was very unstructured; no predetermined ways of doing things. You were pretty much left on your own. I think working for that small company helped prepare me to work here."

Nevertheless, when Joe joined Hanover he was glad to have the help of Tom Sharpe from the Atlanta branch to get him started. "Tom helped to create in my own mind a sense that this is kind of your own thing, that some of the ideas I had were very good. Not that we agreed on everything, but that didn't seem to be very important. It was something to take hold of and do and not be paralyzed by analysis or by over-justification."

Joe quickly learned that merit, openness and localness translated into accountability, competence and trust at Hanover. When one of his supervisors sought his concurrence in establishing a new position, Joe intentionally procrastinated in getting back to him until the supervisor thoughtfully made the decision himself.

The claims procedures at Hanover–Chicago contain little that is standardized. There are standards of service and several standard time frames within which to accomplish certain actions. But, Joe says, every claim is different and deserves individual treatment.

Hanover shies away from developing a standard claim form. "We want people to approach a claim file from what they think it needs. If you don't do it that way, you create robots and automatons. You create paper processors. And a paper processor doesn't give you a very good work product and he really can't do it very long. If he has any intelligence or creativity or enthusiasm, it will wane and he will look for another job. Then you build in a lot of turnover and have problems of job dissatisfaction."

The claims settlement has to make sense to all parties involved, Joe declares. A reviewing supervisor should be interested in learning why the adjuster decided to do what he or she did, not just that the claim was quickly settled. Standard forms, Joe says, may allow for efficiency but they often lead to perfunctory processing and inappropriate settlements.

"Our work volumes are less than other companies. We talk about handling the claims, doing things for the claim, not just processing it. But we've got to make sure they've got the time to do it, to make the extra phone call or make the extra stop." What does that do in terms of Hanover's costs? It costs more in expense dollars to process Hanover claims, but it saves in terms of the larger indemnity dollars that are paid out to settle claims.

Joe has enabled his department personnel to deal with each claim thoughtfully and thoroughly through visioning with them what a properly assembled and investigated file is. He recognizes that everyone in the department cannot be at the same level of competence at any one point. "I think we're all on different levels. But you get people aligned and moving in the same direction. And I think that's what counts."

Doesn't the Hanover approach, which gives employees a large amount of freedom to make decisions without close supervisory or financial controls, lead to a lot of mistakes?

We're willing to make mistakes and take those hits. Even though we know we shouldn't have done what we did, it's important that people are developed to make decisions and groomed and allowed to grow. If you make all the decisions for them, you may get the right decisions, but you haven't grown your people. And I cannot make every decision in this office. Nor can the supervisors. The real decision makers on a day-by-day, claim-by-claim basis are the adjusters in the claims department. And if you aren't developing them to make decisions you're going to take some bad hits that you don't even know you're taking.

Overall, Joe says, using this open approach and constantly re-visioning each year, you develop improvements over how you operated the previous year. Joe believes this approach also provides Hanover a competitive advantage.

I think what happens is you create in the minds of all the people working here that they make a difference. That this claim is their product and that they have certain responsibilities to a lot of people because of this particular thing that's in front of them. We have people who write us letters and say, "We weren't expecting very much from the claims department but here's an adjuster who really took an interest in me. She sent me a check I was worried I wasn't going to get and then called to see if I got it."

I think there are situations where people whom we do

127

not insure come across our claims department, and if the attitude is one of concern and competency, they look at their own insurance and say, "You know, I didn't get that feeling from my company. Maybe I'll switch my business." We have had instances where that has been told to us.

Attracting the appropriate people to Hanover is a challenge.

Sometimes it's very difficult for them to understand what they want out of a job and what we're talking about. But there are others who right away start talking about things that show they are in tune with what we want them to do. You realize this is somebody who may buy in very quickly.

We really take a hard look at whom we are interviewing because we're going to live with them. We talk about ownership: ownership of the files, ownership of the claims department. This is not *my* claims department; it is *ours*. If you get people to buy into that, what a difference it makes in how they approach their job. It's important to them because it is *our* claims department, *our* branch, *our* company.

The employment process at Hanover is lengthy, according to Pat Carey. In addition to numerous interviews with supervisors, an industrial psychologist interviews most candidates. The final decision, however, is made by the person for whom the candidate will be working. Pat herself went through that process several years ago. George Hunt, Hanover's Chicago vice-president and branch manager, had known of Pat and something of her insurance and industrial relations background for several months before asking her whether she'd be interested in coming to work for the company. After months of periodically interviewing and conversing about the position, Pat joined Hanover as the first human resources manager for the Chicago branch.

George Hunt came to Hanover in 1970. "In the first material I read from Jack Adam, the president of Hanover, he said that profit was not the reason for a corporation's being; it was the result of doing other things well. I really believed what he was saying."

George joined the company as state agent in Tulsa where he had been in the property and casualty business with a large direct writer. "That company was very numbers conscious and, as a result, people provided the numbers to management that management was asking for. It became a very political environment, very systems oriented. The numbers drove the organization. It was very tightly controlled."

George had some major disagreements with that approach. He felt it encouraged people to be dishonest so they could look good on paper. He decided to take another job because of the low respect that the employees there had for management because of the dishonesty that was encouraged and the pressure to bring in the numbers.

"I believed that you had to provide either a better product or a better service. And you did that through people, through the type of environment you created. So I immediately subscribed to Jack's theories. We had an organization that was in dire need of being turned around. And it has taken us a long time to inculcate that type of culture in this organization. But I've always believed in that and I've been given the freedom to pursue excellence in this organization where I wasn't in my prior company."

After two years at Hanover, George became a regional marketing manager. He was then transferred to the Chicago office, which was the regional headquarters for eight branch offices covering 19 states. Over the next five or six years, the company decentralized. Chicago then became a major branch office without responsibility for any other branch and George Hunt became the Chicago branch manager.

"If you went to different branches throughout the organization [today], you would see that all of them are different. We have a local flavor. We understand our market and we operate within each market in a different way." Common values, however, are shared at and among all locations. "I think that's one of the strengths of our organization. We're all able to adapt to our local needs." It's also another example of the Hanover value of localness.

Within the Chicago branch, George has seven direct reports, each a manager of his or her department. George sees his job as being the developer of these managers, helping them become better managers of their people. Together as a team they develop the overall plan for the branch and monthly they review with each other how they are doing against that plan.

Each department manager in turn patterns his or her method of operation similarly. Every group of department supervisors is a team and each supervisor has one or more teams that he or she works with. Cross-functional teams also exist. For example, teams composed of underwriters and marketing people plan how they will relate to groups of independent agents. Each such unit also develops a vision of what it intends to become.

This approach to management takes a different kind of person, George says in agreement with Joe Rovito. "I firmly believe there are a lot of people who really don't feel very secure in this type of environment. They don't want this amount of freedom. They'd rather live in a very autocratic, planned, controlled type of environment. That's one of the big drawbacks you have in an organization like ours. There's a tremendous amount of ambiguity here. That's difficult for people who don't tolerate a high level of ambiguity."

But, George says, people who do fit develop a high level of expectation which makes it difficult to hire supervisors or managers who have not grown up in a Hanover-type environment. As time goes by that problem is becoming even more acute.

> As a person becomes less dependent upon authority, managers have to change their roles. If you're helping people grow you see your role as a builder of good decision makers. It's a totally different role than being the decision maker. So the directive approach to management doesn't work. It isn't appropriate for this environment. Listening would be. Asking questions would be, suggesting some options but not dictating options. And it's safe in our environment to say, "I don't know. Let's look at it together and see what we come up with." We learn together. The learning environment is the real important thing, I think. Hanover stresses in its value system making decisions on merit, which requires a learning environment. It's not a political environment and not an authoritarian one.

Within the Chicago branch, Pat Carey helps facilitate and keeps records regarding the technical training done by people in the operating units. However, she conducts Merit, Openness and Localness (MOL) training sessions herself whenever 12 to 15 new people have come on board. George participates in each MOL session. They last a full day.

All salary increases at Hanover, not surprisingly, are based on merit. The compensation system includes a progress sharing program covering all employees. Fifty percent of the annual award is based on national results and 50 percent on local branch results. George doesn't view this profit sharing as a motivator. He believes people want to work for an organization that is a winner, one whose overall purpose they believe in, although he agrees that the elimination of the profit share could be a de-motivator. "But it's not the amount of money, it's job satisfaction that's the most important thing."

George also does not believe that formal management courses have much value. "You can't teach management skills," he says, because management itself is a process of learning and relearning. That's why he has found his career at Hanover so satisfying.

"I've been very happy at Hanover. I enjoy the style. I enjoy my own growth and I have grown considerably since I've been with Hanover. It's exciting to be involved in a company that allows and encourages your personal growth. That's what we're trying to do throughout the company, to have an environment that helps people grow to their maximum potential."

Where did this philosophy of business success through employee growth come from? Who were the architects and when did the effort begin?

History

In 1969, after 117 years in business, the Hanover Insurance Company, based in New York City, was in "near terminal" condition on virtually any scale you might choose to measure it. In that year, State Mutual, a life insurance company, bought controlling interest in Hanover in order to enter the property and casualty business. State Mutual then moved Hanover to its home city, Worcester, Massachusetts. Jack Adam, a casualty insurance executive, then became president of Hanover.

The early days following the purchase were full of challenges. Expenses had to be slashed, and business re-underwritten. In 1971, William J. O'Brien joined Hanover as vice-president of marketing and the decision was confirmed for Hanover to market its own products. In 1979, following Jack Adam's retirement, Bill O'Brien succeeded him as president and C.E.O.

Bill was born in the Bronx and raised in New Jersey. An only child, following parochial grammar and high school, Bill went to Fordham University, graduating in 1954 with studies in philosophy and business. After serving in the army, Bill went into the insurance industry. Beginning in collections he went on to administration, then to underwriting and finally to marketing, through five companies overall.

Most of my early experience was in how not to run a business. Incidentally, I have never been able to complete a traditional management book. They have exceeded my attention span. All of my learning as a business leader has come from other sources, like agriculture. How you grow a plant is not too different from how you grow a department or a corporation. I found myself constantly going back to nature, to family and to my theological belief system for the navigational answers I needed to run a business. I think in many instances the use of what I call "linear approaches to an organization" has been destructive. Things we wouldn't ever think of doing to our kids, businesses have done [using linear approaches] to their employees. Those have been my reference points.

Philosophy

Jack Adam and Bill O'Brien sparked each other's creativity from the start. They believed in the same things.

We had a bottom line. We believed in the potential of people to do a lot more than they were doing. I think we both had a very strong dissatisfaction with the status quo. We had a collaborator relationship with each other.

We didn't set out to build a philosophy. We didn't set out on any social mission. In fact, quite the opposite. We thought the company was pretty sick and the most important thing we had to do was to make it a good insurance company.

In the early 1970s we saw two worthy principles contradicting one another: economic success and practicing the higher virtues of life. It was never said that clearly, but the general thinking was that these two things were opposing principles. You lived your life at work from Monday through Friday and then you went to church on Saturday or Sunday. Life was a set of tradeoffs. Jack and I both believed that instead of tradeoffs, an organization ought to get both. In fact, the more economically successful you were, the better you could practice the higher virtues of life. The better you practiced the higher virtues of life, the more economically successful you could be.

The original problem was how to enlist the people in the front lines in the enterprise's mission, then how to take young people enlisted in the enterprise's mission and to grow them all through life.

In the late 1960s and early 1970s, Bill says, management teaching revolved around "tough-minded men," with the implication that achievements were wrought in business by those who were willing to step on people—to cut back, to fire people, to lay them off, to get ahead.

"When you think about that whole set of beliefs that was underlying the business system, why would anybody on the front lines get turned onto business? For example, earnings per share don't mean anything to the person who is a claims adjuster in Milwaukee."

In 1970–71, Jack Adam laid out the three-part purpose for the organization noted previously, after receiving input from others:

- We want to provide property and liability insurance to as many Americans as we can at a price they are willing to pay.

- We want to provide the environment in our organization so each person can grow to what he or she can become to fulfill their potential.
- We want to earn a profit for future growth and to reward our investors.

We had that purpose in place for six years or so and it was really going nowhere. It took us a good six years to realize that the purpose had to be extended into a vision. We needed to build a vision so we could enlist the people. Extrapolating the present into the future by multiplying everything by 12 percent a year by 10 years motivates nobody but the guy who likes to play with his calculator. So we drew some word pictures—what it was that we wanted to become in terms of perceptions that we wanted people to have of us; the experiences we wanted to have; what our position would be relative to other companies we admired. We needed that to enlist people. But the second thing we needed it for was to set scale. What do I mean by "setting scale"? If you are building a company that's on the bottom and you want to go to the top, you've got to communicate just how good you want to be.

In my first year as president, I went across the country and I talked to every single employee in every branch of the company. I told them what my vision was for the Hanover Insurance Company. Now a vision is an intensely personal thing. Your vision gets you out of bed to go to work in the morning. My vision gets me working. My vision doesn't do a lot for you. So, we don't have a lot of meetings on what should be the vision of the company or what should be the vision of a department. We encourage our people if they run an operation to have a vision for it. And then, when they are facing live, real situations, act in a visionary way. I have never seen a vision come out of a committee. I have heard people say, "Here is what I believe and here is what I think we can do. What do you think?" That kind of process will build some visions.

My vision for the company is not that we discover

some policy that everybody wants to buy but never has any claims. My vision isn't that we develop some computer program that will surpass Travelers or Aetna or State Farm, because they'll copy us six months later. Rather, my vision is that if you could drive from Worcester to the West Coast and visit every one of our offices, you would find a group of people in each of those offices who are tops in their field, the property and liability business; that they possessed a very high degree of self-direction; that they were relatively free of procedural and bureaucratic controls; but that there was a strong common thread of oneness among them based on vision and values. You could identify this common philosophical thread but outside of that you would see a lot of diversity and freedom. Ultimately I would like us to achieve unquestionable superiority in the property and liability business.

We encourage every single department to build its own vision of what it wants to become. When we first did it, everybody thought we were going to have chaos! But there is remarkable harmony between what a branch or department envisions and what a company sees.

At Hanover, the visioning process is never-ending. It is open and continuous in every department and branch. "It's a dynamic, living idea. It was never committed to granite. Our purpose is not on any plaque. Our vision is not in any official version."

During Hanover's recovery period, management was mindful of principles that were essential to creating the company they wanted to become. They had never thought about specifically creating a philosophy of management. Late in the decade, however, it was clear that identifying and disseminating the company's values were necessary. There are seven of them. The three primary values, merit, openness and localness, have been described previously. About merit Bill says: "The plain hard facts are that most companies run on politics and bureaucracy. [At Hanover] we saw merit as an antidote to the enormously destructive politics and bureaucracy that were going on. To have merit in the company you need a strong purpose and vision and values. Otherwise merit becomes what the highest ranking person believes ought to be done." An elaboration on merit entitled "Building a Merit Environment" has been compiled and published by Hanover and is available through the company.

The second value that we built into the culture was openness. Way back in the early days, both Jack and I believed that managers who were open had a much higher level of productivity than managers who played their cards close to their vests. We always widely disseminate information. My reports to the board, for instance, go right down into the middle management of our branches. They are available to anyone.

The third value we developed was localness. It really goes back to the principle of "subsidiarity." It is a disruption of the right order of things for a higher level to intervene at a lower level in something that the lower level is competent to do themselves.

With localness in decision making, Bill says, you get much better decisions. "When you first do it, you get some disruptions. It is like dealing with teenagers. They go through an adolescent period. Mistakes are made while they develop the maturity to handle responsibility. But once they go through that, it is so much more valuable."

The fourth value at Hanover is *what they believe about people.* In one pamphlet by Bill, "A Philosophy to Work By," it states:

- Hanover values the full potential of its people.
- Hanover is a teaching company.
- The environment stimulates my growth.
- The company brings out the best in people.
- It is a demanding but rewarding environment.
- Our people are among the best in the industry.

Hanover's fifth value is *leanness.* "There is a tremendous temptation in corporate life to get fat before you get tall, particularly when you're spending other people's money. We've never seen anybody get great by getting fat first." Bill's pamphlet reads:

- We run a tight ship.
- We pay well and make possible steady advancement.
- We don't spend money on appearances or show.
- Every buck works for us.

The sixth value is Hanover values *responsible customers* and treats them responsibly.

- The Hanover's an effective competitor for good business.
- We won't touch poor business.
- We practice more "risk" than "class" underwriting.
- Hanover goes the extra mile to satisfy customers.
- Our business has high renewal retention.
- We settle claims promptly and fairly.

Finally, it values *quality agents* and treats them responsibly.

- Hanover is very careful in making appointments.
- We're very slow to terminate, exhausting all means to rehabilitate.
- Our underwriting market is comparatively stable in all cycles. We write a balanced book of business and are good at all lines we write.
- We offer a consistently high level of service.
- We're dependable.
- We're helpful.
- Hanover helps to bring business into an agency, not just take it out.

Bill acknowledges,

This is no instant formula to be plugged in. We are in our 17th or 18th year. It was trial and error. What we have done is homegrown. Every bit of our philosophy emanated from a problem that faced us.

What I think has happened in this organization is that

we made a commitment to perform a very mundane business in a superior fashion. That doesn't mean we do it, but we try to do it in a superior fashion. We made a commitment that work could be an important vehicle for each person's growth and development. We made a commitment to being economically successful. Those were the three commitments we made in our purpose and we talk about them. We eventually grew lots of other people who talk about them. I think we get people in the organization who say, "This is consistent with my own beliefs and this is the kind of company that I want to work for."

Although Hanover management focuses its energies on living up to its purpose, vision and values—on positively impacting the lives of its employees, agents and customers—traditional business measurements as well indicate that something very good has been going on in the company.

The Hanover Companies now employ over 5,000 people with less than 10 percent of them assigned to national office positions, a very low percentage for the insurance industry. From 1969 to 1988 Hanover's market value increased from $34,196,000 to $495,019,200, an increase of 1,348 percent. For the same period Standard & Poors 500 industry average increased 197 percent. In premiums written each over the preceding year, Hanover has exceeded industry performance in 10 of the last 12 years, the last four by sizable margins. Hanover's combined ratio (loss and expenses vs. premiums) has bettered the industry's for 11 of the last 12 years. Also, $34,000 invested in Hanover in 1969 was worth $492,253 on 6/30/88 (not too bad for being in a mundane business).

* * *

Attempts at Transformational leadership have been made by dedicated persons in companies for many years. Some have succeeded. It is as true now as it was in the past that pioneers are often in for a rough time. Success for them is different from the success of those who follow. It takes a rare combination of attributes to be a pioneer. We meet one next in the person of Bruce Copeland.

LIGHTNING STRIKES A TRANSFORMER

Bruce Copeland
Resource Development Group

Trying to be a Transformational leader doesn't carry with it any guarantees. This holds true whether you are the boss, as seen in the profile of Hal Bolton's challenge, or not, as was the case with Bruce Copeland. Transformation is an uphill battle in established firms with a history of bureaucratic systems of management and hierarchical structures.

The Bruce Copeland story is included here as a bit of reality, of learning to be shared and to be taken seriously by those who may be tempted to rush ahead without first counting the cost.

Bruce is a true business statesperson by the definition employed here, a pioneer who continues to be committed and dedicated in his role as a Transformational leader.

History

Being a freelance real estate broker in Evanston, Illinois, on the surface at least, didn't seem to indicate much potential in the way of virtuous leadership. Bruce did some "bread-and-butter" real estate business, as he says, but his real mission was to create opportunities for those socially downcast and outcast to live in comfort and dignity. But Bruce and his wife, Carol, are in their 60s now, with four grown children and five grandchildren, so there's a bit of history here that bears disclosure.

There was nothing very dramatic about growing up in a midwestern family, or about being in a V-12 unit at Oberlin College during World War II, or even about graduating from Muskingum College in 1947, a boom year for graduating discharged veterans. In fact, for the next 16 years, the Copeland story reads pretty much like hundreds of thousands of others: getting married, starting a career, starting a family, moving from Connecticut to California, then back east to Pennsylvania as the job required.

Bruce began his career in the insurance industry, working for a national firm headquartered in Connecticut. He started in the home office, then after being a very productive salesperson he became the successful manager of a new West Coast office. Avocationally he was involved with the United Way and the YMCA and was an active churchgoer but "getting what I call 'Boy Scout Ethics' from the pulpit—not prophetic in terms of helping me on the job."

In 1963, however, things began to change in Bruce's life. First, the sales vice-president of his company became president of another old-line insurance company on the East Coast and asked Bruce to join him there. The new firm had some 1,000 employees nationwide and around one-half billion dollars in assets.

Second, several forces began to converge on him to dramatically alter his view of his life's purpose. First, he became aware of voices during the 1960s calling for change in how minorities and women should be treated in our society. His own children began to ask him, "What are you doing about this, Dad?" Later in the decade, a young southern radical, highly skeptical about the legitimacy of a business vocation, was to add her influence in altering his perspective.

But the "Aha!" moment came for him during a meeting of about 20 business people who were members of the Business Sector group of Metropolitan Associates of Philadelphia (MAP). An industrial mission organization, it is no longer in existence. The group was being addressed by Dr. Jitsuo Morikawa, who was then involved in urban ministry.

> Basically, his theme was that if you believe in social justice, then you must understand the powers in our society or in our institutions; they are the ones that determine the value systems and the lives of our people. They are the ones that basically create the injustices. So if you believe in wanting to change this, if you really want to be a change agent, then you must be a part of changing institutions. The new evangelists are going to need to go about the world preaching the gospel to all the institutions. He was basically saying, "Now what you need to do is go back into your company and change it."

Causing Change

Bruce had previously participated in several community change projects. One involved trying to change housing patterns in north Philadelphia and another focused on welfare system reform. "All of my focus had been on the outside, which had little systemic influence. But that was the best I knew how to do. So then I started in and spent a couple of years on my own trying to change that institution."

In thinking through what areas to focus on and how to proceed, Bruce was assisted by a member of the MAP staff. Bruce by then was a second vice-president in the sales department of the firm, one of several dozen officers who managed the company's business day to day. Because of the close relationship he had with the president, Bruce began his change effort by encouraging the president to consider new forms of socially oriented investments and new management styles that involved the participation of more employees in being responsible for running the company.

This effort, attempted over a period of several years, didn't seem to be accomplishing much. It became evident that he could not get much done by himself.

So over a period of probably a year, I gathered together four other people at various levels of the organization into a change agent group. We called ourselves the "Resource Development Group," which was sufficiently ambiguous to allow us flexibility of movement. Then I got myself called the vice-president of resource development. I had some marketing things, I had training, personnel and finally data processing. I sort of became the trouble shooter in the company. I would identify the most serious problem areas and go to the president and say, "This is what I think needs to be done and I think I'm the one that needs to do it. Here are the resources I need. What do you think?" And he'd say, "Fine, go to it." So I'd spend a year or two cleaning up a situation, train up a manager to take over and I'd move on to the next thing. In the midst of this, MAP came into the picture saying I needed to put a much heavier value orientation into what I was doing.

The Resource Development Group then began to focus on the

rights of women and minorities within the company. Two women members of the group led a two-hour meeting, to which all the women in the company were invited, to discuss what things needed to be changed to enhance the opportunities for women in the company. Of the 300 women in the company, 50 attended the meeting. Five proposals arose as the result of the meeting and were presented to the appropriate corporate officer. Three of the proposals were adopted immediately, another at a later date.

"So we started moving. I had maybe half of the company under my jurisdiction [by then] and we were developing more and more of a planning/participatory style of management which was definitely counter to the rest of the organization."

In the rest of the organization, a traditional style of business management persisted. All decisions went to the top of the pyramid for approval and each department head needed and wanted to continuously know the details of what was transpiring in his area of responsibility. Turf was important and turf prerogatives were jealously guarded.

Meanwhile the Resource Development Group proceeded with conscious intention to enhance the opportunities of all employees to participate in running the business and to improve the effectiveness of the organization.

"We moved in a variety of areas and had some successes and some things that didn't work."

The group used an envisioning process to help it decide what to tackle, how far to push it and to play "what if" games in developing its strategy. One of their images was:

> How close can we go to the edge of the cliff without getting pushed over? . . . so we would do some things and say, well, when is it we're going too far and then we would pull back.
>
> Another approach was to act like the revolution had already occurred. In other words, you didn't proclaim it, you just acted like there wasn't any hierarchy, like everybody had an opportunity to make input on any decision affecting their lives, such as secretaries or file clerks, or people in other departments. You just began to act that way

and not make a big deal out of it and see what happened. The object was to change the institution, you know, with justice being the goal and still being effective.

One of the members of the Resource Development Group was named Julie. Early in her career with the company she challenged Bruce and the company's intentions particularly regarding opportunities for women. Then 22, fresh out of the South, she told Bruce that she thought that the direction he said he wanted to push the company in was just a bunch of crap and she was ready to chuck the whole thing.

Bruce said, "I'm going to make a deal with you. We are going to put together a written contract and I'm going to sign it and you'll sign it. What we are basically going to be saying is that we will be treating each other as equals, that we will use each other as consultants. But each of us, no matter where we are in the organization, will give the other the right to make the decision, whatever, and we will support it." At the time, Bruce was a vice-president and Julie was a mid-level technician and obviously a very competent person. They shared the same values and trusted one another.

Sometime later it became evident that the data processing department required a change in leadership. Both Bruce and the president recognized that it was the most difficult job in the company. Bruce selected Julie for the job. She was by then 24.

The protests were that she would lose all of the good people, particularly men, in her department, and she wouldn't be able to recruit good people. Well, the fact is she kept all of her good people and turned a lot of people loose to do things that they'd never been able to do before. She insisted that they make some of their own decisions and move on. She became a company consultant to them instead of deciding for them. And she brought in some real good people and moved that department around from the worst data processing installation in the Delaware Valley into the best in probably about 18 months.

On another front, Bruce attended the senior officers' meeting every Monday morning. The Resource Development Group met beforehand to help Bruce plan how to impact the officers regarding the consideration of values in decision making.

> We owned a lot of common stock. They'd come up with stock resolutions. "Well, how are we going to vote on these issues?" The assumption always was to go along with what the top management of the companies recommended. Everybody would nod their heads. Then I would raise my hand and say I really thought that we ought to consider having them do it some other way, to support the resolution that was being proposed by the Episcopalians or National Council of Churches or somebody, on [for example] the question of South Africa or the question of farm workers and all the issues that were beginning to emerge in the early and middle '60s.

Although his views were continually rejected, Bruce kept plugging away.

When the company built a new home office, Bruce suggested that they put a clause into the construction contract that a certain percentage of the work be done by minority contractors. The responsible vice-president said it would cost 2 percent more in construction costs if minority contractors were involved. In the end, the project cost 50 percent more than first estimated with no minority contractors involved.

During those years in Philadelphia, Bruce and his family attended a church that sponsored a lay ministry unit, a support group of persons who reinforce each other in their ministries of intentional service carried out through their secular vocations. About 10 people in the congregation of several hundred were involved. "We'd talk about our work experiences. One was a school teacher trying to change the school system around hierarchy and values and so on. Each Sunday we would take one person's situation and talk about it and strategize and then they'd come back the next time and tell us how they made out. They were feeling powerless; even people fairly high up were saying, 'I really don't have any power.' In those days it was a very significant church where we voted to mortgage the church for $100,000 to [help alleviate] the urban crisis." Several members of the MAP staff were also members of that church.

MAP was eventually brought into the company to do some consulting on facilitating group process and on developing problem-solving skills, primarily for the units that Bruce was assigned. All senior managers throughout the company, however, were scheduled to have a one-day session with MAP trainers during which they were to play a series of business "games." Unfortunately this program was dropped as the games exposed some of the managers to their own autocratic style, disclosed their dependency on the president for decision making and their own reliance on control as their primary managerial tool.

One of the women members of the resource group was approached by the president one day and asked why she commuted two hours a day each way in order to work at the company when she could get a job much closer to home. The president just didn't understand, she said, that the resource group provided her, for the first time in her life, with an opportunity to really contribute, to have input into how the work would be done in her area. And so the gulf widened.

A student intern from Drexel University really uncovered how wide and deep it had become when he conducted an informal organization development survey. The delegation of responsibility and authority by Bruce and his managers to the people doing the work was becoming deeply resented by senior managers in other parts of the company. Their employees began asking them why they couldn't be responsible for decision making in their areas. Seeing female and minority faces in Bruce's "cabinet" was also a sore point.

One Friday afternoon, Bruce suggested to the president that it would be a good idea to get all the senior managers together with him to talk about instances of racism and sexism that were apparent in the company, to see how they could work together to help each other resolve them. The president rejected the idea, indicating that the company was not a democracy but a monarchy and that he was king.

The following Tuesday afternoon, after 10 years with the

company and two recent promotions including two large pay raises, the president told Bruce that it was the most difficult thing he had ever had to do but that Bruce was through. The following day, Julie was also terminated and a small purge began during which traditional management practices were reintroduced into the units that had been assigned to Bruce.

These actions were devastating but not a total surprise. For several weeks afterward Bruce and Julie debriefed with the MAP staff for everyone to understand more fully why the results came out the way they had. Members of the MAP staff felt particularly badly because they had inspired Bruce's actions to begin with. The conclusions they reached have become fundamental principles for organizational change efforts since that time:

1.   It is essential that the effort have the full and active support of the head of the organization.
2.   A change group needs to be established. It should be made up of persons of unquestionable technical competence in the work of the organization, persons with shared values, having a high level of trust and compatibility among them.
3.   The change must be institutionalized; it must become a new way of life for the organization. Enough people and subgroups in the organization must be aligned with the change so that it can sustain any blow that may come along attempting to derail it, including the departure of one or two of the prime leaders supporting the change. [In other situations this has been called "a critical mass."]

Within six months of his termination Bruce Copeland became president of a small life insurance company with about 100 employees, headquartered in Chicago and owned by a Swiss firm. He was told that the way he was to accomplish his responsibilities was up to him. The owners were only interested in getting the proper business results. At least in this situation, his bosses were neutral as opposed to being against his participative style and his interest in social justice.

Given that autonomy, within three years, half of the middle and upper management positions, including the number 2, 4 and 5 positions, were filled by women and minorities. A participative planning process which included secretaries and filing clerks as well as managers was initiated to chart the firm's long-range future, that is, what they wanted the company to become and how they wanted it to be run.

To effect other changes in the culture of the company, Bruce turned his large office with its imposing furniture into a conference room and moved into a more modest room with a worktable in the corner without making any pronouncements. He merely acted and talked participatively and verbally considered values when discussing issues with other managers and administrative employees.

On one occasion he was invited to appear before a group of insurance company presidents on a panel regarding social responsibility in corporations. "One of the panel persons got up and said how much they gave to the United Way. Another person in the group said how their employees were volunteering in the community and so on in the traditional kind of things. I had a couple of charts and I just said, 'Here is what it was three years ago and here's what it is now, in staffing the company in terms of women and in terms of minorities, at all levels.' I let the charts show what happened in those three years."

He indicated to them that he felt business in general was involved in window dressing, employing token women managers, then not allowing them to manage anything important. Then the questions came up, "Why are you doing this? Why do you think it's important to do this?"

I was perhaps representing the smallest company in the group. And I said, "Well, there are three basic reasons: One of them is because I think it's the right, fair and just thing to do. Second, it's because in the long run it's going to benefit the company. You're going to have more effective, productive, happy employees. And the third reason is if you don't, you're going to get nailed by legal action eventually." I gave some examples of companies who had already been nailed for some $5 million to $10 million. A few other questions were asked and I sat down.

At that time, Bruce had in mind developing a change agent group among insurance companies. However, he was forced to go down another path, one that he could not foresee.

In his first year as president of the company, Bruce was diagnosed as having lymphoma, a type of cancer. Each day for six weeks before going to work he underwent radiation therapy. He does not recall missing a day of work during that time, although he lost all of his hair and most of his voice. After about three months, the lymphoma disappeared. About two years later the cancer suddenly reappeared and chemotherapy was required. Bruce stayed on the job but had to miss work a day or two out of each three-week treatment period.

Three months or so after the chemotherapy began, Bruce contracted a case of shingles in his left leg and it continued with intense pain for about a year. He was finally forced to stop working and go onto the company's disability pay plan. Shortly thereafter his condition worsened, going into thrombophlebitis with other complications.

After being on disability pay for about two years, Bruce resigned from the company. He had made a conscious decision to pursue a different career, one that didn't require a daily nine-to-five work schedule. That was over eight years ago now and he appears to have recovered completely from all of his ailments.

"I was thinking about what I should do next, and to make a long story short, I ended up in the real estate business as a place where I could be on my own and operate fairly independently."

Sometime after they moved to the Chicago area, the Copelands joined a small church in which Bruce began a lay ministry group in cooperation with the pastor. It was an activist church—involved in women's issues, gay rights and so on—as well as a sanctuary church. Annually its 100 members signed pledges on Covenant Sunday to raise the $70,000 to $80,000 required for the budget. No wealthy persons belong to the church and no other fund-raising was required during the year.

Early in their membership, a liberation theology advocate from Costa Rica who attended the church from time to time suggested to Bruce, "The third world is in Evanston. It's not just in Central America. You can't influence Costa Rica or Nicaragua. You can influence Evanston; that's where you ought to be working. So find the toughest problem."

That was the beginning of Bruce's work with the disadvantaged, the handicapped and other socially stressed persons of north side Chicago and of Evanston.

His first project involved working with four members of his church to create a storefront drop-in center for ex-mental patients, called Acorn. It now operates seven days per week and has several dozen volunteers and a staff of 10. It serves over 700 homeless and chronically mentally ill persons from the Evanston area. Next Bruce formed a limited partnership known as the Friends of Acorn to buy and manage the Acorn building.

Through persistent efforts, Bruce developed a very economical way to put limited partnerships together around not-for-profit corporations. This led a neighborhood group to establish housing partnerships in the Rogers Park section of Chicago which controlled 120 apartment units. It is planned that these will eventually be turned into co-ops, to be owned by the tenants.

He has also been involved in helping other groups establish limited partnerships for similar purposes. In recent years he has worked with four or five nonprofit groups, helping them to rent or purchase property for low-income, handicapped and developmentally disabled persons, including scattered site apartments. He did this as a professional real estate operator, not as a volunteer. But the services he provided his nonprofit clients extended far beyond those offered by any regular real estate broker.

In deciding not to volunteer his services, Bruce's reasoning was that the services volunteers provide frequently are those that they have time for after they have completed the work required to make a living. Also, frequently the volunteer, if he or she permitted it, was overused and burned out. So Bruce preferred being paid for his services as a real estate agent, accepting a commission from the property seller and providing his unique skills to assist his clients in the process. With the same reasoning he frequently rejected becoming a board member of nonprofits seeking his knowledge and assistance. Instead he worked with them on a real estate commission or, if necessary, a consulting fee basis.

Carol Copeland, now that the children were raised, had an IBM PC and helped Bruce preplan various ventures to determine what it would take to make them feasible. She had other clients as well and several organizations for whom she did volunteer work using the computer to provide monthly financial reports.

The words you are reading now are not the first time the Bruce Copeland story has been told. Bruce has been asked by a number of organizations to tell his story over the past few years.

One person hearing Bruce tell of his journey was a physician from South Carolina who said his total outside time was given to serving the church on a number of boards and agencies and as an elder. Bruce suggested to him that if he got nine other doctors in South Carolina together and planned that in the next 10 years they were going to make health care available to everybody in South Carolina regardless of their ability to pay, they could do it. The doctor protested that then he wouldn't have time for his church-related board activities. Bruce replied,

> You tell them, "I've given you 20 years of my life and now it's time for me to get out and start working on the injustices that I have some control over." And the doctor turned away and quietly left. I don't believe you have to give away all your wealth. I don't think that's what the Bible meant; I think it's stewardship. It's using your talents for justice, to the limit of your abilities. It's not just to enhance the Presbyterians or the United Methodists. That's not the only thing that you're in this life for. If you can help them along a bit, fine, but there are loads of other people who love that kind of thing.
>
> Why don't people get involved in change? It's fear. I've thought about that a lot. Why are there so few people willing to risk even their jobs? Because as a society, we're trained to play it safe. We are trained to look to the author-ity figure for decisions. Play it safe, play it safe. The church enhances that, most of the time. They don't talk about those parts of the gospel where Jesus speaks of working for justice—and how to connect that to daily life and oppres-sive systems. Along with other institutions I think the church has helped perpetuate systemic injustice and has helped enhance it in many cases. There are a few spots

where they've been a prophetic voice, but not a lot, in recent years.

Several years ago Bruce said he hoped to spend more time with his family and on recreation and travel in the years ahead, so he was training others in the skills he had developed to establish limited partnerships. He may still have that in mind. In the meantime, however, he and Carol have moved to Charleston, West Virginia, where Bruce has joined his brother's human services consulting firm. He is now developing community programs and residential facilities for mentally handicapped, homeless and low-income people, which he was doing on a smaller scale in the Chicago Northshore area. Bruce is also co-chairing a new committee to provide housing for people with AIDS, a controversial but necessary task. The effort is sponsored by Covenant House, a drop-in center for abused women and the homeless, on whose board Bruce serves.

* * *

Bruce Copeland was never able totally to achieve the extent of social pioneering he set out to accomplish within the companies he was with. That did not stop him, however. He created his own opportunities to enhance the lives of those most in need of social justice.

Chapter 7
Transforming the American Enterprise: In Milwaukee, Ann Arbor and Dallas

PERHAPS BECAUSE HE owns the company, Vic Hunter's experience, in seeking many of the same business and social goals as Bruce Copeland, has been different. Vic Hunter presides over the most unusually structured organization of the companies studied. Hunter Business Direct is dedicated to the growth and development of its stakeholders, especially its employees, and monthly gives 10 percent of its net before taxes to employee-selected causes in the community.

Bill Bottum at Townsend and Bottum and Jack Lowe, Jr., at TDIndustries are successors to their fathers as C.E.O.'s. But each has led his company through periods of major growth and of crisis. Virtuous leadership has played a role in both the success and the survival of their enterprises.

Virtue in Business, Milwaukee Style

Victor L. Hunter, President
Hunter Business Direct, Inc.
A Member of the Barnabas Group

In our contemporary secularized society, it is surprising to discover a business that openly professes Christian values and then clearly exhibits comparable behaviors. In fact a visit to Hunter's storefront location in a strip shopping center north of Milwaukee is full of surprises. Hunter personnel are practical, straightforward and unpretentious. They project a sense of purpose. Their candor in describing the unique character of the company and in disclosing areas still under development is disarming. With each person met, you feel you're in the presence of an owner of the business.

The owner of Hunter Business Direct is Victor L. Hunter, president. Vic received a B.S. from Purdue University in 1969, majoring in physics and mathematics, and an M.B.A. from Harvard Business School in 1971. But such credentials do little to disclose a personal history as unique as the company he founded in 1981.

Hunter Business Direct is a member of the Barnabas Group. The "Group" is composed of three autonomous corporate entities which occupy the same office location and work in close cooperation with each other. The other members are W. H. Younger and Associates, Inc., and E. C. Runner and Associates, Inc. All three entities provide management consulting to business clients nationwide, primarily in sales and marketing. Hunter also provides business-to-business direct marketing services to its clients. As opposed to Hunter's 100 employees, Bill Younger and Ed Runner operate solo enterprises.

The name Barnabas comes from the New Testament. Barnabas assisted Paul in establishing the early church. He was a bold encourager and counselor of others. Vic Hunter and Bill Younger have been meeting with others in a monthly businessmen's luncheon group of a similar name, the Barnabi Group, since the late 1970s. The purpose of the luncheon group is to provide mutual support and encouragement. Participants are from different backgrounds, ages, denominations and professional callings, but all are Christians. The Barnabas Group (the businesses) has developed a "creed":

> We, the Barnabas Group, are a spiritually based association of Christian businessmen, drawn together to support, strengthen and more fully develop our God-given talents and gifts. We recognize the work of the Holy Spirit within our lives and within this Group.
>
> We have chosen our name from the man, Barnabas, described in the New Testament book of Acts, who was a bold and visible encourager of others. Like Barnabas, members of our Group support, encourage and assist one

another while serving business clients.

Our mission of encouragement and witness will be tested by the standards of God and the business world. We will blend our abilities as we strive for excellence.

Philosophy

Vic sees no conflict between the standards of God and of the business world when the focus of business is on nurturing long-term relationships and applying mature business wisdom. "The creed and our statement of beliefs were developed to protect our values. Values are extremely important to each one of us and drive both our personal and business lives." The symbol of the Barnabas Group is also used as the Hunter logo. It is a white cross formed by the positioning of four chevrons.

Despite its obvious Christian moorings, Hunter Business Direct is not an evangelistic enterprise. Hunter employees are Christians, Jews and agnostics, perhaps even one or two atheists. But their personal values are generally quite compatible with the culture that the Hunter organization has developed.

The following statement of beliefs describes the foundation of its culture. It was developed by employees being trained for positions in the operating area of the company and presented by them as a gift to management after their first two weeks of training as their understanding of what Hunter was all about:

> We, Hunter Business Direct, being a goal-oriented and growing company, believe in maintaining high ethical standards and providing honest service for our clients, customers and personnel, leading to long-term growth while remaining on the edge of new business technology.
>
> We, Hunter Business Direct, with our open-door policy, wish to promote happiness in a clean, pleasant environment where work is fun, communication is maximized and where every employee is a member of the family.
>
> We, Hunter Business Direct, believe that employee participation, dedication and pride are the prerequisites which developed the high level of trust in existence within

this company. Believing this trust to be our backbone, we encourage the full development of each individual's potential by designing work to promote self-direction, allowing for stewardship, rewarding performance and enriching people's lives through thoughtfulness and sensitivity.

We, Hunter Business Direct, believe that every person who cleaves to our goals will, through diligence, achieve tangible benefits in every aspect of work and life.

The mission statement of the company is summarized as:
1. To assist organizations in understanding and implementing business-to-business direct marketing.
2. To provide our employees an environment which encourages growth and personal fulfillment.
3. To improve our community by sharing corporate and personal resources.

In a more lengthy elaboration on this mission, the company indicates its intention to provide a high level of performance for clients and specifies an organizational social purpose emphasizing its responsibility for the personal development of its employees and in the welfare of the community:

> In assisting *organizations* with direct marketing, we will provide standard products such as lead qualification, profiling, installed base, order processing, audit reviews, research, marketing and business planning, software, database design, seminars, field training and fulfillment. The full range of standard products will be stressed. We will establish quality standards and consistently achieve standards that exceed client expectations. We will mutually agree on product performance with the client at the beginning of a project and we will regularly compare results with the measurable objectives. And we will have external and internal evaluation programs to assure highest quality performance.
>
> Regarding our *employees*, we will assist with career growth in the following areas: Education such as night

156

school, seminars, and correspondence courses will be encouraged. We will aid career planning by explaining future Hunter Business Direct plans and individual opportunity, job assignments, skills development and promotion from within the company. Compensation will be fair at average or above levels. It will be related to performance. Our fringe benefit program will be generous. We will have a pleasant environment. We will build a structured organization around standard products. We will emphasize the stewardship programs of time and money. We will provide performance evaluation through regular reviews and feedback based on set personal expectations. And we will encourage good communication throughout the company.

In the *community*, we will exercise our stewardship skills of time and money. We will contribute by creating jobs and we will be sensitive to the special needs and opportunities for helping others such as the handicapped. We will present a highly ethical and professional organization.

As indicated in its mission statement, Hunter Business Direct not only consults with clients regarding business-to-business direct marketing, it provides a full range of direct marketing services for clients. The company uses telemarketing as its primary operational tool.

Qualifying leads for its clients is also an important service the company renders in addition to making direct sales to its clients' customers. It uses a highly developed set of computer programs to accumulate and process the data it receives.

Organizationally, Hunter is structured as a three-dimensional matrix. One dimension is composed of four work areas to which the bulk of Hunter employees are assigned: marketing, information systems, operations and administration. Each area is headed by an area leader and is composed of groups, and, the groups, of teams. These work areas are cost centers. Employees receive work assignments, plan with their supervisors for their development, have their performance measured and receive their compensation in their work areas.

Another dimension is composed of account managers and

project managers. They operate profit centers. Their "hands and feet" are the employees who reside in the work areas who are assigned to the accounts and projects of the account managers and project managers. Employees may work on only one account or project or be assigned to several account and/or project teams. Assignments are made on the basis of the needs of the client, the skills of the employee and/or what the employee can gain from exposure to a project to which he or she is assigned.

The third dimension of the matrix is the product manager. A product is a standard service or a packaged set of services that can be provided a client because of the skills, knowledge and other requisite resources (usually human resources) available to particular Hunter managers.

This structure means that area leaders, except when they're acting as project or product managers, perform quality assurance roles, ensuring that their people are successful on their projects.

Vic believes the matrix form permits optimum freedom for people to contribute and to grow. "I look for activities that move people up in quantums, not linearly, that move them from one level to an entirely different level of activity."

Anyone in the Hunter organization theoretically could be on any account, project or product team and any manager could be an account, project or product manager. Vic Hunter is on several teams but leads none of them. "As the president, I work on projects for other people. I have a project manager who is my boss. He has an account manager who is his boss, and I get reviewed on how I do, how I manage my time, and the quality of the product that I produce."

Vic's unique role in the company is to be a coach and oversee the character of the enterprise. Formally, he heads one function in the organization, the planning committee. It is composed of the "head people in the company," and is responsible to pull together the strategic vision and annual business plan. Vic also sits in on staff meetings with area leaders and monthly council meetings of account and project managers. Both of these are information exchange and coordination meetings.

There is a defined hierarchy of responsibilities in the company and an organization chart which is used in talking to clients. Titles are used only to identify functions and to communicate with people outside the company, however.

Jim Kurtz, a marketing consultant, likes the matrix design and the otherwise unstructured way of operating. "I enjoy that kind of environment because it gives you a lot of opportunity to be creative." Jim joined the company in 1987 and was surprised at the extent of creativity the Hunter system allowed. "At the same time there are some downside effects to that also, in trying to build consistent quality with people doing things along the same line. We're working toward becoming more consistent, at the same time trying to retain that creativity and not stifle people."

When Jim Kurtz considered joining Hunter, the company put him through a series of interviews with four or five key managers. The interviews were held periodically over two to three months. Jim's experience is typical of the care the company takes in considering candidates for new positions. Vic credits Bob Scheid of Milwaukee's Humber Mundie and McCleary with having developed the successful selection process the company has used since its founding.

Regarding Hunter's religious roots, Jim says,

> At no time during the employment process was I asked what my personal beliefs were. I think the main criteria we are looking for are people that have good sound experience and want to join us and feel comfortable in this type of environment. It's a close group. There's a lot of sharing of information and ideas between people, not only on a day-to-day business basis, but outside in their personal lives. There's a lot of concern in the company for the community and also for individual spiritual needs. That's quite different [from] the type of environment I was involved in before.

The nurture and development of Hunter employees is the primary mission of the area leaders. They identify functionally where people need and/or want to be developed and accomplish that through work assignments, reviews and coaching. John Eben, one of those area leaders, worked in information systems until 1985 when he became head of the operations area. "I found that although I liked the challenge of working with computers, it was difficult for me not to be around and working with people. If you're in information systems, it's hard to move into something else. You're looked at as a technician. You're not looked at as having business or people skills. When an opportunity came up to move into operations, I pushed it pretty hard. I've enjoyed it a lot more."

"I have all my supervisors on performance standards and I sit down with them once a month and review those." Annually, John's supervisors are reviewed against performance standards and various qualitative measures which tie into their compensation review. "I believe for the structure to really work, people need to have expectations and know how they're doing against those expectations."

One of John's counterparts as an area leader is Jim Berry. With a background in consulting and information systems, Jim heads the marketing and information systems areas. Both the account management functions and computer operations are Jim's responsibility, with other aspects of the technological side of the company thrown in as well. Jim joined Hunter because it promised him the opportunity to contribute the skills he had developed, to learn some new ones and to bring the spiritual dimension into his work life. "I believe that this environment gives me a great deal more, not only responsibility, but authority to define the environment as I choose to make it. And that is very important considering this spiritual dimension that I'm trying to incorporate into my career."

Jim's concern for the company at this point is with its rapid growth. Special efforts have to be made so that all employees readily identify how their efforts are affecting company results. With rapid growth and getting new employees to an appropriate level of contribution, some of the spiritual dimensions he'd like to pursue get squeezed out in the pressure of time. "I also recognize that I don't know where else I could go to have more opportunity to do this than I do here, so that's a very affirming thing. I believe that we want to succeed in both dimensions, both the spiritual dimension as well as being a very high quality business that provides significant opportunity to its employees. If I were interested only in the spiritual, I might choose to join a different organization."

Typical of Hunter, as the company has grown, the need for a new function has been identified by an employee. Elayn Ross, who headed the data entry team since the company began, spent most of 1987 documenting the need for and identifying the scope of a proposed human resources group. She did this by discussing her proposal with area leaders and unit managers within Hunter and by visiting other firms and industries in the area to define clearly the work of the proposed group. Its mission would be to coordinate the administrative functions for personnel and to help area leaders, managers and supervisors to perform their employment and developmental responsibilities without doing their work for them.

When Elayn first came up with the idea to form the group, Vic met with her to help her think through a process to get others involved in specifying the need. He also suggested resources outside the company for Elayn to contact to learn how other companies managed similar functions. Once every company unit concurred in its formation and to the plan Elayn developed, it was expected that she would organize the function and become its supervisor within the administration area of the company.

Stewardship

Throughout the preceding review of Hunter Business Direct, reference has been made to *stewardship*. Stewardship is no idle word in the company. At Hunter it is the acknowledgment that the resources of the company, its time, talents and funds, have been provided for the company to use for the benefit of each of its stakeholders, its employees, its clients and its community, particularly those with special needs.

For one hour the second Thursday of every month, all interested employees at Hunter meet as the Stewardship Committee, as Vic described:

Everybody in the company is invited. At any one time maybe 30 people will come, and if you look at three or four meetings, maybe 60 percent or 70 percent of our employees will have participated. The officers of the group are elected by the group every year. Every employee is encouraged to bring community needs to the group to consider funding. They are then discussed, and each suggestion is voted up or voted down. One of the requirements from the beginning has been that every time someone brings a recommendation to the Stewardship Committee and we decide to fund it, a different individual from the committee has to go out and determine how that money was used. So we get at least two people involved in every program. Half of those people don't have any idea of what the program is about when they go out to do the review and they get involved in it and become very active in its development.

Through this employee-run, community-oriented stewardship program, Hunter annually disburses 10 percent of its net profits before taxes. Beneficiaries of the program have been a McDonald's program for kids with cancer, the Campus Crusade at Yale University, a TB clinic in the hills of Mexico and various specialized ministries to the disadvantaged and handicapped in Milwaukee. Additionally, Second Harvesters, a Milwaukee-area program that collects and distributes 20,000 pounds of food daily to needy persons, has received assistance from Hunter personnel in setting up a data and management system. At the time of the Mexico City earthquake, a Hunter employee volunteered to take her vacation there to help out. She was sponsored by her church for the mission, which was funded by the Hunter program.

A recent president of the Stewardship Committee is Kim Albrecht. Kim joined Hunter in 1984 when it had 32 employees. She is an operational service manager on the company's Amoco account. A telemarketing operation, her group contacts Amoco dealers regularly to sell them tires, batteries and accessories. It also bills them, pays vendors and accounts for all transactions. The total operation is done by telephone and computer.

Kim likes her work, but her enthusiasm is unrestrained when she talks about stewardship. "We have a lot of organizations that we contribute to. And we have just now begun to use our people time in various types of volunteer work. In the last few years we've really focused on getting more knowledgeable about the organizations that are in our community, what they spend their time doing, which of the organizations are very good at what they do, which need support or guidance. Now we're getting to the point where we want to do more, have a bigger impact on our area and our community."

That "doing more" is a new stewardship venture, known as the Mission Project. The idea behind the project is to marshal the extensive time, talent and financial resources available at Hunter behind one effort to make a real difference in an area of community need.

To develop the project, the committee reviewed the organizations they had had previous contact with and interviewed people from another 25. They identified the needs of each and finally narrowed the field down to one organization. That organization, the Silver Spring Neighborhood House, was chosen to receive major amounts of volunteer assistance from Hunter employees. The selection was based on the needs of the benefitting agency and the matching skills and talents of Hunter personnel. The agency serves a large number of families, most of them single-parent, on Milwaukee's north side. Many of the families are on welfare and the adults have only an eighth-grade education. A group of four or five dedicated teachers at the agency has been working to enhance the education and employment opportunities of their clients for the past several years.

Kim described how Hunter volunteers expected to proceed:

In the initial phase we're going to focus on employment and education. The biggest demand that this organization has right now is trying to find employment for people. And we feel we want to combine education with that so that possible employment will be easier for them. We'll be helping them with communication, with telemarketing skills, possibly getting into word processing and typing. Maybe six months down the road we will want to get into other personal areas, woodworking, sewing, tutoring; it could be a number of things. We might run workshops on Saturday and we'll have volunteers to take care of the children while parents participate. I think it's now up to 30 different items [skills, talents] that people in our company would like to contribute.

In conjunction with neighborhood house personnel, Hunter employees have approached this project as they would any business project. They've developed a business plan targeting clients' needs and defining objectives and standards of performance. This has brought both agency and company personnel into a close and mutually reinforcing working relationship.

In addition to the company's 10 percent grant and its employee volunteerism, the company sponsors a monthly food drive to help out a particular food pantry and two to four clothing drives per year. Sometimes the food drive gives money collected in the company from the sale of baked goods donated by employees, adding another dimension of enthusiasm to the stewardship effort.

A purely internal program is conducted by the Hunter Entertainment Committee. Its major focus is on the monthly "birthday luncheon" held in the company lunchroom. Everyone is invited. The cost is between $2 and $4 per person. Birthdays, anniversaries and other noteworthy events are celebrated. The theme, motif and decorations are determined by whatever holiday, if any, occurs during that month. The Entertainment Committee has also established a company choir and coordinates a couples dinner and dance at Christmas, a Family Christmas Party, a summer picnic and an annual trip to watch the Brewers.

History

Now, what about the uniqueness of the company's founder? Victor Lee Hunter grew up in Garrett, Indiana, a town of 3,000 near Fort Wayne. Its early history was tied to the development of the B & O Railroad, of which Vic's father was a lifelong employee. His parents embraced a strong work ethic, but were not well educated in a formal sense. They were very encouraging in everything Vic tried to accomplish. He also had a scout leader who supported and encouraged his efforts all the way through Eagle Scouting. As he was growing up, Vic became comfortable with a religious orientation to his life.

While at Purdue, he was an academic tutor for the Boilermakers football team and taught Sunday school in a local church. In his sophomore year he met Linda, a freshman he enlisted as his co-teacher for the next three years. From their earliest relationship to the present, Linda, now Mrs. Hunter, has been Vic's closest encourager and friend. With her help, his sensitivity to others, his feelings and clarity of values have been enhanced, making him a committed person. Together with their four children, Vic asserts, his family provides the foundation and cornerstone of his life, giving it meaning, purpose and reinforcement.

By the time he was a senior at Purdue, Vic planned to go into a Ph.D. program and become a researcher and professor of physics. However, he decided that he wanted to be much more in contact with people, and that a business career would provide him that opportunity. His mentor in the physics department at Purdue urged him to apply to the best business schools in the country and he was accepted at Harvard. His pastor in Lafayette agreed with that course of action, saying that Vic could use his sensitivity and concern for others most effectively in the marketplace.

While at Harvard, Vic did staff projects for Harvard Business School faculty members and fill-in teaching in other business school programs. Again, it looked as if he were headed for a teaching career. But his Harvard mentors urged him to go into the business world for a few years at least to get practical experience before deciding.

When he received his M.B.A. in 1971, Vic joined Krueger Metal Products in Green Bay, Wisconsin. For the next several years he charged into the opportunities the company gave him to set up a marketing department and develop new products. Gradually he began to settle down to the real world of business thanks to coaching he received from key Krueger managers and executives.

During his time in Green Bay, Vic and Linda and several other couples formed a mutual support group, which met periodically with a Transactional Analysis consultant, Dick Chartier.

In 1975, with Krueger's blessing, Vic became president of Business and Institutional Furniture Company (B&I) in Milwaukee, a direct mail seller that was in serious financial trouble. For the next several years, Dick Chartier helped Vic reorganize the company around a values-based model that considered people to be the most important element of the business. The model fit Vic's spiritual orientation well.

The company became very successful under Vic's leadership. Then its controlling stockholders decided to sell it to finance other ventures they were more interested in. At that point, Vic left B&I with the intention of looking for a company to buy and run himself. After several months of doing consulting for several friends, which he complained kept him from finding a company for himself, he was convinced by the members of the Barnabi luncheon group to go into consulting full-time. This led to the founding of the Barnabas Group (the businesses) and Hunter Business Direct.

"As I look back, I continually have been reassured of God's presence through what has happened to me outside of my awareness and control. At the time, I didn't understand why things were going as they were but they obviously have built a solid way to go. I've been well taken care of."

Another Barnabas Group principal, Ed Runner, has remarked that the ethical operation of a business "takes that strong leader, who sets standards and sets a personal example, because I think an organization doesn't have a separate personality of its own. It's generally the reflection of the leader, or an extension of what that leadership demands." When he said it, he must have been thinking of Vic Hunter and of the unique organization he has created.

* * *

Vic Hunter and Bill Bottum, uniquely among the Transitional leaders profiled, have most consciously based their business leadership on religious principles. Whereas Vic Hunter has done so from the start of his career, Bill Bottum generated his theology of leadership in parallel with his development as an exemplary leader. We next learn how this effort unfolded.

FOR EVERYTHING, A TIME AND A SEASON

C. E. (Bill) Bottum, Jr., Chairman
Townsend and Bottum, Inc.

In recent years, many old and respected names in American business have been severely challenged by changes in our economy. Radical surgery has sometimes been required, resulting in financial reorganization, downsizing and the termination of loyal, experienced personnel.

Often the necessity for these actions has been misunderstood both by those being directly affected and by the public at large. For those responsible to make the best of a deteriorating situation, however, such actions are agonizing episodes. The managers involved often feel a very personal and pervasive sense of failure. The almost absolute value that our society has placed on current financial success can only deepen this psychological depression.

The generalization regarding current financial success, however, needs to be challenged. The life of an organization, especially one that has persisted profitably over many years, is like the life of a person. Both are ultimately mortal, with a mixed bag of pluses and minuses, of successes and failures filling the time between birth and death. It is only at a particular moment in time that a specific situation can be declared to be a success or a failure. Viewed historically, such certainty is far less appropriate in judging the life of either a person or an organization.

Townsend and Bottum

Townsend and Bottum (pronounced *boat-em*), Inc., traces its corporate lineage back to 1908 to the Benjamin Douglas Company. For the next 60 years until the 1970s, under the names of the R. E. Townsend Corporation (1925) and its successor in 1938, Townsend and Bottum, Inc. (T&B), the company built approximately 50 percent of the power plant generating capacity for the Detroit Edison, Consumers Power and Ohio Edison companies. During that period T&B regularly consisted of up to 50 permanent employees. These employees supervised several hundred local union craftspersons on two or three public utility construction projects at any one time, except during the Great Depression when utility construction ceased altogether.

Beginning as a construction contractor, the firm broadened in both self-perception and expertise over time to become a construction services organization, initially serving the electrical public utility industry. From the late 1960s until the early 1980s, Townsend and Bottum revenues grew rapidly. The company acquired several other firms in the utilities construction field and established new companies, wholly owned spinoffs of operations developed from within the core business. During the 1970s, T&B's employment increased over 15 times the prior base, peaking in 1978 at about 750 staff employees, with another 4,000 local craftspersons employed on job sites in the field. Through 1985, the corporation had a record of continuous profitability extending back over 20 years.

By 1986, T&B companies consisted of 19 business units, including several subsidiaries, operating throughout the United States and Canada and in Saudi Arabia. These units were engaged in activities involving both very traditional and very contemporary high technology. T&B continued to act as construction managers for fossil fuel, nuclear and solar power generation facilities. They also provided construction management and operation and maintenance services for a variety of large complex facilities; designed and installed computer-based management systems for construction, engineering and publishing activities; did nuclear plant inspection, decontamination and operational consultation; designed and constructed foundation underpinning and earth retention systems; and did underwater maintenance and salvage work including nuclear diving, chemical waste and waste water diving, to note a few. The Saudi Arabian unit managed an industrial power generation facility and a refinery and petrochemical plant.

Impressive as the scope of its operations was, the really distinguishing character of Townsend and Bottum was its culture. Some of the attributes of that culture were:

- No reserved parking or special privileges for any executive or employee.
- Conference rooms utilizing round tables promoting equality of participation.
- The encouragement of open discussion of employee concerns (e.g., where individual interests and organizational interests seem to be in conflict).
- Team building as a way of life, not only involving internal personnel in improving departmental and interdepartmental relations and productivity but also involving supplier and client personnel to optimize project effectiveness.

- Twenty-five percent of net profits before taxes annually set aside for profit-sharing and employee bonuses.
- An insistence on absolute honesty and integrity in all company dealings, even if it was to the disadvantage of the company to do so.

The company mission statement established the tone for how business was to be conducted at T&B (Figure 4).

Figure 4

MISSION STATEMENT

Townsend and Bottum's family of companies' mission is to develop and maintain clients by a commitment to serving clients' real needs and values with integrity, team effort, and innovative management which results in:

- Lowest cost for required quality
- On time projects
- Non-adversarial relationships
- Excellence in client communications
- Objective problem solving
- Mutual economic gain
- Mutual professional growth
- Creating a better business world

That these statements were not merely words but were lived out daily in the life of Townsend and Bottum is due to C. E. (Bill) Bottum, Jr., who spent most of his time seeing to the building, nurture and reinforcement of the T&B culture.

History

After receiving a bachelor's degree from Iowa State and a master's in civil engineering from the University of Michigan, Bill Bottum joined Townsend and Bottum as a full-time employee in 1949. Other than a brief second stint in the navy during the Korean conflict, Bill has spent his entire career at T&B in a variety of increasing responsibilities. His unique brand of leadership, however, only began to be indelibly imprinted on the firm in the late 1960s.

Bill's father had established T&B as a solid construction services organization for the electrical public utilities industry over the preceding three decades. His father's often-repeated phrase characterizing the firm both then and later was, "We have built our business on the principles of the motto, 'Skill–Responsibility–Integrity.' Always remember that the greatest of these is Integrity." The company translated integrity to mean: "Absolute honesty in all dealings and an emphasis on quality service to our clients and respect for our people."

Bill's mother was inspired by the writings of Emerson and Thoreau. She influenced Bill in this regard and to this day he frequently visits Concord, Massachusetts, a place which has come to have a very special meaning for him as he has established his own personal philosophy and life purpose. Although he had never been involved heavily in church affairs, for many years Bill debated whether to enter the ministry or continue to pursue a career in business. The issue was settled for him one day walking on a path near Walden Pond. The answer came to him, as it were, out of the blue that he should remain in business, that business leadership was to be his ministry.

Initially, as he was establishing his vocation as a business leader, Bill pursued a parallel path of intensive Bible study. He had accepted an assignment from his brother to teach a junior high Sunday school class in 1949. Soon Bill began a quest, believing that the teachings of Christ had to be applicable to everyday living. Subsequent studies convinced him that the Beatitudes, portrayed in Matthew's account of the Sermon on the Mount, held the key to this search.

He also read extensively what philosophers, Christian theologians and writers from other religious cultures had to say about the attributes identified in the Beatitudes. The study culminated in a book, *Within Your Reach*, which he first completed in 1967 and revised twice since then.

Philosophy

Certainly not a religious zealot, Bill never forced his beliefs on anyone either within the company or outside it. He charted out the Beatitudes, however, in their religious terminology and then translated them into secular language. The latter appeared as "Guiding Principles and Attributes" for T&B and were used in informing employees as well as persons outside the company regarding T&B's expectation of itself (Figure 5).

From this foundation Bill molded and shaped Townsend and Bottum into a unique organization. He assumed the responsibility of chief executive in 1973 when his father died. From that time on, Bill engaged a number of outside resources to assist him in the process of developing the company.

With its rapid growth during the 1970s, the need for closely integrated and cooperative working relationships among company personnel became apparent. Paralleling the growth and facilitating the integration of new personnel, Human Resource Development Associates (HRDA), the consulting firm of Ron Lippitt, Ken Cowing, Ron Phillips and others, was employed by the company in 1974. The close maintenance and extension of the company's historic climate of integrity was felt to be critically important during that period.

As Bill stated in an article that he co-authored with Dr. D. Joseph Fischer in 1982, "Our objective was to create a climate of openness, sincerity, integrity and trust which would permeate the organization, resulting in a network of trust relationships among fellow employees, clients, suppliers, subcontractors and all that touch the organization."

The primary contribution of HRDA was to train key personnel to improve their communication skills, including sympathetic listening, checking for understanding, conflict resolution and team building. The effort was quite successful. It subsequently was also used to facilitate a major restructuring of the company in which its operations were decentralized and diversified with the objective of achieving greater effectiveness and ability to adapt to changing market needs.

On the external front, working with constructors, subcontrac-

Figure 5
Guiding Principles and Attributes

1 Self-Transcendence	2 Service—Sensitivity to Needs of Others	3 Commitment to Values	4 Achievement, Productivity
Open, teachable; Flexible, adaptable; Able to change, so able to grow (Bias for action—try it, change it)	Service to customers (Close to the customer)	Commitment to ideals; Beyond self—toward making the world better. The business entity must stand for something—have a corporate culture that gives meaning and purpose to its endeavors	Achievement oriented; Productivity; Enthusiasm; Goals, objectives; Focused will (Autonomy and entrepreneurship) (Stick to the knitting)
Humility; Unselfishness; Self-actualization; Self-transcendence; Servant-leader (Simple form, lean staff)	Compassionate understanding of co-workers; Empathetic listening		

5 Nurture Positive in People	6 Integrity	7 Team Building/ Peace Making	8 Growth through Adversity, Endurance
Overcome prejudice and antipathy; Nonvengeful; Nonjudgmental; Control anger; Forgiveness, no grudges; See positive in people; Recognize talents and capacities of people (Productivity through people)	Genuine, sincere; Open, authentic; Trusting and trustworthy (Simultaneous loose–tight properties) Quality of products and services; Total integrity	*Individual:* Equanimity, overcome anxiety; Calm, sure, serene, yet enthusiastic *Organizational:* Conflict resolution; Team building	Growth through adversity; Learning, teaching, training; Courage; Steadfastness; Dedication; Perseverance; Endure to the end (hands-on, value driven)

Attributes in parentheses are described in *In Search of Excellence* by Thomas J. Peters and Robert H. Waterman, Jr.

tors and other related parties, T&B had four major occasions to build and to enhance a climate of trust in recent years. Utilizing its human resource consultants, it replaced the historic adversarial relationships among external parties with cooperation and collaboration, permitting these projects to be completed on time or ahead of schedule and at lower than projected cost. This was achieved on projects valued at over $1.5 billion, saving several hundred million dollars in construction costs overall!

In the 1950s, Bill Bottum read Kelso and Adler's *Capitalist Manifesto*[8] and became enamored with the employee stock ownership plan (ESOP) as both an egalitarian ideal and a practical way to motivate personnel and to insure the continuation of a privately held company. Bill was stayed in his enthusiasm by his father, however, who had only recently secured voting control of the company from surviving stockholders who were no longer interested in the company's operations or welfare.

Bill was mindful, however, that one-half of the G.N.P. in the United States and one-half of private-sector employment was and is provided by privately owned family businesses. He knew that historically only 30 percent of these companies continued to be privately held into the second generation and only 10 percent into the third generation of the founding family because of a variety of reasons including estate tax problems and the disinterest or incompetence of progeny. Even those companies that did make it into the third generation were frequently in a state of chaos, he believed, because nonfamily employees felt secure neither about their future employment nor their current status of exclusion from the favored few.

Until 1970, it had been the policy of T&B to reward a limited number of key contributors with stock ownership. This practice was discontinued, however, in anticipation of discovering a more satisfactory answer to the issue for both the employees and the company. For an interim period an annual discretionary cash bonus pool was used to recognize individual employee performance along with the regular pension plan and profit-sharing trust in which all employees shared.

An in-depth, long-range planning process in 1979 produced a series of subsequent actions that moved the company into many new markets and caused a major decentralization of its operations. A series of important questions to be dealt with over time was also spawned by this effort. These included how key contributors should be compensated in decentralized operations and how the continuity of the company and its culture could be assured.

In 1980, an Income Distribution Unit (IDU) system was implemented to reward key contributors with an individual target percentage of the annual profits of the company in excess of a minimum threshold of earnings. This plan permitted participating employees either to receive their awards in cash or to have payment deferred until termination of employment or retirement. Deferred payment funds were invested in a portfolio of mutual funds balancing growth and income. The IDU also permitted the company to compensate key personnel in a manner that equated to participation in company stock ownership.

In 1983, T&B adopted the Plan for Continuity. Its major component was the establishment of Townsend and Bottum Capital Fund, Inc. This nonstock, for-profit trusteeship was designed to own the stock of all T&B operating units, protect the corporation from unwanted takeovers, remove short-term concerns for earnings per share from determining company decisions and permit capital to be allocated to those ventures appearing to be most promising.

Secondarily, the T&B Capital Fund trustees were to ensure that the company's values and culture would be sustained. The plan reads in part:

> It shall be an organization operating with the highest principles of integrity, service to society and clients, in an environment of trust which will nurture growth and development of employees so that they become stronger, more autonomous, and more serving of their fellow men and women. Leadership development is to stress serving rather than power, status, or prestige-seeking. Teamwork and cooperation are to be stressed in all relationships with clients, recognizing that clients can best be served in an environment of trust where team building is done between the client's organization and T&B so that common goals can be achieved.

174

The mention of leadership development that stressed serving rather than power, status or prestige seeking was derived from Bill's exposure to the concept of servant leadership developed by Robert K. Greenleaf, ex-director of management research for AT&T. (Bill is now a director serving on the board of the Robert K. Greenleaf Center.)

When the Plan for Continuity was adopted, Bill said, "We think we unleashed the entrepreneurial spirit in our family of companies where our people are given the chance to have their individual efforts make a difference. We think that is what the entrepreneurial spirit is rather than ownership. And by sharing in the profits that they generate they are treated equitably and as well as they would be if they had ownership."

Bill strongly believed that the T&B model provided for the liberation and rejuvenation of the free enterprise system, enabling managers to focus on the fundamentals of the business, the health of the organization, the development of its people and serving client needs, rather than being concerned over earnings per share or the redemption value of their stock. An English firm, Scott Bader Co., Ltd., has used a similar organizational model with considerable success for several decades.

Bill Bottum took the Plan for Continuity and the concept of servant leadership very seriously; he gave up 80 percent voting control of the company when the trusteeship plan was adopted.

Results

What were the "real world" results of all of this for T&B by the end of 1985?

- The company had an enviable reputation for complete integrity with those who had done business with it.
- It had an excellent record of earnings growth stretching back several decades.
- It was actively reorienting its operations to develop new markets during a period of major economic change.
- It had attracted an employee group that was unusually dedicated, motivated and of substantial personal integrity.

It also had generated some skeptics and doubters along the way. Even some insiders in the past had voiced their opinion that "you can't run a company this way, especially in the construction business." Outsiders had also voiced doubt that Townsend and Bottum people could be tough enough, "especially with the unions," when they really had to. Despite these critics, T&B officials claimed that no contracts of consequence had ever been denied them because of T&B's adherence to its stated principles.

In early 1986 the Townsend and Bottum management team members relinquished their operating positions in the company to become Capital Fund trustees, and three new corporate operating officers were elected to succeed them. The new officers were selected for their responsibilities after having served in a number of preparatory positions within the company over the past dozen or so years. Each had prior relevant experience with other companies before joining T&B during the 1970s, having been drawn to the company by its reputation.

When the new operating team was named, one member, Fred Rueger, described Bill Bottum's actions: "Bill stepped back and out of our management meetings. He was present in the company but would give us no input on how things were being run. He wouldn't be the decision maker. After we clearly established ourselves as a team, Bill came back on an availability basis. He would not impose his views on us."

As 1986 unfolded, however, the reorganized Family of Companies began to encounter difficulties. By midyear several units were in deep financial trouble. By year's end the corporation in total had suffered its worst loss in history.

During the year, Julian Moody, a long-time organization development consultant, came out of retirement to help diagnose the problems at T&B. In December, he facilitated a three-day workshop involving the top 30 managers of the corporation. As the result of the meeting, several immediate steps were taken:

- An administrative council was formed bringing together the heads of most business units monthly to plan, coordinate and control operating decisions for the Family of Companies. The council reported to the board of trustees.

- Bill Gay, who had previously been elected president of the Family of Companies, headed the council.
- Hank Vaughn, previously vice-president of operations, became president of T&B, operating the traditional construction services unit of the corporation.

In other moves, two smaller business units were shut down and another sold to an ex-T&B manager.

When a cash flow crunch occurred in early 1987 the construction services unit was forced to reduce its staff of 107 down to 34 people. Half of the reduction required terminations, the other half, reassignments to other operating units. The overhead at T&B Computing also was reduced 25 percent. Employees with 25 to 30 years of service were terminated. Bill Bottum reported in a talk before the ASTD Convention in Atlanta in June 1987 that this crisis really tested the values of the organization.

During a previous reduction-in-force in 1984, a policy was established that each supervisor terminating an employee would be personally responsible for seeing that the ex-employee found a new job. This policy was continued in 1987. The company also provided terminated personnel a range of outplacement services including the assistance of an outplacement consultant. The reservoir of trust and good will the company had developed with its employees over the years made it possible for these terminations to happen without their incurring serious bitterness or acrimony.

Throughout 1987, other actions were taken to reduce costs and realign the company to face new market realities. At year end, however, the losses continued. To remove his salary as a burden to the company, Bill Bottum resigned as an employee, though he remained indefinitely as a consultant at a lower level of compensation and also remained chairman.

During 1988, two particularly significant actions occurred to save the company from declaring bankruptcy. First, T&B executives initiated a team concept involving the company, its bank and its bonding firm. This three-party arrangement has enabled the company to meet its current financial obligations and to optimize the potential return to its long-term creditors.

The second action involved Thomas Monaghan, founder of

Domino's Pizza and owner of the Detroit Tigers. Because of the compatibility of the T&B culture with Monaghan's business principles, he agreed to assist T&B financially and to provide management consulting to assist the company in resolving its problems. As the result, T&B Computing, a major company unit, was purchased by the Monaghan organization and communication continued on other ways the Monaghan people might help T&B.

It is now clear that the decline in T&B's traditional business, the construction of public utility electrical generating capacity, was more severe and had greater consequences for the corporation than was ever anticipated. The company's decentralization into many autonomous operating units had to be accomplished too precipitously. Studies of new potential markets and the preparation of technically experienced personnel for new management responsibilities was inadequate.

T&B historically had been accustomed to managing a few very large projects at any one time on incentive fee contracts. Controls and systems to monitor the progress of such contracts had been well established. During 1986, however, all T&B units together were working on 40 smaller projects, each contracted on a firm-price basis. Cost controls and systems to monitor the progress of such a proliferation of smaller projects were yet inadequate. When just a few ran into severe difficulty, the entire organization suffered the consequences.

Prior to 1986, a number of smaller contracts had been profitably completed, but the cost of maintaining the sizable central staff, which had been covered by the previous success of several major units, was not yet apparent. In 1985, for example, the company received $5 million in one incentive bonus payment for the early completion of a long-term utility construction contract. Such payouts obscured the necessity of overhead reduction and the close monitoring of costs on smaller fixed-price contracts.

By late 1988, it appeared that Townsend and Bottum would survive, albeit looking much different than it did even two years previously. Certainly the strategic plan to reposition the company in the face of the disappearance of its traditional market was well founded. The difficulty of implementing such a plan was not foreseen, however. In the rush to implement it, which was felt to be necessary, critical problems arose.

How then are we to view Townsend and Bottum at this time?

Certainly it would do the company and its leadership an injustice not to recognize its many years of financial success and contributions to society. Thousands of persons benefitted financially by being employed on T&B projects. Millions more have been served by the facilities it constructed.

But perhaps most important has been the culture of the organization providing personal growth for its employees and a model of integrity for an industry that needed such a model. Even in its struggle to survive, it continued to live by the motto, "Skill–Responsibility–Integrity. And the greatest of these is Integrity."

* * *

The decline in the need to build more electrical utility generating capacity has had major implications for Townsend and Bottum. A radical decline in the production of domestic petroleum likewise affected TDIndustries of Dallas. The company was in the position of being able to diversify geographically, however, doing what it knew how to do best in other growing areas of the country. How it developed under the guidance of two people with the same name completes our review of Transformational leaders.

THE JACK LOWES OF DALLAS, TEXAS

Jack Lowe, Jr., Chairman and C.E.O.
TDIndustries, Inc.

- The sign at the front of the corporate offices of TDIndustries reads: "An Employee Owned Company."
- This wording appears on a plaque located next to the entrance to the building: "This building is dedicated to all Texas Distributors people—and we include our families. It is a symbol of our commitment to each other in a partnership of the spirit."—1974
- On an announcement board near the reception desk this was a recent message:
  "All Real Management is Self Management."

179

You hear about two Jack Lowes in Dallas, Texas: Jack Lowe, Jr., current chairman and C.E.O. of TDIndustries, and Jack Lowe, Sr., his father, whose heart ceased functioning on Thanksgiving Day in 1980 but whose spirit lives on within the company today.

When Jack Lowe, Sr., died prematurely at age 67 in 1980, the company he founded as Texas Distributors achieved $56 million in annual sales. By 1980 it was, and is today, the market leader in Texas in the distribution, installation and maintenance of residential and commercial air conditioning systems.

Among the regional and national companies headquartered in Dallas, TDIndustries ranks among the smaller ones, even at its peak sales level in 1985 of $135 million. But the figure of Jack Lowe, Sr., cast a shadow of community influence far greater than the business base from which he operated. Jack Lowe, Sr., was a leader of leaders.

Jack Lowe, Sr.

A native Texan and a graduate of Rice University, Jack, Sr., worked briefly for General Electric and then spent the war years in the army before establishing Texas Distributors. At its inception in 1946 the company operated out of an auto supply store owned by Jack's aunt and the Lowe family occupied one-half of the aunt's duplex. The company's army surplus trucks were parked in the yard behind the house each night.

When Jack, Sr., went into business, he focused on selling, installing and servicing residential and commercial central air conditioning equipment. At that time a list of home addresses in Dallas with central air conditioning took up less than two type-written pages.

Over the years since then, Texas Distributors has grown with Dallas and beyond it to encompass all of Texas and parts of New Mexico and Oklahoma. Today its new construction-oriented operations extend even beyond this geography into the southeastern states, with a few isolated projects in both eastern and western parts of the country.

Beginning as a single operating entity, its scope of activities soon required divisionalization. In 1982 the corporation was reorganized again to establish separate company units operating under separate names, such as Texas Distributors, TDService, TDMechanical, Tempo Mechanical, Tempo Service and TDI Air Conditioning and Appliances, and the corporate name was changed to TDIndustries. These separate operations now sell central air conditioning equipment through franchised dealers; operate parts and supplies stores; install and service air conditioning and plumbing systems in large commercial and multifamily residential buildings; provide energy management systems and services for Dallas area commercial facilities; and operate dealerships, selling, installing and maintaining air conditioning and major appliances in several East Texas communities.

But the financial success and visible growth of the company are the results of efforts that were accompanied by some unusual dynamics. Jack Lowe, Sr., was, as Jack, Jr., says, "born generous." He believed from the beginning that any benefits accruing to the company because of its success belonged to everyone in the company according to their contribution to that success. During the company's very first year, he instituted a retirement plan and set up a profit-sharing plan where 25 percent of the company's net earnings were to be shared annually with employees. Soon he began providing ownership shares for all the managers in the company and in the early 1950s established a stock purchase plan whereby every employee could own a part of the business. Today nonofficer employees own over 65 percent of TDIndustries. Harriet Lowe, Jack Lowe's widow, only controls approximately 8 percent of the shares as the company's largest single shareholder.

Employee stock purchases are made by individual voluntary payroll contributions of up to 7 percent of pay with company annual matching contributions depending upon profitability. Historically the value of these company contributions has averaged 28 percent of profits before federal income taxes. In 1985, company contributions again exceeded employee contributions to the Profit Sharing–Savings–Stock Plan.

Majority ownership by employees means that TD directors and officers are subject to an annual vote of confidence by the employees. For the past half-dozen years, employee stockholders have been asked to suggest the names of other employees to be candidates to serve on the board of directors. Through 1988, no nominations were made by employees. The slate suggested by company management, essentially the officers of the corporation, has been accepted by the shareholders annually.

But financial ownership by employees of TD is just the beginning. You know there is something different about the company when you visit its corporate offices today. Three walls in a large employee lounge and gallery behind the reception area are a visible clue. They contain the pictures and names of every current TD employee who has served the company for 5 to 10, 10 to 20 and over 20 years.

Asked what made Jack, Sr., the way he was, Jack, Jr., said recently,

> Until the last five or so years of his life, Dad was almost disinterested in profits, and was never interested in personal wealth. He sort of had the attitude that the kind of company we want to be just doesn't allow us to make much money. I tell people when I recruit them, "Now, if you're looking for a place to get incredibly wealthy, this is not it, because we just share too much."
>
> Dad had something that changed him. In 1955 he had TB. He was isolated in an upstairs bedroom in our home for a year. Mother and the doctor went in there but we couldn't. He read a lot; studied the Bible; studied nature; he had binoculars and studied birds and trees. It changed him. He had a really close relationship with his pastor, Bill Dickinson, at Highland Park Methodist Church. He was his closest friend. They [also] went through some family trauma together.

The "change" that occurred in Jack, Sr., was eventually felt both inside TD and throughout Dallas. Within the company, in the early 1970s Jack, Sr., felt they had lost some of their earlier people orientation, some of the character that had made them successful. So, with the apprehension of his management, he started a series of meetings out at his house, all-day sessions, with 20 or so employees in each session from a cross-section of the company. No one's supervisor was to be present. As Jack, Jr., recalls, "They would sit and talk all day. The pass-out for that [meeting] was Bob Greenleaf's 'The Servant as Leader.' They read it before they came." All employees were eventually included. It took over a year to accomplish. Harriet Lowe fixed lunch for everyone.

> Out of it, a year or so later, came what we called the "People Objective." It said something like: "People are important; we want this to be the kind of place where people can grow and succeed in their own way, and every failure is an important failure." Something like that. It refocused some of the kinds of things that were going on. No heads rolled or anything like that.
> A year or so later people started hitting him up saying, "We don't have a situation like we did then, but it was kind of a neat time. Couldn't we do something like that again?" So we started what we call "Breakfast Sessions." They last almost up to lunch. Everybody who's been here a year or over gets invited to one of those every other year.

Jack Lowe, Jr., attends every one of these breakfast sessions.

The sessions, held 16 to 20 times a year, with groups of 20 to 25 employees in each, meet at the company headquarters in Dallas in a large meeting room. Pay and benefits always come up for discussion and issues raised by an employee survey process are explored. These issues often arise from a survey section that asks, "If you could change three things in the company, what would they be?"

The employee survey process has been underway some four years now. Everyone attending a breakfast session fills out a survey form which deals with 29 separate issues ranging from satisfaction with pay to agreement with company values. Questions regarding adequacy of training, supervision and recognition for accomplishments are also included. The survey was installed by a national firm that gathers data from companies who, in total, employ several hundred thousand persons. Hence, national norms are established annually for TD to check itself against. A group of questions uniquely TD-oriented are included and watched for changes from period to period.

In the recent economic downturn, a series of changes was initiated influencing some employee job content and working conditions. Survey results, expectedly, showed a decrease in aggregate employee satisfaction within the company of some 10 percent, from 79 percent to 72 percent. Interestingly, regarding a specific issue, satisfaction with pay, only about 50 percent of TD employees ever indicate that they are satisfied there, showing that pay satisfaction is certainly not the only, or perhaps even the primary, reason for employees to appreciate working for the company.

Interviews with employees indicate that the quality of human interactions throughout the TD system is its hallmark. Denny Henderson, a veteran field supervisor for Tempo Mechanical, reported, "When I met Jack he remembered my name from then on. The people that manage the company make the difference. Every year it becomes a better company in one way or another."

Graham Moore, manager of engineering and fabrication for TDMechanical, joined the company in 1979. At first he didn't believe the company could be successful by being more concerned about its employees and its customers than its profits. When pondering a decision regarding design specifications or the assignment of crews, he said the question always was, "What would Jack Senior do?" That meant, do it right for the customer and the employees. It takes new personnel six months or more, he indicated, to realize what the company is really like, that it means what it says about the importance of people. "This place breeds openness," he declared and added, "You can voice your opinions to your supervisor and it won't hurt you."

"You can just about do what you want to here. The company provides people the support to try things," according to Larry Taylor. The vice-president and manager of Dallas–Fort Worth operations for TDService, Larry has been with the company for 16 years. On the other hand, he says, "We are hard to work for because we don't give people black-and-white rules to follow. We give them a picture frame and tell them to do what is right, treat your fellow employees and your customers right, and that is tough for them. There is no way for them to turn to page 27 and get the answers. The people that stay here, however, stay because of that."

In the Dallas community, the previously mentioned "change"

in Jack, Sr., had broad implications. Additionally, Jack, Jr., believes that a very personal experience within the family taught his father tolerance for people who thought differently from himself. "He sure had strong opinions about things. But he really honestly considered other people's opinions and was influenced by them. He wasn't 'dug in' anywhere so you just couldn't move him. He never did get that way."

In the wake of civil rights legislation, Dallas was ordered by the federal court to come up with a desegregation plan for its public schools. The first plan developed was bumped back to the school board by the court as being inadequate.

About that time, a group was formed called the "Dallas Alliance," representing a cross-section of the community, to deal with areawide problems of race and poverty. The group specifically said it was not going to get involved in the school desegregation issue. The first chairman of the Dallas Alliance was Jack Lowe, Sr. With little progress underway on the school desegregation issue, the judge requested that the alliance and Jack Lowe get involved. Chairing a task force, Jack Lowe led the effort.

A few weeks before the task force was to finish its work, Jack Lowe, Sr., became ill and went to the hospital. His irregular heartbeat required the insertion of a pacemaker. Progress on the desegregation plan ceased until Jack, Sr., was able to work again. Within a few weeks, he was back and the plan was completed and accepted by the court. "Nobody in the whole group liked every bit of it; there was a lot of bussing in it; but the community accepted it and we didn't have any riots or stoning buses or any of that kind of thing," Jack, Jr., relates.

Jack Lowe, Sr., spent about half of his time on community-related work while continuing to run Texas Distributors. He worked long hours, but then to him, his family, his business and his community were all one. He didn't intentionally divide his time among them. They were all a part of each other in his way of thinking. There is no question that Jack Lowe, Sr., molded the character of TDIndustries just as he strongly influenced the development of Jack, Jr.

Jack Lowe, Jr.

Likewise a graduate of Rice, Jack, Jr., did his military service at the Houston Manned Space Craft Center in the 1960s. He has been with TD since 1964, and he has been chief executive officer since 1980. No mere caretaker of the company his father founded, Jack has moved it in new directions, extending the systems of employee training and involvement as well as the products and markets it serves.

Philosophy

Employees who have been with the company the longest (anyone over five years) compose a group known as the Oak Room Council and are brought together whenever crucial issues face the company. When the company's name was changed to reflect better its current scope of business, Jack sought a new logo and settled on one that he thought was appropriate. When he discussed it with the Oak Room Council, however, they rejected it and commissioned a new design which even Jack agrees is a vast improvement over his original selection.

In 1985, the council met to consider what to do about a key issue related to the stock ownership plan. Plan provisions require that all shares be sold only to the company and the company agrees to buy back all shares tendered to it according to a repurchase formula. That year, owing to a variety of factors including several retirements, a situation arose in which the company wasn't able legally to buy all shares tendered to it for repurchase. The council was called together to decide what should be done about it. Out of the meeting came an apportionment plan determining what shares would be purchased when, an increase in the voluntary contribution levels that employees could choose in order to buy shares and a one-time sale of shares of up to $10,000 to any one employee. From these sources, the problem was resolved.

In early 1987, the Oak Room Council was asked to consider a revision of the company's mission statement, which initially was brought up for discussion at a management retreat. The key issue was whether the statement should begin with a focus on employees or customers or profitability, acknowledging that each is essential to the success of the business and must be a part of the statement.

Graham Moore volunteered that some employees consider the Oak Room Council sessions so important that even though they are stationed outside of Dallas they will fly in at their own expense to attend these meetings.

Another employee group, the TD Employee Committee, meets periodically to review ideas presented to it through idea boxes placed throughout the company, to follow up on the feasibility of the ideas and to respond to the people who submitted them.

The company has no formal grievance procedure. It has, however, a universal open-door policy. Anyone with an issue can talk to anyone else in the company at any time without jeopardy. That includes talking to Jack. In the corporate office the open-door policy is carried to an extreme. There are no doors on the offices. Architecturally an open office concept, all "walls" are movable partitions.

There are no executive or management perks at TD. The only difference in employee treatment is the salary level, based on market forces and individual responsibility. All benefits are the same and everyone assigned a company car because of business necessity drives an equivalent automobile—recently, Buick Centuries that then were two years old.

TD Industries is a training-oriented company. Historically, there have been regularly scheduled, semi-annual mandatory management development sessions for all supervisors and managers coordinated by the main office "People Department" (now really the People Person), which reports to Jack. Periodically, outside resources such as Tom Peters have conducted workshops at TD on effective management and leadership. Several key managers also attend the annual Drucker Seminars at New York University.

In 1981 and 1982, Jack compiled a Basic Values–Mission–Leadership document that sets out the principles which have guided the company's relationship to its individual employees, customers and communities in the past and for the future (Figure 6).

Figure 6

We recognize that actions are vastly more important than words. However, to perpetuate the character that is the essence of our organization, we will try to reduce to words:

- The Basic Values that we strive to uphold in all of our relations
- The Mission of our organization, and
- our ideas of Leadership.

BASIC VALUES

At TDIndustries, we try to follow these Basic Values in all of our relations with customers, with suppliers, within our communities, and among ourselves:

CONCERN FOR AND BELIEF IN INDIVIDUAL HUMAN BEINGS
The basic character of our group is, above all, a concern for individual human beings. We believe that the individual has dignity and importance, that people are basically honest, and that each person wants to do a good job. We believe that no one has ever really found the limits of human ability. If we draw our strength from the uniqueness of each individual, together we can become greater than the sum of our members. TDIndustries is best thought of as a group of individuals—not as an impersonal "company." We, as a group, own it and do its work.

HONESTY

BUILDING TRUSTING RELATIONSHIPS
We believe people react positively when trust and confidence is placed in them and when the best is expected of them. We try to reflect this belief in all our relationships.

FAIRNESS
Fairness includes equal treatment and equal opportunity for everyone.

RESPONSIBLE BEHAVIOR
We have high expectations of each other. We expect people to act responsibly and to work for group goals. We expect them to be dependable and to work hard.

HIGH STANDARDS OF BUSINESS ETHICS

MISSION

A relatively high level of profits is necessary for the continued existence and future growth of our company, as it is for any business enterprise. This requirement, however, is not a measure of accomplishment of our mission as an organization.

Our Mission is:

SERVICE TO OUR CUSTOMERS

Through high quality goods and services, and value—as determined by our customers—we must continually earn and re-earn the right to serve our customers.

OPPORTUNITIES FOR REWARDING EMPLOYMENT

A building block of our philosophy about people and business is the belief that the goals we share as a group need not conflict with the goals we seek as individuals.

We believe that each person wants to grow—to do a good job; to be proud of what he has achieved; to receive not only material reward, but also the respect of others. These individual goals are in harmony with company aims for high quality, fair price, excellent service, and thus increased value and satisfied customers.

In order to provide growth opportunities for the people of TDIndustries, we plan to continue to grow our business.

We believe that our group benefits by building and strengthening the judgments of individuals. We cannot order good judgment, but we can provide the environment in which it grows. We favor those practices that encourage each individual to make judgments that meet both company and personal needs. We believe it is better to educate than to command.

We know each of us should think and act as a manager. Even if you supervise no one else, you have a responsibility to manage your own job. When making decisions, you should ask yourself, "How would I handle this situation if I owned TD?"

SERVICE TO OUR COMMUNITIES

We believe the most important way we can serve our communities is by sustaining an organization which accomplishes our first two mission statements with excellence. However, we also believe we have important responsibilities as individual citizens and as a company to be involved in our communities on a volunteer basis, in addition to giving generously of our money, goods and services.

Our organization is committed to the accomplishment of this mission over the long term. We do not believe in seizing short term benefits to the detriment of our long term mission. We believe in continuous, intense "people-development" efforts, including substantial training budgets. We believe in investing in the tools, equipment and facilities that enable us to better accomplish our mission.

LEADERSHIP

If our organization is to live up to its Basic Values and Mission, a key ingredient will be Leadership from a very large number of us. Simply and plainly defined, a leader is a person who has followers. He has earned recognition and respect.

- The leader is first a servant of those he leads. He is a teacher, a source of information and knowledge, and a standard setter; more than a giver of directions and a disciplinarian.
- The leader sees things through the eyes of his followers. He puts himself in their shoes and helps them make their dreams come true.
- The leader does not say, "Get going." Instead, he says, "Let's go!" and leads the way. He does not walk behind with a whip; he is out in front with a banner.
- The leader assumes that his followers are working with him. He considers them partners in the work and sees to it that they share in the rewards. He glorifies the team spirit.
- The leader is a people builder. He helps those under him to grow big because he realizes that the more big people an organization has, the stronger it will be.
- The leader does not hold people down, he lifts them up. He reaches out his hand to help his followers scale the peaks.
- The leader has faith in people. He believes in them. He has found that they rise to his high expectations.
- The leader uses his heart as well as his head. After he has looked at the facts with his head, he lets his heart take a look, too.
- The leader keeps his eyes on high goals. He is a self-starter. He creates plans and sets them in motion. He is a person of thought and a person of action—both a dreamer and a doer.
- The leader is faced with many hard decisions, including balancing fairness to an individual with fairness to the group. This sometimes requires "weeding out" those in the group who, over a period of time, do not measure up to the group needs of dependability, productivity and safety.

- The leader has a sense of humor. He is not a stuffed shirt. He can laugh at himself. He has a humble spirit.
- The leader can be led. He is not interested in having his own way, but in finding the best way. He has an open mind.

Asked whether the values statement has affected TD's relationship to its suppliers and customers, Jack related, "We don't preach it, but we are very customer oriented. Our employees know how important they are. Our customers see it in the quality of our folks and how they perform for them. Two of our divisions have a party once a year for our suppliers and we are fanatical about paying our bills on time."

At TD, volunteering for community service is encouraged. Employees can arrange through their supervisors and the main office to spend time on community activities. In addition to normal service club and business association activities, company officials have been active in the Dallas Private Industry Council, Council on World Affairs, St. Paul Hospital Board of Trustees, United Way and others. Jack is a member of the Dallas Salesmanship Club, which doesn't really have anything to do with salesmanship. It supports programs for severely emotionally disturbed children and their families by sponsoring an annual Dallas Cowboys preseason game and the Byron Nelson Golf Classic.

"One of our strengths is that Dallas is a business-run community and people know who is taking leadership on community issues. That's appreciated by the business community. People want to do business with us. They know we are a leader in some of these areas. A lot of our customers want us to succeed. People like what we stand for." As a matter of policy, TD is also very aggressive in seeking out minority suppliers to service the needs of the company.

Reflecting on the underlying reasons for the company's overall perspective, Jack, Jr., shares his father's view that we're all together here on "spaceship Earth." Particularly focusing in on the civil rights issue, "Unless society as a whole is treated fairly and succeeds, has fair opportunities, ultimately it's going to destroy us. Dad's underlying belief was that it is the basis of democracy to have an informed electorate. If we have an uneducated electorate, democracy is doomed. That's sort of a long view of why we need to get on with the business of educating kids, but that's just kind of the way he thought. I learned something from that and I think our company learned from that. It's also a moral issue. Golly, what's fair here? You have to ask, 'Is this fair?' "

The TDIndustries story is not finished, of course. It continues to unfold. With the decline in the Texas economy owing primarily to the fall in oil prices worldwide, and the subsequent troubles in the regional banking business, new construction of large commercial and multifamily projects has slowed to a trot. TD historically has been tied closely to commercial and multifamily construction and has had to reduce its employment levels very selectively over this period from 1,250 to approximately 950 people. Predictably it did so with care and concern for its people. Those close to vesting in company plans were allowed to stay in the plan until they were vested. Those terminated received severance allowances, extended benefits and outplacement assistance.

With the worst of that behind the company, Jack senses a new energy and spirit emerging in the company to get on with building the business. New projects, previously not considered because of limited size and potential, have been accepted as opportunities to grow new markets. Cooperation between TD companies has become a new norm, with sales leads passed between them and employee-sharing readily accessible to meet customer priorities.

As the company has extended its operations into new areas of the country, a key issue, according to Larry Taylor, is "how we get our philosophy, that feeling, the unwritten word, that caring and concern from this headquarters to a lone guy in Orlando. How do we keep him pumped up and supported? And how does he pass that on to someone who goes to work for him?"

Jack would be the first to acknowledge that TDIndustries hasn't arrived at a state of ultimate perfection. All operations of the company are not yet uniformly successful. He's also continually concerned with how to maintain a balance between being an effective leader and not dictating outcomes to an employee/stockholder group that needs to feel responsible for the future of the company.

He sees changes occurring in the business environment. His

mother and father's generation did not make any distinctions between family, business and community in terms of time spent or personal priorities. Now he sees people making a distinction between business time and personal or family time. Spouses are more demanding of "time away" from work. The individual's sense of loyalty to the company seems to be changing; Jack isn't sure where all this will lead. "Maybe the company was too central in people's lives," he reflects.

Like Bill Bottum of Townsend and Bottum, Jack is on the board of the Robert K. Greenleaf Center. Together, they, along with others, are searching for the appropriate perspective from which to view their roles and for the most effective ways to provide leadership in the future.

SUMMARY

No one profile presented in these chapters has portrayed the ultimate model of the virtuous leader, nor were they expected to do so. All are "in process," dynamic, not static. All are human and not always consistent, subject to diversions and potentially corruptible. But currently each is moving forward, pushing past the frontiers of traditional business social relationships, questioning old assumptions and developing new ones. They are present-day pioneers. The territory they are advancing through is the realm of consciousness. The heights they climb provide a new perspective on the potential of human civilization. In a sense, it is their openness, flexibility and creativity that are the model attributes required for these times.

By their example, there is no longer any validity to the often held belief that successful business leaders must be rugged individualists, or that those who are concerned about others have no significant role to play in the "real world" of competitive enterprise.

Also by their example, there is no longer any validity to the belief that the relationship between owners and workers is inherently adversarial. When workers become owners as well, the adversarial dimension is reduced and/or eliminated, even if by *ownership* is meant the proprietorship that workers are enabled to have in their jobs.

Finally, their example demonstrates that many American workers who have the opportunity to be self-managing welcome the responsibility to work in cooperation with others for the benefit of both their organizations and themselves.

Acknowledging these and other "new truths" and discarding old assumptions are signs of the end of an era. They portend the emergence of a new age although it clearly has not yet arrived.

It is important in this period of change then to foster and nurture leadership in all institutions that is open, flexible, accepting of change and perceptive to the needs of society. Old social arrangements, which previously provided a sense of place and social and financial security as well as points of moral anchorage, are now in disarray. Thoughtful leadership is required during these times so that new human interconnections are established in accord with emerging realities. The ultimate purpose of leadership in any institution is, after all, to serve human needs and not to control a machine or feed a bureaucracy.

But how have such virtuous business leaders come about? What factors have conspired to produce their sensitivity to the human condition? For this we turn now to a summary of what we have learned from these profiles.

Chapter 8

OBSERVATIONS AND CONCLUSIONS

OBSERVATIONS

THE PREFACE STATES the threefold purpose of this book: to identify the human/social concerns these business leaders were addressing, to learn how they were addressing them and to discover what motivated them to do so. By doing this, it was hoped, it would become more apparent how exemplary business leadership could be intentionally developed in the future.

First, speaking to the issue of conscious motivators, most of these leaders specifically cited the example set by their parents as being important in the development of their concern for others. Only a few recalled early educational experiences as being formative of their values. Perhaps the influence of this source was too subtle to be recognized at the time, but was nonetheless present. Even later formal educational exposures were not recalled as being significant in the development of their ethical perspectives. The structure of the educational enterprise has not often appeared to be conducive to the development of virtue in leadership, particularly of the Transformational variety. The leadership example set by the educational system has often been authoritarian, elitist and hierarchical, stressing competition between individuals, eschewing the cooperative effort of persons in teams, with greater emphasis placed on measuring individual academic performance rather than on facilitating relevant learning. Many content elements, as well, essential to appropriate functioning in business, such as the need to understand other people's needs, aspirations and responses, have often been left out of the academic curriculum. The focus has been on increasing an individual's knowledge in a particular subject.

Assessing the importance of religious exposure as a primary motivator of these statespersons is even more difficult. Only a few specifically mentioned church or Sunday church school as being important in their ethical development and social sensitivity. Perhaps early religious influences are no longer remembered, again because of the subtle but repetitive nature of their mediation. In retrospect, for many of the 24 it may now be difficult to separate the influence of their families from the influence of their early religious exposure, as the two were closely joined. What they may remember is that the family which they regard as being ultimately important viewed church membership and attendance as being of high value. Whether this importance was really understood by them at the time is an open question.

Certainly in later years, as young adults, religious influences were of some significance for the majority of the 24. Over half specifically indicated that they maintained their church involvement during that period of their lives, most as a continuation of a pattern established by their families in earlier years. More significant, perhaps, are seven cases where various religious "interventions" were identified as being somewhat influential in establishing their life purposes and direction.

Several volunteered, however, that their present church connections have shown no interest in their vocations nor concern for the problems they face in attempting to be faithful to their beliefs in the business world. Several others expressed outright hostility to organized religion citing personal experiences or observations of institutional failings. Though somewhat disaffected, these few have remained actively interested in the subject of religion and have developed their own personal, and relatively detailed, theologies. Religion then, if not church, has remained an important matter for them.

Viewed from the perspective of the assigned categories, several of the Traditionalists remain committed to orthodox religious communities. The Transitionalists and Transformationalists tended to be somewhat less "churched" and to be more inclusive of other systems in viewing human purposes and values.

In total, 14 highlighted particular critical events or circumstances that caused them seriously to consider the purpose of their lives and what was of most value to them. These "change events" included adversities involving family members, severe personal crises, unusual personal opportunities and "psychic or religious experiences." Many of these "change events" then had the potential of enhancing the sense of empathy that these persons might have for their fellow human beings.

Apparently the most significant factor was the influence of a role model. Sixteen of those interviewed voluntarily identified specific persons whose living examples had profoundly influenced the development of their values and priorities. These role models were people with whom they had very direct personal contact. In several cases the influences were most important during childhood years and the significant persons were relatives. In several other situations, persons whom they had worked for influenced them in their value development. Challenging clergymen who became mentors and close personal friends influenced another few. The remainder were positively affected by the examples set by their in-laws, a blind church school teacher, a seminary ethics professor, a state legislator and, one, by different significant persons in virtually every stage of life.

In 10 situations, both "significant persons" and "change events" influenced the leader's values and priority development. (It would not be surprising if business statespersons were more inclined to be reflective about the meaning of life and about the significance of their experiences than is true of other business leaders.) In total, 19 of the 24 reported that they had been quite consciously motivated by the examples of role models and/or by life-changing events.

CONCLUSIONS

From the preceding review, it appears evident that the concerns and values of these business leaders are the result of a variety of interactive influences throughout their lives. Having watched the early development of fraternal twin grandsons who have totally different personalities and behavioral patterns, I feel the presence of some congenital predisposition on the part of the statespersons themselves must also be suspected. However, from the evidence cited by those interviewed, dealing with serious adversities or very unusual opportunities or being consciously affected by the example of appropriate role models may well have deepened or radically altered such predispositions.

On the one hand, it is quite clear from the data that the "values learning" of this group of leaders was primarily observational and experiential in character. This learning appears also to have required a sensitive, though not necessarily conscious, perception on the other hand.

The development of virtue, then, quite reasonably occurred in stages. It likely began in a *foundation* stage with their parents as primary role models and was modified over time by close exposure to and observation of other important figures and formative experiences. (Childhood peer influences, incidentally, were not mentioned by anyone, although they were undoubtedly present. As adults, several remarked they had peer experiences that helped to sharpen their sensitivity to human concerns.)

Although book learning and classroom instruction were not recalled by many to be consciously significant in the development of their values, the exercise of repetitive disciplines may well have provided a *reinforcing* stage that occurred in more cases than are evident.

The same might be said regarding religious instruction. Its repetitive, subtle influence may have been directly experienced or have been mediated through parental example and instruction and through the observation of others. Certainly if such disciplined repetition reinforced values already apprehended through other experiences and observations, their validity would be compelling. As such, a case can be made for teaching business ethics in the classroom, not necessarily as foundational but as reinforcing. Perhaps even more important among maturing students is the formation of the habit of consciously considering the ethical aspects of otherwise technical issues as a regular part of the educational exercise. The habit of ethical wrestling, not the perfect rightness or wrongness of the specific action to be taken in each situation, becomes the primary objective of the learning.

Significant "change events" and the inspiring examples set by others, then, provided the *capstone* stage for most of these leaders. Having said all of this, however, is to speak more to the form of value development than to the substance. What are the primary issues that these business people have dealt with in their roles as virtuous business leaders?

Overwhelmingly, they have been concerned with the issue of justice and equity. "What's fair?" asked Jack Lowe, Jr. The Traditional statespersons have answered this by their philanthropy and volunteerism, seeking to make amends for what society has not been able to insure through normal participation in the socioeconomic system. The Transitionalists have focused on specific causes such as employing the disadvantaged, involving employees in deciding issues facing their companies, opening new opportunities for women in business and giving special help to those seeking to begin new enterprises because they were viewed as the economic hope of the future.

Overwhelmingly, the Traditionalists have focused on society, on those outside the business system. The Transformers have done the opposite. They have focused on opening up the business system for participation by those employed inside it, to have a major say in how business is conducted, to be accountable for their efforts and to have a "piece of the action."

A secondary concern for these statespersons has been the issue of community enrichment. Certainly the issue of justice and equity has its communal as well as its individual dimensions. This concern relates to the maintenance of community voluntary institutions, the advancement of community cultural affairs and the resolution of major problems that threaten community solidarity such as racial unrest, unemployment, poverty and homelessness, substance abuse, domestic violence and teenage pregnancies.

A subset of this concern for community enrichment has been a concern for the development of the youth of the community, often articulated today as a need to provide alternatives to the traditional institutional mechanisms that previously supported youth development, namely, the family, the schools and the churches. So far this effort has primarily been one of reaction and of defense. At any rate, both the concern for community enrichment and for youth development has mainly been the province of the Traditional statespersons, the philanthropists and the volunteers, again with exceptions.

Finally, an even smaller group dwelt on the issue of what authority they recognize as being the valid source of principles to live by. Certainly this appears not to have been a consciously important issue for the majority of statespersons. Some, however, have spent much energy on the issue and have developed comprehensive answers for themselves and often for their organizations.

Several have generated meticulously researched, religion-based answers; others have consciously based their value decisions on an ethics foundation with the religious roots obscured. Still others have developed their operating principles on the fundamentals of American democracy, on the exercise of personal freedom within a context of responsibility to a larger community. Some seem to have created a mixture of each. Many logos, company slogans and statements of corporate purpose and mission are evidence that the issue of authority may have been considered or that the statesperson has decided merely to posit certain principles as being valid for the business behavior of company personnel and the organization in total.

In particular, the Transformers seem to have varied widely in their claims of authority, citing biblical teachings, natural law, prior personal experience and pragmatic observation. However, the Transformers all apparently have embraced a common view of the nature of humankind: that most people are fundamentally trustworthy and want to do the very best they can given the freedom to do so. The extension of that belief into action directed these leaders to become the enablers of others rather than their controllers. It required them to be open in dealing with employees, not secretive, about the competitive conditions and financial circumstances of the company; to be communicative; to encourage employee participation in managing the work; to trust employee intentions and their capacity for self-management; to believe in employee self-disciplining and accountability; to be more supportive than critical; to recognize that equal treatment of all personnel is imperative for their personal growth and commitment to the firm; and to acknowledge that the equitable sharing of the fruits of organizational success should be a right of employment.

Finally, and perhaps of first importance, they came to recognize that it was their responsibility to articulate an overall inspiring vision of the company, embracing its highest principles, aspirations and values, enlisting the company's personnel in the attainment of that vision for both the success of the organization and the personal fulfillment of each individual employee.

Chapter 9

CULTURE MAKERS AND
CULTURE RESPONDERS

IN CHAPTER 8, the efforts of the 24 virtuous business leaders were reviewed from the perspective of patterns and trends from within the context of the business system itself. But as we said early on, and as many of the leaders themselves declared, it is how business meets the needs and expectations of the society within which it operates that is ultimately important, both for business and for society.

What are the needs and expectations that society has of business? Providing employment, producing and marketing goods and services, obeying the laws of the nation and of its subjurisdictions and, minimally, doing no harm are society's primary needs and basic expectations. But these business statespersons have responded to, indeed have all created, higher standards for themselves and most for their organizations as well.

The actions of the persons studied indicate a kind of give and take between business and society. Society supports business as business supports society. In addition to this instinctive symbiosis, however, very specific business and societal actions have historically affected the other sometimes quite negatively or quite positively.

For many years, in league with science, business has applied technology to create a material revolution, producing a myriad of products and services which Americans have readily consumed at a prodigious rate. But after many generations of ever-increasing rates of production and consumption and ever-higher material standards of living, the social contributions of business-wed-to-technology also began to display other attributes. The industrial machine that once survived on the willing labor of hundreds of thousands of unskilled workers became technologically sophisticated and the unskilled found themselves increasingly unemployed and largely unemployable. The technological system that was supposed to be the salvation of humankind produced whatever it found it could invent, including the most heinous of weaponry.

The distance between top management and employees grew as hierarchical and bureaucratic forms of organization spread, it was said, in order to control far-flung operations. Within such a system, employees were ranked according to status and increasingly felt unappreciated, underutilized and unfulfilled. At the same time the demands of the job on employee loyalty and on their time grew. Work life, family life and community involvement became fragmented, the latter two suffering most in the process.

From still other evidence in our culture, all is not well. Many of us now have a low regard for our traditional institutions. We trust neither our government nor our business leaders very far. We participate in the political arena only through special interest groups. Our knowledge of our freedom, how it came to be and how it must be sustained, is lacking.

With the increase in our private affluence has come public fear: fear of losing what we have, fear of robbery or of violence. Both have increased the felt need to protect personal property and to protect national interests. Our personal freedom is diminished by the security devices with which we must surround ourselves. Our national freedom and security have now grown fragile because we need the resources of many other nations, many of them underdeveloped and historically exploited, to feed our production/consumption machine. This has forced us to extend our police/military power around the globe. Although we are 6 percent of the world's population, we need 30 percent of the world's resources to maintain our economic apparatus.

Our domestic society has seen a rapid deterioration in personal morality. Drug and alcohol abuse and domestic violence abound. Such circumstances are problems in themselves, of course, but they are also symptoms of other changes occurring. Just what is going on?

WHAT HAS BEEN GOING ON?

Robert Bellah and four other researchers have written a profound description of contemporary American culture, examining its current dynamics and tracing its roots in a book called *Habits of the Heart: Individualism and Commitment in American Life.*[9]

The thesis of *Habits of the Heart* is that the typical white, middle-class American has lost the ability to speak about the moral importance of community (our public life in common) because all aspects of our lives have become so imbued with the veneration of individualism. Further, this loss threatens freedom, the central value of most Americans, because it is now thought of as being an individual right, divorced from any personal commitment to public responsibilities. Historically that community dimension was informed by and was composed of our national biblical and republican traditions, our "communities of memory," which provided us with their "second languages." These "second languages" were unique words and phrases that once gave our lives meaning and purpose within the context of community, such as our "calling," the importance of "civic virtue" and of the "public good."

In the words of Bellah (et al.), "Taking our clue from Tocqueville, we believe that one of the keys to the survival of free institutions is the relationship between private and public life, the way in which citizens do, or do not, participate in the public sphere."[10]

At the nation's founding, the authors argue, the importance both of individual freedom and of freedom for groups of persons within which personal freedom was to be responsibly expressed was present. As the nation grew, simultaneous to the development of its industrial economy, freedom became the right of each person to pursue private economic interest without structural ties or moral commitments to any group with which the person might have previously been identified.

Tocqueville, in the early decades of the 19th century, the authors remind us, saw the pursuit of personal economic interests as a threat to democracy and hence to freedom because it shut people off from each other. Religious and political participation, however, put people into cooperative relationships with each other. He saw the American proclivity to establish a variety of active civic organizations as being key to the maintenance of American democracy.

As economic individualism eclipsed communal religious and civic participation in importance, our political system became the province of professionals whose concern was more for effecting compromises between conflicting interests than acting with concern for the public good. Hence, our expressions of civic virtue (of what was best for everyone) were overshadowed by our concern for our personal interests.

The objective of education changed from learning what was right to do in life to learning how to do most effectively what you wanted to do. Parental encouragement went from concern for youngsters doing good to concern that they do well. "Success" became the new objective of individual efforts. Self-fulfillment, empty of a sense of social responsibility, was now the goal.

Not that persons no longer related to each other. But in a world of enhanced individual competition, with everyone seeking to further personal interests, the "ability to impress and negotiate"[11] replaced old-fashioned friendships.

This is not what the founders of our nation had in mind.

[They] all were agreed that a republic needed a government that was more than an arena within which various interests could compete, protected by a set of procedural rules. Republican government, they insisted, could survive only if animated by a spirit of virtue and concern for the public good.[12]

Further on, the authors declare,

The tension between self-reliant competitive enterprise and a sense of public solidarity espoused by civic republicans has been the most important unresolved problem in American history. Americans have sought in the ideal of community a shared trust to anchor and complete the desire for a free and fulfilled self. This quest finds its public analogue in the desire to integrate economic pursuits and interrelationships in an encompassing fabric of national institutional life. American culture has long been marked by acute ambivalence about the meshing of self-reliance and community, and the nation's history shows a similar ambivalence over the question of how to combine individual autonomy and the interrelationships of a complex modern economy.[13]

Although business and government are the most powerful institutions in our society (they observe), our mores, our habits of the heart, can alter culture by changing our consciousness, our attitudes and opinions. It is to initiate that culture-altering process that the authors have written the book.

They then rehearse the degrading of society that we observed earlier in this chapter stemming from the overreaching of our industry and technology. Despite all of this, they say, our "communities of memory," our biblical tradition, persists by reminding us that God and neighbor come first. And our republican tradition is sustained by our annual recall of important national dates, heroes and historic events. The argument of *Habits* is clear: We must take our common history and our cultural institutions seriously and revitalize them so that they can speak relevantly to us today.

Moving toward the resolution of our conditions, they specify that "the litmus test that both the biblical and republican traditions give us for assaying the health of a society is how it deals with the problem of wealth and poverty,"[14] and that "classical republican theory from Aristotle to the American founders rested on the assumption that free institutions could survive in society only if there were a rough equality of condition, that extremes of wealth and poverty are incompatible with a republic."[15]

The answer that the authors suggest is the development of a movement "to transform our social ecology," which would take over where the civil rights movement left off. It would change the relationship between government and the economy, but not in a socialistic manner. Just how the movement would be initiated and what the propellant for change would be is not clear. Presumably it might emanate from a powerful vision orchestrated by a democratically supported, politically oriented statesperson or group.

A summary paragraph perhaps encapsulates the thinking of

the authors in this regard:

> Reasserting the idea that incorporation is a concession of public authority to a private group in return for service to the public good, with effective public accountability, would change what is now called "social responsibility of the corporation" from its present status, where it is often a kind of public relations whipped cream decorating the corporate pudding, to a constitutive structural element in the corporation itself. This, in turn, would involve a fundamental alteration in the role and training of the manager. Management would become a profession in the older sense of the word, involving not merely standards of technical competence but standards of public obligation that could at moments of conflict override obligations to the corporate employer. Such a conception of the professional manager would require a deep change in the ethos of schools of business administration, where "business ethics" would have to become central in the process of professional formation. If the rewards of success in business management were not so inordinate, then choice of this profession could arise from more public-spirited motives. In short, personal, cultural, and structural change all entail one another.[16]

It is particularly interesting to note in *Habits* that the authors' answers to our dilemmas focus on the necessity of developing an inspired social movement that enlivens political debate regarding substantive justice, leading to a transformation of our business system. Such a singular final focus on private business enterprise further supports the argument that how business relates to society is *a*, if not *the*, key influence in contemporary American culture.

In the light of *Habits of the Heart*, how do our 24 business statespersons appear?

To begin with, of course, the 24 have been no less subject than any other citizen to the dynamics of American society that have occurred during the past 200 years. These changes have reshaped our culture from the pattern that our national founders expected would continue or emerge. Unlike the persons interviewed for *Habits*, most of the 24 are upper-income level today, but that was not true of the families from which most of them came. More of them than might have been expected from reading *Habits*, however, continue to identify with "communities of memory," especially the church, and some may still understand its "second language." Several, as well, have articulated their familiarity with their republican roots, but overall few appear to have consciously applied either of these foundations of principle to justify their personal or organizational purposes and values. However, there is a common sense of responsibility to the larger community apparent among them.

As noted in the previous chapter, concern for the issue of justice and equity clearly runs through the vast majority of those interviewed. The specific focus of each leader, however, and how the issue was approached vary widely.

The primary focus of the Traditionalists has been on injustices and inequities occurring in the general community beyond the walls of their enterprises. Basing their actions on historic principles, Al Wilson, David Koch and Miles Barber have each provided generous personal and organizational philanthropy, and a strong commitment to volunteerism, in dealing with the issue of social justice and equity. Their beneficiaries have ranged from traditional community service organizations all the way to particular attention given to specific disadvantaged populations. The processes they employed to achieve justice, although distributive in effect, were voluntary in nature. The problem with such a voluntary effort is that, unlike these virtuous leaders, others have viewed their own actions of philanthropy as matters of private prerogative and discretion. No serious challenge to the structures of a sociopolitical-economic system that may be responsible for the maintenance of substantive injustice or inequitable conditions can be mounted by private efforts if their participation is viewed by those involved as purely discretionary.

The Transitionalists all zeroed in on target populations. Rather than relying primarily on philanthropy, voluntary action was the means of dealing with the issue of social justice, and providing access to institutional participation was the primary method employed. That the development of substantive justice was the intent in these cases is clear. Norbert Berg and Control Data saw the creation of opportunities for permanent employment for the impoverished and the racially underprivileged as a key need and pioneered that effort in multiple locations. Dan May saw that employee access to information about the condition of Republic Airlines and participation in company decision making were essential for both the maintenance of employment and the survival of the organization. Margaret Hansson and Carol Green have fostered entrepreneurism, assisting others in developing access to markets, personnel and financing, and have encouraged and have supported the participation of women in positions of institutional leadership. Meg and Carol have done so both individually, as significant role models, but have also joined with other women in developing an organized effort to achieve those purposes, not in opposition to others, but to challenge structural barriers that have long existed in our sociopolitical-economic system.

The Transformationalists represent a significant departure from the approaches of the Traditionalists in dealing with social justice and equity. Their focus has been primarily, though not exclusively in all cases, on the internal structural mechanisms of their organizations. In each case, the interests of Ken Iverson, Bill Krause, Billye Ericksen, Bruce Copeland, Hal Bolton, Bill O'Brien, Bill Bottum, Jack Lowe and Vic Hunter have been to provide substantive equity: access of their employees to shared authority, to be accountable for their own work and to participate in the rewards of their organization's successful efforts. Although there is no general movement in America to encourage every company to operate this way, and the design of each organization is unique, a number of small voluntary associations of interested employers, such as the Robert K. Greenleaf Center, have arisen in the last decade or so to encourage efforts in this direction. No formal action to reestablish an older conception "that incorporation is a concession of public authority to a private group *in return* for service to the public good, with effective public accountability"[17] has yet been proposed, but it would appear that the Transformational statespersons would agree in principle to the direction of the concept. The problem arises when definition of *service to the public good* is attempted. What and whose standards will apply? Would specifications exceeding some minimal requirement be possible considering the multitude of variables involved in the circumstances of each incorporation? One would hope that the answers to these and other questions could be arrived at by social consensus, which is a doubtful current possibility.

Relative to other points suggested in the *Habits* program of cultural transformation, certainly the role of the manager is changing dramatically in Transformational organizations. The institutionalization of that new role will only be complete when it becomes the model of management taught in the business schools of America and is adopted more widely in companies than it currently has been. The most predominant, though unconscious, current model projected in schools and in industry remains that of "the boss," except in university classes on organizational effectiveness or corporate public responsibility, which are not required courses in many curricula.

The matter of teaching ethics in business schools as well as in all other schools, as *Habits of the Heart* recommends, is of some importance. However, specifically how to teach ethics and how to measure the effectiveness of such teaching requires further effort. To be sure, the methods employed in the past have been found to be unsatisfactory virtually by all parties involved. The findings of this study point toward the observation and coaching of appropriate role models and experiential learning as being the most effective methods. The Transformers, by modeling their virtue and exhibiting both the success of their enterprises and personal growth and fulfillment in the lives of their employees, testify to their commitment in this regard. Their positive ethics, enabling that personal growth and envisioning the achievement of lofty purposes, can inspire the human spirit, which is the locus of values sensitivity—as opposed to logically appealing to the mind, the accepted approach to date. Alas, the primary focus on personal fulfillment within organizations still reinforces the primacy of individualism over community. The central concern of the Traditionalists and the Transitionalists for community and society outside the workplace is an important addition to the Transformers' primary focus if the *Habits* resolution is to be forthcoming.

Finally, the "inordinate rewards," especially those received exclusively by senior managers who supposedly have led their companies to financial success, is an area of concern to the Transformational statespersons as well. In the cases presented in this book, the issue of employee stock ownership and/or of profit sharing, or the use of other methods of distributing the rewards of the success of the business to employees, is a central concern. Some have developed their "final answer." Others are still in process. Participation by all employees in sharing in the financial success of their companies, however, is becoming a standard feature in Transformational organizations.

The real issue now is, what is to be done about justice and equity for those who are no longer employed or employable even in traditional organizations, let alone in the transformed ones? How does a "privatized society" deal with such issues that inevitably affect the "public good"? But we will hold these questions open as we consider our 24 statespersons in the light of another observer of American culture.

In the mid-1970s Willis W. Harman, now president of the Institute of Noetic Sciences, wrote *An Incomplete Guide to the Future*.[18] This book and a talk[19] given by Harman to a management seminar in 1986 are complementary and shed further light on the emerging role of business in society.

Quite obviously, Bellah (et al.) and Harman approached their tasks from different standpoints. Bellah viewed American society from a historical and ideological perspective and Harman, from a futuristic and visionary perspective. They also did not always see the same effects occurring.

Willis Harman's observations cite much of the same evidence as the *Habits* authors regarding the degradation of our culture. However, Harman focuses on all of Western industrial society including the American experience. As a futurist it is his contention that we make current decisions on how we view the future just as much as on our recall of the experiences and principles that informed our history. This perspective then informs him that we are in a period of a major paradigm change, wherein our views of reality are undergoing a radical departure from past assumptions and principles to a new view that correlates more closely with emerging assumptions and principles. Harman calls this paradigm change a "changing concept of consciousness." The old paradigm, that of the industrial era, was based on scientific "facts" and observable phenomena, and the new one, of the transindustrial era, on "consciousness-as-ultimate-reality."

In the old industrial-era paradigm, the scientific worldview and method determined how work was performed. The objective was to divide tasks to increase productivity in order to secure a higher standard of material life. The goal was to achieve technical progress through the predictability and control of every variable. Unlimited material progress was believed to be possible by allowing autonomous units of production to pursue their own ends. The results of this worldview until now have been materially dramatic but are becoming humanly disastrous, according to Harman.

Harman identifies five fundamental failures of the paradigm:

- "It fails to promote one of the most fundamental functions of a society, namely, to provide each individual with an opportunity to contribute to the society and to be affirmed by it in return."[20]

  "The basic problem is that the structure of society has the effect of defining an ever-increasing number of people as 'unneeded.' "[21]

- "It fails to foster more equitable distribution of power and justice."[22]

  "More fundamentally, however, the mechanisms are unsuccessful because the basic paradigm itself contains no rationale for redistribution."[23]

- "It fails to foster socially responsible management of the development and application of technology."[24]

  "A central weakness in the free-market system [is] its inability to place public needs above private gain."[25]

- "It fails to provide goals that will enlist the deepest loyalties and commitments of the nation's citizens."[26]

  "It fails to shed light on the question of *what is worth doing*."[27]

- "It fails to develop and maintain the habitability of the planet."[28]

Improvements in our health system have led to world over-population. With longer individual life spans, we now have the increased problem of providing meaningful lives for our older citizens. Advanced technology has led to the threat of world destruction, through nuclear war, natural resource depletion and environmental problems, and automation has led to dehumanized working conditions and chronic unemployment.

The failures of the industrial-era paradigm and the social conditions they have produced are reflected in four dilemmas facing world society today:

- Growth—"The industrialized countries of the world are structured in such a way that their economies demand growth that the world's finite resources can support only with increasing difficulty."[29]
- Work roles—"The work-roles dilemma is the reverse side of the growth dilemma. The work-roles dilemma charac-teristic of advanced industrial societies reflects a funda-mental inability to provide enough satisfying work roles to meet the needs and expectations of the citizenry."[30]
- World distribution—"We cannot risk the international instability that results from the vast disparities between the rich and poor nations, yet neither of the obvious solu-tions—making the poor nations richer or the rich nations poorer—seems feasible."[31]
- Control—"How can we exercise needed societal control over technology without sacrificing individual liberty?"[32]

From these circumstances, Harman concludes, "those prob-lems are so deeply rooted in the basic industrial-era paradigm, and so intertwined with one another, that they are probably not resolv-able, individually or together, within that paradigm."[33] We are in a period of change that may end up being one of the most dramatic in world history, he believes.

Harman cites four dynamics propelling this change forward: the shift to an information society, the shift to a global perspective, the awakening of the subjugated and the shift in underlying beliefs.

The shift to an information society, he says, inevitably leads to fewer people being required to produce the material needs of society, which forces us to rethink our economic assumptions about work, life purposes and social value. Further, he believes, evidence is accumulating that at some level of mind/spirit we are connected, not separate beings as the scientific-industrial era assumed. If our new paradigm includes this assumption, our emphasis on individual and organizational competition will also be affected.

A global perspective means seeing the problems of the world as *our* problems: nuclear armaments, the shaky world financial situation, environmental degradation and so on. These call for the emergence of world values—commitments to ultimate meaning and purpose—rooted in the religious and spiritual traditions of all nations. Western society, Harman says, in its emphasis on materialism has pushed these traditions aside and needs to reappropriate them in relevant terms for today and tomorrow.

When he speaks of the awakening of the subjugated, Harman is referring to persons in Third World countries and to women. Both bring new perspectives of reality, furthering cultural diversity and balancing our traditional belief in competition and exploitation with the values of cooperation and nurturing.

Finally, the shift in underlying beliefs, Harman says, is evident in the renewed interest in the human spirit and its relationship to a human world ecology. In this shift, belief in scientific materialism gives way to a new universal transcendentalism, which unlike traditional religious practices is more experiential and noninstitutional, less fundamentalist and sacerdotal.

The common thread that runs through Harman's discussion of each of these shifts is the re-emergence of the importance of what he terms the "perennial wisdom" that is at the heart of all of the world's spiritual traditions, not only balancing our view of reality against the assumptions of scientific materialism, but positing that we understand ultimate reality not just through our physical senses but also through our intuitive faculties. Further, we now are beginning to recognize that it is our process of consciousness (including our unconscious creative/intuitive mind) that defines that reality for us. Therefore, if we view possibilities greater than what we previously thought possible, they become a new reality for us. In short, we create reality by our assumptions, beliefs and vision and by our self-imposed limitations regarding any of these.

The implications of this "new consciousness" are considerable in terms of how we view all human relationships, how we reconstitute our fundamental beliefs regarding national interests and global dilemmas and how we structure our political economy to deal with the issues of work, social purposes and the distribution of wealth.

To be sure, the "problems" Harman sees in contemporary society are for him "givens," symptoms of macrosocial dynamics. He has attempted to accept these symptoms/problems as data and, without imposing a bias on them, ask where all of this is leading us. His ideology, if he has one, is that each human being has a mind/spirit composed of conscious, unconscious and intuitive faculties, with unlimited powers of perception which can create the reality that he or she wants to create—given an environment of trust and a lack of fear, the discovery and acceptance of a life purpose, the creation of an empowering vision and being in touch with feedback to modify behavior to align oneself appropriately with that goal.

In his book, Harman indicates that the new paradigm will focus on human growth and development and the institutions that foster this in partnership with nature; in short, on the advancement of human civilization. Further, he describes how private business enterprises, now not subject to direct control by society or operating according to the principles utilized in establishing national goals, nonetheless impose their will on society by their domination of our economy. Hence, for the new paradigm to operate, some formal accommodation to society's needs will have to be provided for in the decision-making systems of business. Harman expects that this accommodation will occur voluntarily as business leaders see that "good business policy must become one with good social policy."[34]

Harman's approach primarily has been to observe the macro-dynamics of contemporary society both in terms of the industrial-era paradigm and the paradigm of consciousness-as-ultimate-reality which he believes to be emerging to replace it. Moving from the macro to the micro or individual company level, the focus quite naturally can become somewhat blurred. The specific, situation-bound actions of virtuous business leaders may not correlate well with the broader perspective of an entire culture in ferment. The appraisal by Harman of the failures and dilemmas of the industrial era are arguable and provide one possible description, which our business statespersons may accept as being accurate of current reality or not. All of them probably would not. Many of the 24 decried the value erosion in American society and speculated as to causes. Some, like Bill Bottum and Hal Bolton, specifically volunteered their conviction that we are in a period "between paradigms."

CULTURE MAKER?

Both the authors of *Habits* and Willis Harman have provided convincing evidence that business has become a greater maker of culture than a culture responder. This assessment appears to be correct. The balance of power in contemporary society has come to rest on the side of business. Witness the commercialization of virtually every aspect of contemporary life. Even the arts, long the bastion of free expression and of creativity, are now increasingly dominated by works commissioned to sell.

Such an unusual degree of power that it can define culture also demands unusual responsibility. That responsibility will either be voluntarily assumed or it eventually will be legally required of business. History has shown that sooner or later democratic societies awaken to debilitating excesses and force changes upon their institutional sources.

It is for this reason that particular attention and support need to be given to exemplary leaders and their companies today. Every citizen is a stakeholder in business whether he or she holds a share of stock or not, is employed in business or not, or buys the products and services of business or not. Just to live in American society today makes everyone a stakeholder in business.

The exemplary leaders portrayed here, and their virtuous peers throughout the country, clearly exhibit that the higher qualities of human life need not suffer because of the actions of organizations. Indeed, such qualities can be enhanced because of the way some businesses are operated.

The interests of business, seen from an appropriate time perspective, and the interests of each individual in society, must be, and are, the same. The conditions of domestic and international peace, of positive interpersonal and intergroup relations, of universal employment and financial security, of lifelong growth and opportunities to contribute and of continuous improvement in the quality of our common life are not utopian ideals. They are practical goals commonly applicable to each citizen and to every company.

To be more specific, the leaders profiled here have demonstrated that businesses need not be depersonalizing; that companies can be structured so that employees can grow, manage themselves, find fulfillment in their work and be very appropriately rewarded for their contributions; that joint efforts between parties once regarded as adversaries can lead to greatly improved productivity and mutual success; that creative attention given to the needs of those existing historically on the fringes of our socioeconomic system can produce positive results for all concerned; and that our public life can be qualitatively enhanced by the concerted action of companies dedicating their attention and a reasonable percentage of profits to common causes.

The pivot point in the character of each leader, it seems, rests between the need to control and the need to share. Behind these needs lie assumptions about the value of persons and how they are motivated, about ownership versus stewardship, about private rights versus public responsibilities, about exclusiveness versus inclusiveness in human affairs and about deserving success versus being grateful for one's good fortune. Certainly, as in all matters, simple statements cannot be made about these complex assumptions. However, where the balance lies, how the pivot point is moved, determines one's ethics, one's morality.

None of our business statespersons obviously could be expected to be a model of understanding and action paralleling the expectations of the authors of *Habits* or of Willis Harman. Several, however, clearly embody elements of the new direction in which Harman sees us traveling as citizens of Western society. For example:

- Bob Gary's work at Texas Utilities on the development of "whole brain" utilization.
- Gene Shea's book, really focusing on the "perennial wisdom," indicating that we are ultimately spirit, not mind or body, in nature.

- Miles Barber's and Bill Bottum's willing admissions that unseen forces dramatically informed their career decisions.
- Norbert Berg's and Bruce Copeland's efforts to include the downcast and outcast as worthy participants in mainstream society.
- The business stateswomen struggling to recast their life purposes and seeking to free others to see new possibilities for their lives.
- The Republic Airlines management group willing, even temporarily, to bring prayer and meditation into the conference room as a legitimate exercise in business practice.
- The visioning of the Transformers, portraying lofty purposes and futures that inspire achievements that benefit employees and organizations alike; also their discarding of old assumptions about the roles and status of people.
- The view of all of the statespersons that all human beings are persons of ultimate worth and of value in themselves.
- The acknowledgment by each of the statespersons that the culture of business needs to provide society with more than material benefits.

Chapter 10

LOOKING AHEAD

THE AUTHORS OF *Habits* declared, "The tension between self-reliant competitive enterprise and a sense of public solidarity, espoused by civic republicans, has been the most important unresolved problem in American history."[35] Within the business system itself, or more specifically, within individual companies in the business system, as illustrated by the Transformational business leaders, some progress in the direction of resolving this problem is evident.

The investment of employees in their work is seen by the Transformers as being of equal importance to that of the investment of their shareholders. Certainly the advent and growth of major institutional investors and of portfolio managers with no long-term commitment to a particular enterprise has helped to reduce the primacy of shareholder rights over those of all other business stakeholders. The positive acknowledgment by the Transformers that employees need to "own" their positions of authority and responsibility in order to be appropriately affirmed and motivated must be seen for what it is: a major revolutionary step en route to economic democracy. Minimally, the Transformers have recognized that the rights of all of the stakeholders of their enterprises must be balanced. Interestingly, in 1946, Jack Lowe, Sr., already knew this when he founded Texas Distributors.

Exemplary leaders like Bill O'Brien at Hanover Insurance, Ken Iverson of Nucor, Billye Ericksen at CAPSCO and Bill Krause at 3Com have also built the employee rights dimension right into the structure of their companies through their compensation and employee-management systems. This "democratic" capitalism implies no spongy or spineless corporate leadership. It requires excellent employee personal performance and accountability to the organization. But it shares the gains received as the result of successful corporate performance in ways that are far more equitable than the traditional capitalist formula.

* * *

The aspect of financial reward aside, Vic Hunter at Hunter Business Direct and Bruce Copeland, as pioneers in participative management, have recognized that employees are far more able to manage their own work than they had previously been given credit for; further, that most want to do so and, with that freedom and accountability, they grow and find dimensions of self-fulfillment and actualization that they have never experienced before, which in turn reinforces their motivation and their commitment to the common cause of their enterprise.

Meanwhile, Hal Bolton at Dahlstrom wanted to share both the rights and the responsibilities of management and to share the benefits of company success with the Dahlstrom work force, which held itself captive to old stereotypes, retaining the false security of the obsolete system of adversarialism.

The Transformers have tried to enhance the participation of company personnel in the internal functions of the organization. To be sure, some of the Transformers have, like the Transitionalists, affirmatively acted to include target groups from the general population in the operation of their businesses as well. Like the Traditionalists, most of the Transformers have personally engaged in forms of community philanthropy and volunteerism. And a few, most noteworthy Billye Ericksen, Jack Lowe, Jr., and Vic Hunter, have reported that their companies systematically encourage and facilitate the participation of employees in community affairs. It is this externalizing of the internal participation of employees in company management that is the link remaining to be forged that will begin to resolve this central problem raised in *Habits*.

On January 1, 2001, the world will not suddenly become a radically different place. As Harman has observed, societies and institutions exhibit continuity. Their outward appearance may remain quite the same as we observe today. However, the assumptions that inform their actions can change dramatically in the period between now and then.

It is hoped that the importance of a fundamental role of democratic government will re-emerge, seeing to the equitable treatment and participation of all citizens, as opposed to listening to and arranging compromises between powerful special interest groups. The social need to be satisfied by such a government is the nurturing of public virtue in service to the common good and the reinvolvement of its citizens at all levels in the democratic process. It can be inspired by a national leader—at best, the nation's chief executive—who raises up a national purpose and a lofty, positive vision of what our nation is at its best, a model of justice and equity for all other nations to emulate. We need this leadership and vision to show us the way to new national greatness in a complex international context whose troubles we have too often compounded through our continuing need to feed our unbalanced production/consumption machine.

Given appropriate national leadership, the not-so-subtle shifts demonstrated by virtuous business leaders can proliferate leading to the eventual recognition that of all institutions in modern society, business, previously regarded as among the most conservative, can be the most significant agent of positive socioeconomic and political change.

Businesses, now operating in an international economy, proceed regardless of borders and most directly face the problems of the world as they seek to foster trade, secure resources and open markets. Unlike the governments of the nations, theoretically businesses remain unfettered from the need to defend parochial and territorial self-interests. Unlike the religious establishments, no competition between deeply felt ideologies forms barriers in transnational business discussions. Unlike educational institutions, which seek to understand and project hypotheses, businesses must develop live agreements between diverse parties and operate appropriate to their contexts in order to survive and to prosper. Certainly there is much room for corrupt practices to be generated today because of the unequal power of the parties involved in international business transactions. Universal moral purity as well will not suddenly appear on January 1, 2001. However, maintaining vast areas of the world and their populations in economic servitude will certainly not move the problem of inequitable power distribution and its resulting corrupting influence toward resolution.

Recently, a group of business, professional and academic leaders (including Willis Harman) initiated a new organization, the World Business Academy. Its purposes and objectives are defined in its brochure, which reads as follows.

WORLD BUSINESS ACADEMY

Leading the way

Beyond Business—
Through Business

"In our era, the road to holiness necessarily passes through the world of action."
—Dag Hammarskjöld

The World Business Academy is an international network of business executives and entrepreneurs who recognize a personal commitment to utilize their skills and resources in the creation of a positive future for the planet. Hence the Academy motto "Beyond Business—Through Business."

THE ROLE OF BUSINESS

- World business leaders have emerged as the first global citizens. They understand that global problems can no longer be resolved solely within any national boundary. Engaged in commerce, business leaders understand the inherent and irreversible interdependence of all nations.
- Business enterprise has been a principal agent of change in creating the world we now live in and can play a significant role in creating a viable world. Through international commerce business fosters economic interdependence and reduces the separation of nations by political boundaries. Through communication and transportation business has helped to create the awareness of one humanity, on one planet, all sharing a common fate.
- Business leaders are trained by their activities to respond to changes in the marketplace or fail. This ability to rapidly respond to changing circumstances is the most critical skill required to deal with the major issues of our time.

THE NEED

- The industrialized world is going through a period of rapid and profound evolutionary change—a change *driven* by a complex of interconnected global problems and *pulled* by an emerging vision of a positive global future.
- Any response to this change requires the world business community to: play a constructive role in creating a humane, realistic and economically viable future; reassess humanity's ecological relationship to the planet; and assist in creating conditions of worldwide peace and common security.
- International business executives already comprise an informal worldwide economic network. *Until now, there has been within this network no deliberative body which encourages its members to address business interests within the context of a broader vision of responsibility for the future of humanity and the planet.*

FUNCTIONS

The World Business Academy's functions:
- The Academy provides a neutral platform for the examination of the relationship between world business activity and the critical intersection of the various economic, social, technological and political forces accelerating the world community to an uncertain future.
- The Academy is a network of business leaders who accept a responsible role in addressing global problems and who are willing to give thought, time, and energy to coordinated engagement.
- The Academy identifies and interprets forces for fundamental change.
- The Academy enables business leaders to articulate the need for resolution of global problems.

THE FORUM

- The Academy provides a forum for continuing dialogue among those business leaders who are convinced that the shape of the future is our choice and who feel a responsibility to help determine the outcome. That dialogue is conducted through:
- *WBA Perspectives,* the Academy's bulletin
- Inter-regional dialogues, symposia, and limited participation forums
- An annual international meeting
- Electronic communication
- WBA is *not* a business lobby, political action committee, economic de-

velopment board or formal educational institution.

- It has no pre-existing "agenda." Nevertheless, its participating executives are "action-oriented" and will follow discussion with action when they deem it appropriate.

MEMBERSHIP

- Academy Members have made a personal commitment to establishing a positive role for business in the creation of a better world future.
- The on-going dialogue of Members is stimulated and augmented by the imagination, background, experience and vision of a number of consultants and analysts who serve as Fellows of the Academy.
- Invitations to participate as Member or Fellow are carefully and selectively administered to ensure a network of congenial, globally aware, practical visionaries.
- Guided by a prestigious Board of Advisors, the business of the Academy is conducted by the Members through its Board of Governors.

WHY WORLD BUSINESS LEADERS?

- The future viability of the planet is heavily influenced by the attitudes and actions of the world business community.
- The growth and future prosperity of business enterprise will be critically dependent on the state of the world in which that business is conducted.
- Business leaders already have worldwide capability and responsibilities.

The World Business Academy provides a meeting-ground where business leaders, entrepreneurs, practitioners and scholars can address the crucial role of business in shaping the global future. To this meeting-ground business leaders bring their unique capabilities to convert vision into reality, and practitioners and scholars bring their skill of interpretation and analysis. It is this interaction which leads us beyond business through business.

"A small group of thoughtful, concerned citizens can change the world. Indeed, it is the only thing that ever has."

—Margaret Mead

To achieve lofty goals, such as those set for the World Business Academy, multiple leadership is required. As we saw in reviewing the motivation of the 24, the example set by others inspired the majority of them. Of course, the importance of political leadership articulately calling us to new common purposes and portraying the vision of a just and equitable society cannot be underestimated.

To be sure, the influence of family values personified by the example of parental actions will continue to be fundamental in the generation of virtuous leadership. In addition the reinforcement that repetitive educational processes can bring to value formation and to the development of life purpose, including the consideration of ethical issues in the classroom, is required. Expecting this action to do wonders, however, is bound to disappoint unless it is more than a didactic exercise. The experience of early and repeated exposure to models of virtue for effecting moral growth is paramount. Only following such observations and/or experiences is the classroom method of any lasting value, and then, most likely, only if it leads to the generation of a self-conscious expression of belief and commitment by the learner.

It is in the realm of the moral dimension that much hope for the growth of business statesmanship lies. The *moral dimension* here means awareness of our essential spiritual nature and the connectedness of all of life. This nature transcends the artificiality of boundaries; the socioeconomic irrelevance of race, color, creed or sex; the tragic misperception that there are natural generic enemies—and includes a recognition that whatever divides us is a barrier that we have constructed ourselves and can as well remove.

Further, it means our acceptance of the fact that we truly are created as equals, and that we are responsible as equals to respect all life and all that supports life. And finally, it means that we have powers of knowing, of envisioning, and of achieving that go far beyond what we have previously realized because we assumed our own limits and they became self-fulfilling prophecies.

This moral dimension can be nurtured by the churches, but it may not be. It is the innate, if often unrecognized, characteristic of all humans. And it can be nurtured, as we have seen, in many other ways, most successfully by exposure to appropriate examples.

Perhaps the most relevant question at this point is, how can we move beyond the current condition of moral drift? Amidst and among our private enclaves of individual material success, nationally and internationally, poverty and deprivation persist; environmental degradation escalates; public concern for common problems seemingly continues to decline; nations continue to pit themselves against each other. How can a new age of consciousness emerge? Must it take some cataclysmic event after which the survival of humankind is in doubt? Or are we finally arriving at a point in history where we can foresee disaster and avert it? Are we willing enough to reclaim the principle of concern for the common good to set aside a sufficient amount of individualism to adopt a new course of human/social action?

Given appropriate and supported national leadership, the inspiration of models of virtue, the positive influence of family examples, the effective reinforcement of education, and the reawakened spiritual perspective of life, a new age of virtuous business leadership can emerge. We can envision *Transcendental* business statespersons arising. Assuming many of the attributes of the Transformational leaders, who were primarily focused on the internal culture of their enterprises, they will creatively apply those attributes to the arenas of the Traditionalists and the Transitionalists, the structures of society that will produce conditions of greater justice and equity for all citizens. Those engaged in international business will then be inspired to extend the range of these concerns to the structures that enable or inhibit equity for persons worldwide.

These new business statespersons then will be Transcendental leaders because their perspective of reality will transcend the limits that people have previously imposed upon themselves. They will be Transcendental leaders because they will portray compelling visions inspiring us to achieve greatness not only for ourselves but for the common good of all. And they will be Transcendental leaders because they will be concerned about the quality of human life everywhere because they accept a transcendent morality that recognizes that the international social economy of this one small world cannot long prosper peacefully under conditions of inequity and injustice prevailing anywhere.

228

APPENDIX

THIS APPENDIX HAS been provided for those who may be interested in some of the research aspects of this book. As a businessman working in the areas of corporate responsibility and human enablement, and with a foot periodically stepping into the social change arena, I generated a wide range of contacts over the years.

When I decided to write about exemplary business leaders and how they came to be that way, these contacts were invaluable. Early on I determined that to eliminate my biases I would only interview candidates nominated by others.

Beginning in early 1986, I soon received enough names to fill several books of profiles. Over the next two years I requested interviews from some four dozen people. Fortunately, some did not wish to participate; others, on closer inspection, were really not involved in for-profit businesses; and in the case of individual local entrepreneurs, I received an overabundance of candidates, many of them located in remote areas, quite inaccessible to a freelance writer on a limited budget. Eventually a total of 27 primary candidates were interviewed.

In the end, two dozen persons emerged as representing a spectrum of examples. They varied considerably in major characteristics: size of business, location, age, family background, education and life experience. Nineteen were men, five were women.

The method employed was to interview the leaders at their places of business, and in many cases to interview others who knew them and/or interview those who worked closely with them or for them. No standard questionnaire was used in the interviews. I said I was interested in knowing their life stories and what events and circumstances had been most important to them. Their narrations, which were taped, of course, led to further questions regarding

229

specific points they raised. In short, the methodology was conversational and in each case I reciprocated with a summary of my life and interests.

In age, the 24 were fairly evenly spread across the three decades between 40 and 70, which is predictable for persons in senior business positions.

Ten achieved their positions of leadership after coming up through the ranks as professional managers. Six were entrepreneurs. Four came up through businesses controlled by their families. Two purchased companies after having been successful as professional managers and two others have had careers in middle management positions.

Eleven of the 24 companies they represented were manufacturing companies. Four provided business services. Three were in the insurance field. Two were in distribution, and one each was in construction services, public utilities, commercial real estate development and transportation.

Five of the firms did less than $10 million in annual business. Six others did over $10 million but less than $100 million. Nine were in the $100 million to approximately $1 billion range, and four were in the $1 billion-plus range. The large firms were all publicly held; the medium-sized were about equally privately held and publicly held; and most of the smaller firms, and all of the smallest, were privately owned.

As children, these leaders came from families of all sizes. Several were only children. Several others came from very large families. They grew up in rural, small town, suburban, medium-sized urban and major urban environments. Half of them lived in the same communities throughout their childhood years. The other half moved from once up to many times. Most came from two-parent homes; however, two persons lived in single-parent situations and one other had parents who were divorced while the person was still in high school.

Slightly over half had fathers who pursued business careers. The others had fathers or mothers employed in a range of occupations from blue-collar to professional positions. Twenty came from middle-class economic circumstances, although a few were poor as children and several were from more privileged situations.

Educationally, all went to college and 10 had advanced degrees, all at the master's level. Nine had undergraduate degrees in engineering. Nine others had degrees in liberal arts and sciences. Six majored in business. Three had M.B.A.s; the other seven had postgraduate degrees in law, industrial management, industrial relations, engineering, metallurgy, meteorology and theology.

It is noteworthy that so many of these leaders had engineering or liberal arts and sciences backgrounds and so few acquired M.B.A.s. This appears to contradict the general belief that most business leaders have an M.B.A. Or it may be an important anomaly related to the development of virtuous leadership.

Twenty-one of the leaders reported being raised in families that regularly attended church services. In two other cases church attendance was only of the Easter/Christmas variety and in one situation there was no relationship. Seventeen were Protestant and six were Catholic. Since becoming adults, only about two-thirds of the 24 indicated that they continued to maintain a church relationship.

In short, the business leaders profiled came from a cross-section of American businesses. They were not a special breed of people determined by some commonality of ancestry or particular circumstance. Several reported that they had siblings who were quite unlike them in their concern for the human/social dimensions of business. Also, they were not all the first born (or second or third) in their families.

Universally, however, they were achievers, very intelligent, more than somewhat introspective, with high energy and an interest in the welfare of other people. Of these five attributes, the first four are common to many people who are successful; the fifth sets them apart as being virtuous, in the traditional definition of that word. In talking with them, I sensed that they felt they had received much in this life and that, therefore, much was required of them. Yet they did not accept this condition as a burden. They accepted it confidently as a responsibility appropriate to leadership in business.

ENDNOTES

1. The words *statesman*, *stateswoman* and *statesperson* appear here-after where they are contextually appropriate. The words *virtuous* or *exemplary* are used interchangeably with them. All designations are meant inclusively.
2. I suspect that someone else coined this phrase, but I have not determined to whom it should be attributed.
3. Robert N. Bellah, with Richard Madsen, William M. Sullivan, Ann Swidler, and Steven M. Tipton, *Habits of the Heart: Individualism and Commitment in American Life* (New York: Harper and Row, Perennial Library, 1986), 254.
4. Bellah, *Habits of the Heart*.
5. Ibid., 271.
6. Carl Bakal, *Charity USA* (New York: Times Books, 1979), 27.
7. Robert Levering, Milton Moskowitz, and Michael Katz, *The 100 Best Companies to Work for in America* (Plume, New York: New American Library, 1985), 4.
8. Louis O. Kelso and Mortimer J. Adler, *Capitalist Manifesto* (New York: Random House, 1958).
9. Bellah, *Habits of the Heart*.
10. Ibid., vii.
11. Ibid., 118.
12. Ibid., 253.
13. Ibid., 256.
14. Ibid., 285.
15. Ibid.
16. Ibid., 290.
17. Ibid., emphasis added.
18. Willis W. Harman, *An Incomplete Guide to the Future* (New York and London: Norton, 1976, 1979).
19. Willis W. Harman, "Creativity and Intuition in Business"

(Speech given at the Shell "Uncertainty in Management" Seminar, Vevey, Switzerland, June 19, 1986).
20. Harman, *An Incomplete Guide*, 25–26.
21. Ibid., 26.
22. Ibid.
23. Ibid., 27.
24. Ibid.
25. Ibid.
26. Ibid., 27–28.
27. Ibid., 28.
28. Ibid.
29. Ibid., 39.
30. Ibid., 51.
31. Ibid., 67.
32. Ibid., 79.
33. Ibid., 115.
34. Ibid., 130.
35. Bellah, *Habits of the Heart*, 256.

BIBLIOGRAPHY

THESE BOOKS ADDRESS various aspects of the subjects covered in *Business Ethics*. It certainly is not an exhaustive list, but it does represent perspectives and persons the author has come to respect.

Ainsworth-Land, George T. *Grow or Die: The Unifying Principles of Transformation*. New York: John Wiley & Sons, 1986 (reissued edition).

Argyris, Chris. *Personality and Organization*. New York: Harper and Row, 1957.

Bakal, Carl. *Charity USA*. New York: Times Books, 1979.

Baumhart, S. J., Raymond. *Ethics in Business*. New York: Holt, Rinehart and Winston, 1968.

Beer, Michael, Bert Spector, Paul R. Lawrence, D. Quinn Mills, and Richard E. Walton. *Managing Human Assets: The Groundbreaking Harvard Business School Program*. New York: The Free Press/Macmillan, 1984.

Bellah, Robert N. *The Broken Covenant: American Civil Religion in Time of Trial*. New York: The Seabury Press, 1975.

————, Richard Madsen, William M. Sullivan, Ann Swidler, and Steven M. Tipton. *Habits of the Heart: Individualism and Commitment in American Life*. Berkeley and Los Angeles: University of California Press, 1985.

Berry, Thomas. *The Dream of the Earth*. San Francisco: Sierra Club Books, 1988.

Capra, Fritjof. *The Turning Point: Science, Society and the Rising Culture*. New York: Simon and Schuster, 1982.

Cheshire, Ashley. *A Partnership of the Spirit: The Story of Jack Lowe and TDIndustries*. Dallas: Taylor Publishing Company, 1987.

Childs, Marquis W., and Douglas Cater. *Ethics in a Business Society*. New York: Harper and Row, 1954.

235

DePree, Max. *Leadership Is an Art.* East Lansing, MI: Michigan State University Press, 1987.

Drucker, Peter F. *The Age of Discontinuity.* New York: Harper and Row, 1969.

———. *The Frontiers of Management: Where Tomorrow's Decisions Are Being Shaped Today.* New York: Truman Talley Books, 1986.

Fox, Matthew, and Brian Swimme. *Manifesto! For a Global Civilization.* Sante Fe: Bear and Company, 1982.

Fruedberg, David. *The Corporate Conscience: Money, Power and Responsible Business.* New York: American Management Association, 1986.

Golden, Clinton S., and Harold J. Ruttenberg. *The Dynamics of Industrial Democracy.* New York and London: Harper and Brothers Publishers, 1942.

Greenleaf, Robert K. "The Servant as Leader." Pamphlet published by Center for Applied Studies and distributed by Windy Row Press, Peterborough, NH, 1970, 1973.

Harman, Willis W. *An Incomplete Guide to the Future.* New York: W. W. Norton and Company, 1979.

———. "Creativity and Intuition in Business: The Unconscious Mind and Management Effectiveness." Speech given at the Shell "Uncertainty in Management" Seminar, Vevey, Switzerland, June 19, 1986.

———. *Global Mind Change: The Promise of the Last Years of the Twentieth Century.* Indianapolis: Knowledge Systems, Inc., 1988.

———, and Howard Rheingold. *Higher Creativity: Liberating the Unconscious for Breakthrough Insights.* Los Angeles: Tarcher/St. Martin's Press, 1984.

———, and John Hormann. *Creative Work: The Constructive Role of Business in a Transforming Society.* Indianapolis: Knowledge Systems, Inc., 1990.

Heckscher, Charles C. *The New Unionism: Employee Involvement in the Changing Corporation.* New York: Basic Books, 1988.

Herzberg, Frederick. *Work and Nature of Man.* Cleveland and New York: World Publishing Company, 1966.

Jones, Donald G., ed. *Business, Religion and Ethics: Inquiry and Encounter.* Cambridge, MA: Oelgeschlager, Gunn and Hain, Publishers, Inc., 1982.

Kelso, Louis O., and Mortimer J. Adler. *Capitalist Manifesto*. New York: Random House, 1958.

Kochan, Thomas A., and Thomas A. Barocci. *Human Resource Management and Industrial Relations: Text, Readings and Cases*. Boston, Toronto: Little, Brown and Company, 1985.

———, Harry C. Katz, and Robert B. McKersie. *The Transformation of American Industrial Relations*. New York: Basic Books, 1986.

Lawrence, Paul R., and Davis Dyer. *Renewing American Industry*. New York: The Free Press/Macmillan, 1983.

———, and Jay W. Lorsch. *Developing Organizations: Diagnosis and Action*. Reading, MA: Addison-Wesley, 1969.

Levering, Robert, Milton Moskowitz, and Michael Katz. *The 100 Best Companies to Work for in America*. New York: Plume, New American Library, 1985.

Maccoby, Michael. *Why Work: Leading the New Generation*. New York: Simon and Schuster, 1988.

Naisbitt, John. *Megatrends: Ten New Directions Transforming Our Lives*. New York: Warner Books, 1982.

O'Toole, James. *Vanguard Management: Redesigning the Corporate Future*. Garden City, NY: Doubleday and Co., Inc., 1985.

Peters, Thomas J., and Robert H. Waterman, Jr. *In Search of Excellence: Lessons from America's Best-Run Companies*. New York: Harper and Row, 1982.

Reid, Peter C. *Well Made in America: Lessons from Harley-Davidson on Being the Best*. New York: McGraw-Hill, 1990.

Senge, Peter M. *The Fifth Discipline: The Art and Practice of the Learning Organization*. New York: Doubleday/Currency, 1990.

Silk, Leonard, and David Vogel. *Ethics and Profits: The Crisis of Confidence in American Business*. New York: Simon and Schuster, 1976.

Swimme, Brian. *The Universe is a Green Dragon*. Santa Fe: Bear and Company, 1984.

Thompson, William Irwin. *At the Edge of History*. New York: Harper and Row, 1971.

Toffler, Alvin. *The Third Wave*. New York: Morrow, 1980.

Tuleja, Tad. *Beyond the Bottom Line: How Business Leaders Are Turning Principles into Profits*. New York: Facts on File, 1985.

Zuboff, Shoshana. *In the Age of the Smart Machine: The Future of Work and Power*. New York: Basic Books, 1988.

INDEX

Index

DATE DUE

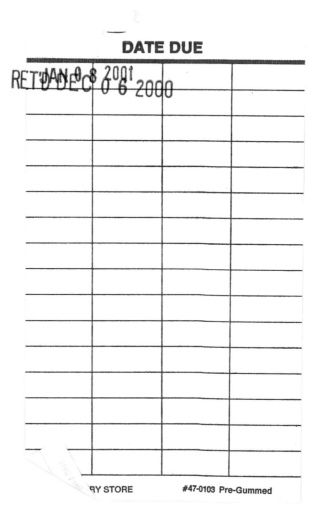

RET'D JAN 0 8 2001			
RET'D DEC 0 6 2000			